THE FAITH WE CONFESS:

AN EXPOSITION OF THE THIRTY-NINE ARTICLES

BY GERALD BRAY

The Latimer Trust

The Faith We Confess: An Exposition of the Thirty-Nine Articles

© Gerald Bray 2009

ISBN 978-0-946307-84-5

Published by The Latimer Trust, November 2009

Cover photograph: © Stephen Finn – Fotolia.com

The Latimer Trust
PO Box 26685, London N14 4XQ UK
Registered Charity: 1084337
Company Number: 4104465
Web: www.latimertrust.org
E-mail: administrator@latimertrust.org

Contents

The historic formularies of the Church of England

The Thirty-Nine Articles of Religion are one of the three historic 'formularies' (constitutional documents) of the Church of England. Along with the Book of Common Prayer and the Ordinal they gave the church its distinctive identity at the time of the Reformation, an identity which has had a formative influence on worldwide Anglicanism. Even if Anglican churches outside England are free to alter their statements of doctrine and patterns of worship, and many have done so, it remains true to say that the English formularies have played an exceptionally important role in shaping the Anglican Communion and that they continue to serve as reference points whenever it is necessary to think in terms of a common Anglican tradition. In the confusion caused by recent developments within the Communion, it is encouraging to see that groups like the Fellowship of Confessing Anglicans have returned to these sources for inspiration and seem determined to bring them back to the centre of the church's life and witness. Whether or to what extent this will become a pattern for the future remains to be seen, but for the first time in many years there appears to be a genuine hunger for both Anglican tradition and sound Christian doctrine in many parts of the Communion. It is to meet this growing demand that this book has been written.

The historic formularies were designed by Archbishop Thomas Cranmer (1489–1556) to give the English Church a solid grounding in the three fundamental areas of its life – **doctrine, devotion** and **discipline**. The Articles provided its doctrinal framework, the Prayer Book settled the pattern of its devotional life and the Ordinal outlined what was expected of the clergy, whose role was the key to the church's discipline. Until the early twentieth century all three formularies functioned in a recognisable way within the Church of England, and although they were modified to varying degrees in other Anglican churches, the family resemblance among them all was still easily discernible. In the past century however, that situation has changed dramatically. Pressure from the Anglo-Catholic wing of the church led to demands for the reform of the Prayer Book, which was undertaken by some Anglican churches, including the Church of England, in the 1920s. Though successful elsewhere, the revised English Prayer Book was rejected by Parliament in 1928, because of its perceived Romanising tendencies. However, many parishes decided to use it anyway on the ground that the church's own representative assemblies had approved it, and so the liturgical unity of the church was compromised. In the 1960s renewed pressures, coming this time from modernisers as much as from traditional Anglo-Catholics, led to a round of liturgical experimentation which culminated in the *Alternative Service Book* (1980), which has since been replaced by *Common Worship* (2000). The 1662 Book of Common Prayer has not been withdrawn, however, and is still used by some people, but it is probably fair to say that most parishes use forms of worship which they have cobbled together out of the liturgical resources available, or preferred to do their own thing. As a result, the devotional unity of the Church of England has been destroyed and with very few exceptions, the younger generation has no experience of the Book of Common Prayer in worship.

The Ordinal has suffered less drastically from modernisation, but it has been undermined in another way. It was intended to provide a framework for the admission of full-time stipendiary men to the church's threefold ministry, and it laid a solemn charge on them to preach the Word of God, to administer the sacraments and to undertake their pastoral duties to the best of their ability. That pattern remained intact until the 1970s, but liturgical reforms that have laid more emphasis on the sacraments than on the ministry of preaching and teaching have increased the pressure to ordain significant numbers of undertrained and part-time people who can perform ceremonies but are ill-equipped to teach congregations. Alongside this, the fusion of many parishes, particularly in rural areas, has produced an irregular ministry in many places. The concept of a professional minister still survives to some extent, but the traditional vicar is a vanishing breed and will probably be quite rare in thirty years' time if present trends continue.

The Articles of Religion have not been revised or supplemented, but if anything they have suffered an even more drastic fate – they have been sidelined and ignored instead! It is true that official church statements continue to make occasional references to them, but these are for the sake of form more than anything else. Few people, even among the clergy, have ever read them properly and almost nobody who is now active in church life has ever studied them seriously. Historians pay attention to them, as they must, but others tend to dismiss them either as antiquated relics or as inadequate statements of the church's beliefs – or both! The fact that they are less comprehensive than the Westminster Confession of Faith (which was originally intended to be a revision of the Articles) is used to argue that the Church of England is not a confessional church and that its doctrine must be sought elsewhere – notably in the Book of Common Prayer! There is little understanding, even among those who support the retention of the Articles, of what they are or of why they matter for the church. This book is intended to show that, despite their apparent shortcomings, the Articles are indeed the church's confession of faith and that they remain indispensable to its mission and identity in the world. It is possible to argue that they should be supplemented by further doctrinal definitions and to regret that they were effectively fossilised in the early seventeenth century for largely political reasons, but that does not mean that they can simply be ignored by modern Anglicans. What they say remains of key importance to us, and in the current identity crisis that we face as a worldwide Communion, the Thirty-nine Articles of Religion give us a clear picture of the framework within which we are called to operate.

Articles as statements of doctrine

The shape and function of the Thirty-Nine Articles reflect a long tradition of intellectual activity that can be traced back to the law schools of ancient Rome. In a world where memory had to be stored in the human head and not on a computer, vast quantities of information had to be compressed into a format that could be absorbed by the average intelligent person. Roman laws were often long and complex in their details, so lawyers had to learn what they contained in general terms, and know where to look for those details if they needed them. As a result, the laws were epitomised in short paragraphs, known as *regulae* (or *canones* in Greek), that were learned off by heart. The early church adopted this practice with respect to the Bible, which was also too long to be memorised as a whole. It developed what was called 'the rule of faith', a series of basic doctrinal points that comes in different (but mutually compatible) versions, out of which emerged the creeds as we know them today. In addition to these, there were a number of canons enacted by various church councils, covering matters of doctrine and discipline. Most of these canons were produced because a controversy had arisen which they were intended to resolve by applying some theological principle to a particular concrete situation. As time went on, collections of canons were made and it was discovered, not surprisingly, that different conclusions had been reached by different churches at different times and in different circumstances. Sorting all this out became a matter of urgency in the twelfth century, when the papacy was trying to unite the whole of Western Europe under its authority, and it was at that time that systematic theology as we now understand it can be said to have begun.

The two most important people in this process were an Italian lawyer-monk called Gratian (*fl. c.* 1140), and Peter Lombard (1090–1160), another Italian who migrated to Paris and died there as its bishop. Gratian wrote what he called a 'concordance of discordant canons' but which we now know as the *Decretum*. His work was soon supplemented by a large number of papal decretals, which were subsequently collected and put in some kind of order by different popes – Gregory X (1234), Boniface VIII (1298) Clement V (1313) and John XXII (1325) being the most prominent among them. This pattern continued until about 1500, when the collections reached their classical form in what came to be called the *Corpus iuris canonici*.

Peter Lombard's work appeared in four volumes and was known as the *Sentences*, the word being used in its legal sense of 'decision' or 'definition' (as in 'passing sentence' on someone.) Like Gratian, the Lombard assembled as many ancient authorities as he could find and organised them in a logical pattern to produce the first truly systematic theology. His magnificent synthesis, which has only recently been translated into English, remained the theological textbook in common use until the sixteenth century, when other works, especially John Calvin's famous *Institutes of the Christian Religion*, finally supplanted it. Of course, theology did not stand still in the interval and men like Thomas Aquinas (1226–1274) produced longer and more detailed systematic theologies that are still widely read today, but the *Sentences* were never lost sight of and most medieval theologians, including Aquinas, cut their teeth by writing commentaries on them.

As the medieval universities developed, it became customary to present new thoughts and initiate controversy in a similarly abbreviated form. Debates were frequently started by asking leading *questions* (*e.g.* 'Did Adam have a navel?') or by publishing short *theses* intended to provoke further discussion, and concluded in equally brief *articles* that summarised the main points of agreement between the parties concerned. Such articles of agreement were also used in legal documents, ranging in time from the *articuli cleri* of 1316, which outlined the sphere of jurisdiction allotted to the ecclesiastical courts of England, to the Articles of Confederation, composed after the American Revolution as a prelude to the union of the states that emerged from it.

This was the world into which Martin Luther (1483–1546), Thomas Cranmer (1489–1556) and John Calvin (1509–1564) were born. They too believed that complex theological arguments could and should be condensed into brief statements that could be memorised and expounded, rather in the way that a professor would now lecture from his class notes. To put it a different way, their theses or articles were meant to be understood as the tip of an intellectual iceberg, giving a clear outline of what lay concealed beneath the surface. From a distance of nearly five centuries it is easy to look at them and conclude that they have little to say, but those who do that are liable to discover what the unfortunate sailors in the *Titanic* found out to their cost – there is more to them that what the eye can see, and to ignore their hidden depths is to court shipwreck.

The Reformation began with ninety-five relatively brief theses that Martin Luther circulated in 1517, in which he challenged the pope's pretensions to an authority that he could not legitimately claim. Debate about this and other related matters soon followed, and before long there was a torrent of literature coming off the presses, including the *Assertion of the seven sacraments*, a refutation of Luther's views written by no less a person than King Henry VIII of England. The pope reluctantly rewarded Henry for his efforts with the title 'Defender of the Faith', which his successors bear to this day, although the content of that faith is no longer quite what was originally intended!

In the early years of the Reformation, there were so many voices wanting to make themselves heard that nobody knew for sure what Luther and his true followers believed. In response to a request for clarification made by the Holy Roman Emperor Charles V (1519–1556), the Lutherans put together a statement of their beliefs, which they presented to the Imperial diet (parliament) at Augsburg in 1530. This was the famous *Confessio Augustana*, or Augsburg Confession, which remains a basic document of Lutheranism to this day. Those who signed it were protesting (*i.e.* confessing) their faith and so came to be known as 'protestants'. When the Church of England broke with the papacy in 1534 and Henry VIII sought an alliance with the Germans, it was only natural for the latter to ask whether the English were prepared to accept the 'protestant' faith – in other words, were they willing to sign the *Augustana*?

This may seem like a simple question to us, but it was politically and theologically complicated. Henry VIII had not broken with Rome merely in order to submit himself to a rival authority in the shape of a group of German theologians. Nor was he persuaded of the truth of the *Augustana*, at least not in every respect. To his mind, opposing the pope did not necessarily mean supporting Luther, and Luther was well aware of Henry's theological deficiencies. The two men were tactical allies thrown together by having a common enemy and those who strove to create a lasting bond between the Church of England and the Lutheran churches of Germany had to take account of that fact.

In late 1535 a small group of English theologians made their way to Wittenberg, where they conferred with Philipp Melanchthon and other Lutherans and eventually agreed on a series of articles of belief. These articles reflected the Augsburg Confession in substance but were sufficiently different from it in form as to appear to be a fresh statement of faith. What happened to these so-called Wittenberg Articles is unknown. Apart from a few extracts, they disappeared from view almost immediately and were not rediscovered until 1904. They were found in Germany however, and it is not known whether a copy of them ever reached England. But soon after the English theologians returned home the Church of England adopted the so-called Ten Articles, which bear some resemblance to the Augsburg Confession and to the Wittenberg Articles, though mainly in the way they divide their subject matter into a doctrinal section (the first five articles) and one dealing with questions of ritual and devotion (the last five articles). It looks very much as if the English theologians realised that they would be unable to persuade either the church or the king to accept anything more radical, and so the Wittenberg Articles were quietly dropped. All that remained was the form – the first doctrinal statement made by the independent Church of England appeared as a series of articles, a pattern that set the standard for the future.

The origin of the Thirty-Nine Articles

The adoption of the Ten Articles in 1536 was soon followed by an extended theological commentary, put out under the authority of the bishops and thus known to us as the 'Bishops' Book' (1537). It was clearly Protestant in tone and Archbishop Cranmer went on to draw up a further series of thirteen articles which were modelled very closely on the Augsburg Confession, along with at least three others which have survived among his papers but whose exact status is unclear. Had things gone smoothly, it is possible that the Church of England would have adopted something very much like the *Augustana*, but before that could happen, Henry VIII had a change of heart. His reformation was moving too fast in a radical direction, and he determined to stop the process by getting parliament to enact six ultra-conservative articles, reaffirming such things as compulsory clerical celibacy and the doctrine of transubstantiation (1539). Four years later he produced a revised version of the Bishops' Book (which we now know as the 'King's Book') that gave a much more traditional presentation of Christian doctrine, though it did not simply restore the old religion as it had been before 1536.

There matters rested until Henry died in 1547, leaving his nine-year old son Edward VI (1547–1553) on the throne. Archbishop Cranmer belonged to the regency council and was put in charge of church affairs, which allowed him to introduce more far-reaching changes than had previously been possible. His first public act was to issue a book of sermons, or homilies, which were designed to teach ordinary people the basic truths of the Christian faith. These homilies were a mixture of theology and practical pastoral counselling, and they were written by a number of different people, including at least two men (Edmund Bonner and John Harpsfield) who were not sympathetic to the Reformation. Nevertheless, the homilies demonstrate the fact that doctrine has to be the starting point for Christian discipleship. Unless we know what we believe and why we believe it, we shall not put it into practice with the consistency and conviction required of true Christians. The homilies were designed to bring that message home to people, and to prepare them for the other changes that were to follow.

The next stage was the composition of a Book of Common Prayer, which provided the church with an English-language liturgy that was authorised for use from 9 June (Pentecost) 1549. Annexed to this book (though not part of it) was the Ordinal, which established the form for making bishops, priests and deacons in the reformed church. The impetus for reform now gathered pace, and within three years Cranmer managed to revise the Prayer Book, produce a set of doctrinal articles and prepare a thorough-going church discipline that would supplement the Ordinal and touch every aspect of the church's life. He managed to get parliament to accept his second Prayer Book, which was in use from 1 November 1552, but there seem to have been difficulties with both the articles of religion and the book of discipline. Exactly what happened is unknown, but it is clear that parliament would not accept the latter when it met in March 1553. Whether the convocation of the clergy of the archbishop's province of Canterbury, which met simultaneously with the parliament, ratified Cranmer's articles or not is unclear. Writing many years later, Matthew Parker, archbishop of Canterbury from 1559 to 1575, insisted that it did, and as he was present in 1553, his testimony may be regarded as that of an eye-witness. However, there is no documentary evidence that this happened, and modern scholarly opinion tends to doubt Parker's statement. Either way, the articles received the royal assent on 19 June 1553, only a few days before the king died.

Cranmer originally composed forty-five articles, which were reduced to forty-two by the simple expedient of combining articles 26-29 on the sacraments into one. In the overall arrangement of their material, they bear little resemblance to the Augsburg Confession and much more to Peter Lombard's *Sentences*, or Calvin's *Institutes*. Of course, as mere articles, they were much shorter than any textbook of theology, but the range of subjects covered (and their order) shows that Cranmer was thinking in terms of a systematic presentation of Christian doctrine. The forty-two articles were not just position statements on disputed points but a general exposition of what he thought the church ought to believe. That this is so can be seen from the inclusion of a number of articles on subjects that were not particularly controversial at the time, but which formed an integral part of the church's overall confession of faith.

It is obvious that the articles were composed in an atmosphere which reflected hostility to the church of Rome, but the nature of this polemic is more complex than most people realise. The papacy had long been in conflict with secular rulers over matters of jurisdictional competence, and the fact that Cranmer generally took the side of the state in such things was not necessarily the result of the Reformation. The Catholic states of Europe, especially France and Spain, were doing exactly the same thing, and papal power over them was often rejected with just as much determination as it was in England. For example, the popes wanted to convene a church council to deal with Protestantism, but they were not allowed to do so until the emperor Charles V could be persuaded to permit it. Charles only gave way after insisting that the council should be held on his territory – at Trent, in northern Italy. The council of Trent duly opened in 1545 and continued off and on until 1563, the year that Cranmer's articles reached their final form. This was not a coincidence. The articles of religion cannot be fully understood except against the backdrop of Trent, which was making its own doctrinal definitions of the Catholic faith. It would be wrong to say that Cranmer and his successors reacted against Trent and contradicted it at every turn, though it is true that Trent tended to produce theological definitions which were deliberately designed to be as far away from Protestantism as they could possibly be. The Protestant churches were therefore forced to deal with this challenge and provide a convincing alternative, and the effects of this are clearly discernible in several of the surviving articles.

It is harder to say whether or to what extent the forty-two articles consciously set out an 'Anglican' position in relation to churches other than the Roman one. Cranmer was aware of the Eastern Orthodox churches but on the points where they disagreed with Rome, he tended to side with the latter because those differences had emerged at a time when the English Church was still in communion with the pope. The main exception to this was the doctrine of the papacy itself, where Cranmer was obviously closer to the Eastern position, though this was an accidental circumstance rather than the result of a deliberately pro-Orthodox policy on his part. With regard to continental Protestants, Cranmer tried to weave a middle course (the famous *via media*) between the rival factions, looking for formulas that would be acceptable to as many different Protestant groups as possible. The one strand of continental Protestantism that he had no sympathy for was Anabaptism, which he openly denounced, though it is interesting to note that many of his references to the Anabaptists were removed from the articles when they were later revised.

Cranmer composed his articles in Latin, the theological language of his day, and the English translation was only an approximation to that and had no formal authority of its own. It is important to understand this, because Latin terminology was subsequently absorbed into English and may seem more natural to us today than Cranmer's translation does. For example, in the first article we read that God is 'without...passions' which is somewhat ambiguous (at least to a modern ear), but the Latin is *impassibilis*, or 'impassible', which makes the meaning immediately clear – to a theologian, at least! Modern students whose Latin is shaky or non-existent must therefore be especially careful not to read meanings into the English version of the articles which the official Latin text cannot support. On the other hand, English was obviously the mother tongue of those who composed the Articles, and so it is not unreasonable to think that the translation can shed light on the true meaning of the Latin whenever the latter is ambiguous or obscure.

The revision of the Articles

The death of Edward VI on 6 July 1553 and the accession of his sister Mary I (1553–1558) was a disaster for the Protestant cause. Cranmer was soon imprisoned and was eventually put to death, as were a number of other leading Reformers. The second Prayer Book went officially out of use on 20 December 1553, though no doubt it had disappeared some time before that, and the forty-two articles were stillborn. Mary did her best to put the clock back to 1534 and if she had lived, or produced a credible heir, she might have succeeded. As things turned out however, she died before any real reaction could set in and her persecution of leading Protestants won sympathy for their cause among the general population. This enabled her successor, Elizabeth I (1558–1603) to restore the position that had existed at the death of Edward VI, though she took the opportunity to make some changes along the way. In particular, the 1552 Prayer Book was slightly modified to make it more acceptable to traditionalists, and the forty-two articles received a more thorough overhaul.

The revision of the articles was entrusted mainly to Matthew Parker, the archbishop of Canterbury and to John Jewel, bishop of Salisbury, both of whom were Protestant in their sympathies. Many of the changes they made were cosmetic and of little or no doctrinal significance. This is particularly true in those cases where only the English translation was altered, or where modifications to the Latin were not enough to force any change in the English. In several cases, the text was reworded or rearranged to make it flow better, but there was no significant alteration in meaning. The most important changes were those which involved the deletion of Cranmer's text and its replacement by something else. This happened, for example, in article 7, which deals with the Old Testament, where the revised version is completely different from the original, even though it covers the same subject matter. Also in this category are articles which were added by the revisers, like article 5 on the Holy Spirit, or simply deleted, like articles 39-42 which discussed eschatology, an ever-controversial subject about which the divines of the English Church evidently decided it was best to say nothing at all.

The revised articles, now numbering only thirty-nine, were brought to the convocation of Canterbury on 29 January 1563 (1562 according to the old calendar then still in use) and signed by its members on 5 February. But when the queen was asked to ratify them, she struck out article 29, probably because she thought that it might offend the Lutherans. It was only in 1571, after the pope had excommunicated her, that Elizabeth allowed the issue of the articles to be reopened, and the opportunity was taken to make several more revisions to them. Among other things, article 29 was restored and the Cranmerian text of article 7 was put back alongside (rather than instead of) the 1563 version. In this form, the Thirty-Nine Articles were approved by the Canterbury convocation on 4 May 1571, after which they remained unchanged. The clergy were expected to subscribe to them at ordination and on admission to a benefice, a requirement that was formalised in canon 36 of 1604. That requirement remained in force until the late nineteenth century, after which it was progressively watered down so that today it is only necessary for the clergy to affirm general assent to the historical traditions of Anglicanism, of which the Articles are one representative text. As a result, it is still possible to claim that the Articles are an integral part of Anglican identity but difficult, if not impossible, to prosecute anyone who dissents from them for heresy.

Theological debate did not cease in 1571 of course, and nobody at the time thought that the Articles were immutable. When controversy erupted over predestination in the 1590s, Archbishop John Whitgift produced nine articles on the subject which were signed by him and a number of other bishops on 20 November 1595, but these so-called Lambeth Articles were rejected by the queen for reasons that remain unclear. She probably objected to the idea that her bishops could act without her prior consent, but may also have felt that a statement on such a controversial subject might undo her hard-won settlement of the church.

The next occasion for reform came in 1615, when the Church of Ireland decided to adopt its own articles of religion. The Irish Church had gone along with the English articles, more or less by default, but by the early seventeenth century some Irish theologians felt that a more thoroughgoing revision was needed. They took the Thirty-Nine Articles as they stood (though with the notable omission of numbers 34-36 and 39), added the Lambeth Articles and filled in the rest with subjects that the English articles had not touched on or which had been deleted in the 1563 revision. The result was a text of 104 articles which became the official doctrinal statement of the Church of Ireland and which many hoped would be adopted in England as well. The most important innovation of the Irish Articles was its change of theological method. Whereas the English ones followed the medieval tradition of starting with God the Holy Trinity, the Irish ones adopted the pattern first found in the Second Helvetic Confession of 1566, whereby the doctrine of Scripture claimed pride of place and was followed by the doctrine of God. The reason for this was that our knowledge of God is derived from Scripture, even though in the absolute sense, God exists independently of the Bible, which he gave to us.

The subsequent history of the Articles was determined by the reign and policies of Charles I (1625–1649). Charles wanted to restore the church to what he believed was its former glory and to that end he did his best to go back at least to 1559 and perhaps earlier. In December

1628 he issued a curious declaration forbidding discussion of theological points like predestination, which had become the subject of bitter controversy within the church, and imposing the Thirty-Nine Articles on the church as definitive for all time. A few years later he tried to extend this policy to Ireland, but although he got the Irish to accept the Thirty-Nine Articles in place of their own ones, he could not persuade them to rescind the latter and they remained available for use at least up to the outbreak of civil war in 1641. Only at the restoration were they definitively retired, but even then it would be more accurate to say that they were in abeyance and not actually revoked.

The revolt of parliament against the king had deep religious causes, and so it is not surprising that in 1643 an assembly of theologians was called to meet at Westminster, in order to hammer out a common confession for the churches of England, Scotland and Ireland. The Thirty-Nine Articles were the agreed starting point, but it soon became apparent that they would need considerable supplementing, as the Irish experience in 1615 had already demonstrated. The resulting Westminster Confession of Faith, which like the Irish Articles, also starts with the doctrine of Scripture rather than with the doctrine of God, was finished in 1646 and imposed by parliament on the churches of the three kingdoms, only to be rescinded at the restoration in 1660. Further turmoil led to the Scottish rejection of episcopacy in 1690, at which point the Scots adopted the Westminster Confession as their doctrinal standard. In England and Ireland however, the Thirty-Nine Articles remained in place, with the curious declaration of Charles I prefixed to them as a reminder (and a warning) to anyone who might want to reopen the question of their adequacy.

In the eighteenth century John Wesley reduced the number of articles to twenty-five by omitting the ones he did not like (like article 17 on predestination) or felt were irrelevant, and many of his Methodist followers went along with that, though it meant leaving the Church of England. After the American revolution the remnants of the Anglican church in that country regrouped themselves and adopted a slightly pruned version of the Articles, omitting those with political references and doctoring a couple of others, notably the one on the creeds, where mention of the Athanasian Creed was removed (1801). Since that time, other emerging Anglican churches have either accepted or rejected the Articles as a whole. None has attempted to modify them and the 1571 text remains their standard as far as it is applicable to their circumstances.

Those who wish to study the history of the Articles in greater detail are referred to the books mentioned in the bibliography which deal with the subject. The intention of this book is to take them as they now stand and interpret what they mean for us today. Historical circumstances cannot be avoided completely and will be mentioned as necessary, but the main emphasis here is theological. What do the articles say about what we believe and how should they be understood and applied by us today? Read on!

The structure of the Articles

Do the Articles possess a clear structure in the way in which they are set out? This is a difficult question to answer, and the Articles themselves give us no clue as to how (or whether) they can be subdivided according to theme, although various commentators have tried to construct a rationale for them and there are certain things which point in a particular direction. For example, it is clear that the first few articles deal with the doctrine of God, and that the sacraments are grouped together later on. Whether this is enough to produce an overall pattern is less clear, but for our purposes the following subdivision seems to be the most appropriate.

1.   The Catholic doctrines

This is covered in articles 1-8, which deal with God the Holy Trinity (1-5), the Holy Scriptures (6-7) and the ancient creeds (8). The order is the right one, in that God inspired the Bible and the creeds summarise its teaching, and on the whole, the contents of these articles can be regarded as pan-Christian. The only exceptions to this are the list of canonical books in article 6 and the inclusion of the Athanasian Creed in article 8, but these are minor. In the first case, the canon given is that of Jerome which had a strong claim to catholicity even though it was rejected by the council of Trent. In the second case, the Athanasian Creed was never accepted in the eastern churches, but although this may be an issue in modern ecumenical dialogue, it was not so in the sixteenth century, when most people believed that it had originated in the east with Athanasius and would not have understood the objections to his authorship that are put forward today.

2.   The Protestant doctrines

This includes articles 9-34 and forms the main body of the Articles taken as a whole. This is hardly surprising, given the fact that both Thomas Cranmer and the later revisers were mainly concerned to expound the Church of England's teaching in the light of the Reformation and to chart a course that would keep it firmly allied with both the Lutherans and the Reformed, even though they were falling out with each other. The main thrust of these articles is directed against Rome, which was perceived to be the chief opponent of orthodox Protestant views, but there was also hostility to the kind of radical reformation usually associated with the Anabaptists. However, it is noticeable that in the course of revision, hostility to Rome remained unabated whereas adverse references to Anabaptism were modified and often deleted entirely.

Within this section, there are seven subdivisions as follows:

a. the need for salvation (9-10)
b. justification by faith and the place of good works (11-14)
c. the Christian life (15-18)
d. the church (19-22)
e. the ministry (23-24)
f. the sacraments (25-31)
g. church discipline (32-34)

Each of these subdivisions follows on logically from the preceding. We begin with sin and the fall of mankind, which is the inevitable starting point, since if that had not happened, the Christian message would have been unnecessary. From there we move on to how things are to be put right, which is by faith and not by works, however good and even necessary the latter may be in their proper context. After that, we look at the Christian life as the imitation of Christ, who alone is sinless. Our relation to him is established by pointing out that we are still sinners, but that we have been called and chosen by God for a particular purpose, which can only be fulfilled in Christ, our unique Lord and Saviour.

Next we move on to the church, which is the body of all who believe in Christ and which exists in both invisible (perfect) and visible (imperfect) forms. The invisible church is not our concern because it is directly in the hand of God. At the same time, God has committed the government of the visible church to us, and we must rule it in a way which furthers his divine and invisible purpose. The authority of the visible church is clearly delineated, and the pretension that it can extend to souls after death is denied. From there we move logically to the ministry and the way in which it is called to function in the church.

After that come the sacraments, both in general and in particular, with various abuses singled out for special treatment. Finally, there are three articles dealing with matters of church discipline – clerical marriage, excommunication and tradition(s). None of these has the status of an official doctrine but each of them affects the way the church lives in the world and so they are dealt with together.

3. The Anglican doctrines

These are found in articles 35-37 and deal mainly with matters specific to the Church of England or to the civil order. Included here are the *Homilies*, issued for the instruction of the people but confined to the English Church, the threefold order of ministry, which again is seen as something practised in the Church of England but not necessarily of universal application, and finally the relationship of church and state. The last two articles (38-39) are not specifically 'Anglican' or even 'Protestant', but because they concern matters of civil government, they are logically appended to the article on church-state relations.

Understood in this way, the Thirty-nine Articles have a logical and harmonious symmetry, starting with what is universal and going on progressively to what is more particular, first to the protestant world in general and then to the specific circumstances of the Church of England. The passage of time has brought changes to some of the individual provisions contained in the Articles, but the basic structure is sound and shows that, at the time of their composition, the Articles of Religion were the most systematic and comprehensive concise statement of faith that the Reformation had up to then produced.

A NOTE ON THE FORMAT OF THIS BOOK

Each article is treated individually, with some questions for group discussion and suggestions for further reading appended at the end. The lists of books are not intended to be a definitive guide to their subject but only an introduction for those who want to pursue the matter further for themselves. Some of these books are important contributions to their subject but their authors do not share the same Evangelical faith as the members of the Latimer Trust, which does not necessarily endorse every view expressed in them.

Bibliography

THE THIRTY-NINE ARTICLES

Commentaries on the Articles have been written since the late sixteenth century, but few of them are readily available now. The classic one is by Thomas Rogers (d. 1616), which first appeared as *The English creed* (1585). Rogers later revised it substantially and republished it as *The faith, doctrine and religion professed and protected in the realm of England* (1607). This edition was reissued in 1854 by the Parker Society, with the title *The catholic doctrine of the Church of England.* The most important commentaries still in use today are:

Bicknell, Edward John. *A theological introduction to the thirty-nine articles of the Church of England.* London: Longmans, Green and Co., 1919. Repr., 1955.

Browne, Edward Harold. *An exposition of the thirty-nine articles: historical and doctrinal.* London: Longmans, Green, Reader and Dyer, 1874. Repr., Philadelphia, Pa.: Classical Anglican Press, 1998.

Griffith Thomas, William Henry. *The principles of theology: an introduction to the thirty-nine articles.* London: Longmans, Green and Co., 1930. Repr., London: Vine Books, 1978 and Grand Rapids: Baker, 1979.

Also of interest, though not commentaries in the strict sense, are:

Bridge, G. R., ed. *The Thirty-nine Articles.* Charlottetown, PEI: St Peter Publications, 1989.

Hughes, P. E. *The theology of the English reformers.* London: Hodder and Stoughton, 1965.

O'Donovan, Oliver. *On the thirty-nine articles: a conversation with Tudor Christianity.* Exeter: Paternoster, 1986.

Packer, J. I. and Beckwith, R. T. *The thirty-nine articles. Their place and use today.* Oxford: Latimer House, 1984. Repr., Vancouver, BC: Regent College Publishing, 2007.

Proctor, W. G. C. *The teaching of the Church of England following the thirty-nine articles.* Worthing: Churchman, 1987.

Subscription and assent to the 39 articles. Report of the Archbishops' Commission on Christian Doctrine. London: SPCK, 1968.

There have been few detailed studies of the Articles by non-Anglicans, but one of the most interesting and remarkable, for those who can read

Greek, is the detailed commentary by Professor K. Skouteris.

Skouteris, Professor K. Τὰ 39 ἄρθρα τῆς Ἀγγλικῆς Ἐκκλησίας ʽυπὸ τὸ φῶς τῆς Ὀρθοδόξου συμβολικῆς παραδόσεως - (The 39 articles of the English Church in the light of the Orthodox creedal tradition). Athens: G. K. Parisianos, 1982.

OTHER ANGLICAN SOURCES

The writings of the English Reformers were collected, edited and published in the mid-nineteenth century under the auspices of the Parker Society. Many of them are still available for purchase second-hand, and most good libraries have a set of them.

Bray, G. L. *The Anglican canons 1529-1947.* Woodbridge: Boydell and Brewer, 1998.

Bray, G. L. *Documents of the English reformation.* Cambridge: James Clarke, 1994. Repr. with corrections, 2004.

Bray, G. L. *Tudor church reform.* Woodbridge: Boydell and Brewer, 2000.

The homilies appointed to be read in churches. Edited by John Griffiths (1859). Rev. by Ian Robinson. Bishopstone: Brynmill and Philadelphia: Preservation Press, 2006.

NON-ANGLICAN SOURCES

Calvin, John. *Institutes of the Christian religion.* Edited by John T. McNeill. Translated by Ford Lewis Battles. 2 vols. Philadelphia: Westminster Press, 1960.

Decrees of the ecumenical councils. Edited and translated by N. Tanner. London: Sheed and Ward, 1990.

Luther, Martin. *Works.* English translation. 55 vols. St Louis, Mo.: Concordia, 1955-1986.

Maurer, Wilhelm. *A historical commentary on the Augsburg Confession.* Philadelphia: Fortress, 1986.

Peter Lombard. *Sentences.* Translated by G. Silano. 4 vols. Toronto: Pontifical Institute for Mediaeval Studies, 2007-10.

Reu, J. M. *The Augsburg Confession: a collection of sources with a historical introduction.* St Louis, Mo.: Concordia, 2005.

GENERAL WORKS

Davies, J. *The Caroline captivity of the church. Charles I and the remoulding of Anglicanism.* Oxford: OUP, 1992.

Dickens, A. G. *The English reformation.* 2d ed. London: Batsford, 1989.

Heal, F. *Reformation in Britain and Ireland.* Oxford: OUP, 2003.

MacCulloch, D. *Thomas Cranmer.* New Haven and London: Yale, 1996.

MacCulloch, D. *Tudor church militant. Edward VI and the Protestant reformation.* London: Penguin, 1999.

Neill, S. *Anglicanism.* 4th ed. Oxford: Mowbray, 1977.

Podmore, C. *Aspects of Anglican identity.* London: Church House Publishing, 2005.

Quantin, J. L. *The Church of England and Christian antiquity: the construction of a confessional identity in the seventeenth century.* Oxford: OUP, 2009.

The Articles

I.   *Of Faith in the Holy Trinity*

There is but one living and true God, everlasting,
without body, parts or passions;
of infinite power, wisdom and goodness;
the maker and preserver of all things both visible and invisible.
And in unity of this Godhead there be three persons,
of one substance, power and eternity,
the Father, the Son and the Holy Ghost.

This article (arranged here in clauses in order to bring out its underlying structure) is taken almost word for word from the first article of the Augsburg Confession. The only significant difference is the addition of the word 'passions', which is something of a puzzle. The Lutherans agreed that God is impassible, and so its presence here cannot be interpreted as a distinctively 'Anglican' addition. It is probably due to nothing more than a rhetorical sense of the desirability of expressing things in threes, which the Augsburg Confession achieved by appending 'body' and 'parts' to 'everlasting'. Cranmer rearranged the sentence and put 'everlasting' with what went before, rather than with what came afterwards, and therefore he needed a third element to round off the other two. 'Passions' was a logical choice, and that probably explains why it occurs where it does.

Otherwise, it must be said that the Augsburg article is much longer than this one, with a preamble stating that it is taking its doctrine from the Nicene Creed and an additional paragraph denouncing the heretics of the early church by name, including even Muslims among them. In contrast to that, the Anglican article omits any reference to the ancient heresies and says nothing about the Nicene Creed either, perhaps because the only line which undoubtedly comes from it is the one that describes God as the maker 'of all things visible and invisible'. The Latin text makes it clear that 'maker' is to be understood as 'creator', the difference being that God has created everything out of nothing, not made it out of some pre-existing matter. The Creed also stresses that God has created invisible things like angels and demons, who tend to be overlooked in most accounts of creation, including the one found in Genesis 1. In the Nicene Creed this statement is made about the Father only, and not about the Godhead as a whole, so Luther was extending the creedal statement to include both the Son and the Holy Spirit in the term 'Creator'. This is fully in line with ancient theology, but it was not so expressed in the Creed, which may be another reason why Cranmer omitted any reference to it.

In some respects, the language used in this article is more reminiscent of the so-called Athanasian Creed (also known as the *Quicunque vult,* from its opening words in Latin) which uses the triadic pattern to describe both the oneness and the threeness of God, than it is to the Nicene Creed, but the attributes chosen for inclusion here are different. It should be said that in most triadic formulas, the first element is the key one and the others are to be understood in relation to it. This is true of the Trinity, for example, because the Father is not derived from the other persons, whereas the Son and the Holy Spirit are both portrayed as deriving from him in some way – the Son by generation and the Holy Spirit by procession.

Luther apparently thought that God's eternity was his most important characteristic, and regarded his incorporeality and indivisibility as somehow implied in his eternity. The Anglican article treats his eternity as a separate concept and describes his divine being as incorporeal, indivisible and impassible, regarding the last two of these as consequent on the first. This makes good sense in purely logical terms. A body obviously has parts that can be cut off and presumably it can also suffer harm in different ways, but neither of these things is true of God and so in saying that he has no body, it is logical to add that he has no parts or passions either.

In modern times, the notion of divine impassibility has come under attack by those who claim that God must be able to 'feel our pain', to suffer alongside us. Anything less than that, this argument goes, makes him a cold and remote deity, and not the loving Saviour revealed to us in Scripture. There are two things wrong with this assumption. First of all, 'impassibility' was never intended to make God remote from human concerns but rather to insist that his power and sovereignty can in no way be diminished by a suffering inflicted from outside himself. It is there to remind us that he cannot be weakened by any disability which might call into question his power to save us, nor can he be deflected from his purposes by knee-jerk emotional reactions. The other thing wrong with this point of view is that it assumes that a Saviour must share the suffering of the person he is trying to save, which is false. A doctor does not have to have his patient's illness in order to cure him, nor would it be very helpful if someone intending to rescue a person who has fallen down a hole were to jump into it in order to demonstrate his solidarity with the victim. God in his love for us alleviates our suffering, overcomes it and will eventually eliminate it. He cares for our pain without having to endure it himself, which is what makes him our Saviour and not just a fellow sufferer.

It is true, of course, that the Son of God came into the world to suffer and die for us. Suffering and death were experiences which he assumed voluntarily, out of love for us and a desire to put us back in the right relationship with God. It was precisely because he could not do this in his divine nature alone that he assumed a human nature which was capable of experiencing our pain and death. As Christians we believe that the divine person of the Son of God suffered and died in his human nature, and in that sense we can say that 'God suffered and died on the cross.' That it was not his divine nature that suffered is plain from the fact that his divinity is shared with the Father and the Holy Spirit, neither of whom suffered and died for our sins, although both of them were present with the Son in his unique suffering and death. The doctrine of impassibility is not meant to obscure or diminish God's compassion for us, but to safeguard his ability to bring victory out of suffering and new life out of death.

The second triad speaks of God's infinite power, wisdom and goodness. The first element stresses his sovereignty over all things, including sin, death and hell. It is impossible to escape from the controlling hand of God, however hard we may try to do so. As the Psalmist put it: 'Where shall I go from your Spirit? Or where shall I flee from your presence?' (Psalm 139:7). God is everywhere and nothing in the universe can resist him. Even the forces of evil are able to act as they do only because he allows them to do so – for a time and within limits. It is said that all power corrupts, and that absolute power corrupts absolutely, so it is important to understand that God's infinite power is exercised in both wisdom and goodness. Wisdom is a quality of the mind, the knowledge of how to use the resources at one's disposal. Goodness is a moral virtue, seeking to ensure that power is used for the right purpose. As our sovereign Lord, God is both wise and good, pondering carefully what is right and using his power to achieve it.

God is not merely the creator of all things; he is also their preserver. This is an important principle, because it avoids the danger of what is now called 'deism'. Deism is the belief that God set the world running according to its own inner laws and then abandoned it to its own devices. In such a world, prayer is meaningless, because the mechanics of creation cannot be interfered with. The best we can hope to achieve is to understand what those mechanics are and act accordingly, so as to avoid the fate of those who ignore or defy the natural law. We believe that God controls the universe according to a pattern which we call the law of nature, but we also maintain that he is sovereign over it and can overrule it if he wishes to. God's purpose is to preserve his creation in being and so he is actively present and involved in everything that happens in and to it, not a remote deity who does not care about it one way or the other.

There is only one living and true God, but within the divine unity there are three persons, the Father, the Son and the Holy Spirit. They are all equal because they all share in the substance, power and eternity of the one God. The key term here is 'substance', which translates the Greek word *ousia*, or being of God. God reveals himself as the great I AM, the ultimate and absolute Being. The use of the word 'substance' for this is perhaps somewhat unfortunate – 'essence' or 'being' would be more accurate – but the meaning is clear. The being of God is an active power and it will not fade away at some point in the future. God can act anywhere at any time because his substance permits him to do this. Furthermore, each of the persons of the Trinity is equally capable of acting in this way, which is the ultimate proof that all three of them are God. When they do so however, they necessarily act together with the others because there is only one God, so it is not possible to experience one of them apart from the others. As Jesus said: 'He who has seen me has seen the Father' (John 14:9) and 'I and the Father are one' (John 10:30).

Questions for discussion:

1. What are the most important attributes, or characteristics, of God?

2. How can the Son and the Holy Spirit be equal to the Father but different from him?

3. Can God suffer, and if so, in what sense?

Key Bible Passages:

Genesis 1; Psalm 19; Isaiah 40:28-31; Isaiah 45:5-23; John 10:30-33; John 14.

For further reading:

There is a vast literature on the Christian doctrine of God and on the Trinity in particular. Good introductions to the subject are:

Bray, G. L. *The Doctrine of God.* Leicester: IVP, 1993.
Letham, R. *The Holy Trinity.* Phillipsburg: Presbyterian and Reformed, 2004.

Of special interest for the question of the suffering of God is:

Weinandy, T., *Does God suffer?* Edinburgh: T. and T. Clark, 2000.

2. *Of the Word or Son of God, which was made Very Man*

The Son, which is the Word of the Father, begotten from everlasting of the Father, the very and eternal God, and of one substance with the Father, took man's nature in the womb of the Blessed Virgin, of her substance: so that two whole and perfect natures, that is to say the Godhead and manhood, were joined together in one Person, never to be divided, whereof is one Christ, very God and very Man, who truly suffered, was crucified, dead and buried, to reconcile his Father to us and to be a sacrifice, not only for original guilt but also for all actual sins of men.

Like the first article, this one is also taken more or less word for word from the Augsburg Confession (article 3) and is much more obviously derived from the Nicene Creed, though with touches of the Chalcedonian definition of the person and natures of Christ and also of the Apostles' Creed. Only the last line, mentioning the sacrifice for human sins and guilt, goes beyond the creedal statements, though not beyond what they imply and certainly not beyond the teaching of the New Testament.

The name 'Son' is meant to underline the identity of nature between him and God the Father, because just as a human son is a man in exactly the same way as his father is, so the divine Son is God in exactly the same way as his Father. The Son of God is called the Word, a somewhat inadequate translation of the Greek *Logos*, which is found in John 1:1-14. The normal Greek translation of 'word' is *lexis* (a lexicon being a dictionary, or list of words), but *logos* implies speech and reason, as is implied in the term 'logic'. It might be better to say that the Son is the revealed plan and purpose of God, the one through whom we come to understand who God is and what he has done for us. The fact that his connection with God is not an abstraction (as 'Plan of the Mind' would be) but a relationship that has affinities with human relationships makes it possible for us to understand that our God is a God of love who wants to share his inner relationships with us by reconciling us to himself.

The first of those inner relationships is described by using the term 'generation' – the Son is 'begotten' of the Father. This language is Biblical (John 1:14) but it caused confusion in the early church because it was taken literally. As a result, many people came to believe that there had been a time when the Father was alone, before the birth of the Son which came to be regarded as the first act of God's creation. Of course, these people believed that the Son was a *divine* creature, but that was a contradiction in terms, because something that is divine cannot have been created. In 318 a preacher in Alexandria called Arius was accused of teaching that the Son was a creature born in time, and the ensuing controversy led to the summoning of the first council of Nicaea in 325. That council decreed that the Son was 'eternally begotten of the Father', a verbal paradox which underlines the fact that the relationships between the persons of the Trinity, although they are described in human terms, cannot be understood in that way. We have to transpose our language from the world of time and space to the world of eternity, a process which is known in theology as 'analogy'. The Father-Son language describes a relationship which is best understood in the context of Jewish law. The terms 'only-begotten' (John 1:14) and 'first-born' (Colossians 2:9) which are used of the Son in the New Testament, mean that he is the heir of all things, the Father's co-creator and now co-ruler with him of the universe. As the second person of the Trinity he has always been there, and did not emerge from the Father at some point in time. We are not told how he came to be related to the first person of the Trinity in a way that can be described in terms of Father and Son, but we must assume that it was a voluntary decision on their part and not something imposed on them by unavoidable circumstances.

In order for us to be able to share in this divine relationship, the Son must first become a man. This he did by entering the womb of the Virgin Mary and taking on her human nature without losing his divinity. How the humanity and the divinity of Jesus Christ interacted with each other was the subject of a long debate that was not resolved until the council of Chalcedon in 451 (and even then, there was considerable dissent from the final declaration.) On the one side were the Alexandrians, who stressed the fact that as a human being Jesus Christ was still very much the Son of God and those who met him on earth met God and not just a man. Their most articulate spokesman was Cyril of Alexandria (d. 444), who defined the incarnation as making two natures one in Christ. For that reason, Cyril's followers are often known as Monophysites, proponents of the view that Christ had only one nature *after* his incarnation. In reaction to this, theologians in Antioch stressed that Jesus was fully human, since otherwise he would not have been fit to take our place on the cross and die for our sins. The chief proponent of this view was Theodore of Mopsuestia (d. 428), but it has come to be associated more with Nestorius (c. 381–451) who became

Cyril's great adversary and whose theology was condemned at the council of Ephesus in 431. Both sides in the argument believed that the doctrine of salvation was at stake, and feared that any concession to the other point of view would compromise this. The Monophysites and the Nestorians were both so locked into their respective positions that neither of them could accept the solution proposed at Chalcedon, but the rest of the church has done so and modern ecumenical discussions have made it clear that Monophysite and Nestorian objections are more formal than substantial.

What Chalcedon did was to give priority to the notion of the person. Instead of thinking of a person as the manifestation of an underlying nature or substance, it saw things the other way round. A person, in Chalcedonian theology, is a concrete reality in possession of a nature or substance, but not necessarily defined or limited by it. It was therefore possible for the Son of God to add a second nature to his divine person without compromising his divinity. Each nature functions within its own parameters and neither is directly affected by the other, but the one person of the Son has full control at all times over both and can use them separately or together as he sees fit. In order to suffer and die for us, he had to acquire a nature that was capable of suffering and dying because he could not do either of those things in his divinity. On the cross in other words, the divine person of the Son of God suffered and died in his human nature.

For those who find it difficult to see how a person can be so distinct from a nature or substance, it may be helpful to reflect that as human beings we are also called to pass from one nature to another. Our flesh and blood will die because it cannot inherit the kingdom of God, but we shall be raised from the dead with a new nature that will be ours in eternity (1 Corinthians 15:50). However, we shall still be the same persons that we are now, since otherwise salvation would have no meaning. The parallel between our resurrected state and the incarnation of the Son is not exact of course and must not be pushed too far, but at least it shows that it is possible to think of the same person having two different natures.

Curiously, article 2 does not say that the incarnate Christ was sinless, although this is clearly implied in what follows. It is important, not only because Christ had to be the spotless Lamb of God in order to be acceptable to the Father as the sacrifice made for us on the cross, but also because it reminds us that sin is not inherent in human nature. Our first parents were created good, that is to say, without sin, and the sinfulness that we have inherited from their disobedience is a corruption of our humanity, not an integral part of it. Great harm has been done by the misuse of the term 'nature', which can be traced back at least to the fourteenth century and which is enshrined in the classical translation of 1 Corinthians 2:14: 'The natural man knoweth not the things of the Spirit of God', which the English Standard Version renders as: 'The natural person does not accept the things of the Spirit of God', which is even worse! After all, Jesus was both a natural man and a natural person, but this statement clearly does not apply to him. The Greek words that lie behind these translations are perfectly clear and unambiguous – they are *psychikos anthropos* and the meaning is that human beings who are untouched by God's Spirit do not understand him. The trouble is that we have no word to translate *psychikos* accurately. We cannot say 'psychic' because this implies some kind of crystal-ball gazing or the like, nor can we easily use the Latin equivalent, which is 'animal'. 'Soulish' might be possible but it does not exist in normal English, and so the translators fall back on 'natural', oblivious to the fact that the Greek word for that (*physikos*) does not imply a sinful or unregenerate state any more that 'physical' does in English. If an ancient Christian writer wanted to use the concept of nature in this context, he would have described the *psychikos anthropos* as the 'unnatural man', not as the natural one. As for the term 'person' it has a theological meaning that is not conveyed by *anthropos* and should at all costs be avoided when 'human being' is what is meant.

The expression 'reconcile his Father to us' is interesting because today we would most likely put it the other way round and say 'reconcile us to the Father'. The difference is a subtle one, but the article's version is a reminder that God has rejected us because his holiness cannot bear to live with our sin. By dying on the cross, the Son paid the price for our sinfulness. By making a satisfactory atonement for our disobedience he removed the Father's anger and made it possible for him to accept us back into his fellowship. In dying for us, Christ atoned not only for the original sin of mankind in Adam, but also for every sin committed by Adam's descendants ever since. In other words, both the root cause of our separation from God and all its after-effects have been dealt with on the cross, so that it is not now possible to sin in a way that cannot be forgiven by the shed blood of Christ.

It should also be said that the article speaks of Christ's paying the price for *sins* rather than of his taking the place of *sinners*. This is an important distinction, because while Christ's death is sufficient to atone for every sin, it does not mean that every human being is therefore forgiven and saved. Neither forgiveness nor salvation would be possible without the atoning sacrifice, but the sacrifice is no guarantee that everybody will be forgiven or saved. There have always been many people who have rejected Christ (or at least failed to accept him) and it is hardly surprising that people want to know why this is so. Do we have the freedom to choose or to refuse the offer of salvation, or has God decreed from the start that it will only be given to those whom he has chosen – to his elect? The first option is desirable but it compromises the sovereignty of God by giving human beings a veto over it as far as they are concerned. The second option is the only one consonant with God's majesty and power and it is the one found throughout the Bible, where salvation is of the Jews, who are presented as God's chosen people. Hard as it is for human pride to accept, it is God's prerogative to grant salvation to those whom he wants to save and to withhold it from everyone else. We cannot fathom the logic behind his choice, which often seems strange to us (1 Corinthians 1:26-29) but the fault lies in our limited understanding, not in the sovereign will of God (Romans 9:19-29).

Questions for discussion:

1. Did Jesus have a human will and a human mind in addition to his divine ones?

2. Why were people healed when they touched Jesus, or even just his clothing?

3. Did Jesus die for every sin ever committed by anybody?

Key Bible Passages:

John 1:1-14; John 3:14-21; Romans 3:20-30; Philippians 2:5-11; Colossians 1:15-20.

For further reading:

Letham, Robert. *The work of Christ.* Leicester: IVP, 1993.
Macleod, Donald. *The person of Christ.* Leicester: IVP, 1998.

3.   Of the going down of Christ into Hell

As Christ died for us and was buried, so also it is to be believed that he went down into hell.

The text of this article is clearly taken from the ancient creeds, with no significant alteration. In its original form, it contained an additional sentence which said that Christ's body lay in the tomb for three days but that his Spirit went to preach to the spirits in prison, or in hell, as I Peter 3:18 says. All reference to that was dropped in 1563, for reasons which are unclear but may have had something to do with the extensive treatment of this doctrine by John Calvin in his *Institutes* (II, 16.8-12). Calvin did not rely on the Petrine text but preferred to base his exposition on Ephesians 4:9, which situates the incident in the broader context of salvation history.

The descent into hell is one of the least understood aspects of Christ's earthly life, and the paucity of Biblical references to it has brought it under suspicion in many quarters. Modern commentators tend to focus on the idea of 'hell' which they are determined to make as innocuous as possible by saying that it means no more than 'the place of the dead' or by substituting words like Hades and Sheol for it, which are misleading and meaningless to most people, but do not excite the negative emotions often provoked by the mention of 'hell'.

Despite its obscurity, the descent of Christ into hell has always been part of the Gospel proclamation. There are two main reasons for this. On the one hand, it was necessary for Christ to suffer the full extent of human punishment for sin, which he would not have done if he had not gone to the place of eternal punishment. On the other hand, it was also necessary for him to do battle with Satan on his own turf. The power of evil would not have been overthrown, or even seriously challenged, had he not taken the fight into the heart of the enemy camp and (as Ephesians 4:8 puts it) 'led captivity captive'.

In medieval times it was common to believe that Christ had descended to hell in order to preach the Gospel to those who had died before his coming and to set them free. This was known as 'the harrowing of hell' and there are many paintings which show the Saviour leading Adam and Eve by the hand as he comes back from the dead. Whether there is any truth in this is hard to tell, because even I Peter 3:18 says only that he *preached* to the souls in prison, not that they responded and were delivered. That may have been the experience of some, but we have no reason to suppose that it was universal and should not make such a claim without any evidence to support it.

The precise nature of hell is another difficult subject. Obviously nobody likes to talk much about it and we cannot rejoice at the thought of millions of souls suffering in eternal torment. But the unpleasantness which surrounds hell does not mean that it has no foundation in fact, and we must not be misled by a false desire to make it sound less awful than it really is. At one level, hell is clearly a place of the dead, but not all the dead go there. This is plain from the New Testament, where Jesus tells the thief on the cross that he would be with him in paradise that same day (Luke 23:43). The Apostle Paul also wrote to the Philippians that for him, to die was to go to be with Christ, which would seem to exclude any thought of an intermediate state in some 'place of the dead' (Philippians 1:20-23). On the other hand, we are told in the New Testament that there will be a general resurrection at the end of time (1 Corinthians 3:11-15) and that those who have died will rise first (1 Thessalonians 4:14-17). The key to reconciling these statements appears to be that the former relate to the transition from time to eternity that we experience when we die, whereas the latter refer to the end of time which will occur at some point in the future after many Christians have died. From the perspective of those still alive at that time, there will be a resurrection of those who have 'fallen asleep in Christ' as Paul says, but this does not mean that we shall experience centuries of being frozen in some kind of limbo (or purgatory!) before we get a chance to be with Christ in eternity.

Most of what we are told about hell is in the New Testament, and most of that comes from the lips of Jesus himself. There can be no doubt that Jesus issued dire warnings against the danger of being eternally separated from God, and he was not afraid to invoke images of torment to describe this. Whether these images are figurative or literal does not really matter, because the true horror is to be cut off from the Lord for ever. The notion of eternal torment faces the objection that God would not inflict needless punishment on people. From this perspective, the lost either live in a kind of semi-conscious limbo where they feel little or nothing, or else they are eventually wiped out so as not to have to suffer any longer – a kind of euthanasia beyond the grave.

The difficulty with annihilationism, as this interpretation is called, is that it is based on sentiment rather than on evidence. God hates nothing that he has made, and there is no reason to suppose that the rebellious spirits in hell will be annihilated any more than Satan and his fellow demons have been. If the devils believe and tremble (James 2:19), it is entirely possible that the lost will do the same, as the story of the rich man and Lazarus seems to imply (Luke 16:19-31). The torments of hell, whatever they are, may be self-inflicted, as some Eastern mystical theologians have suggested. After all, if a rebellious spirit wants to get as far away from God as possible and God holds him back from achieving that desire, the spirit in question will probably feel such restraint as torture, when in fact it is the love of God that is preventing his final destruction. That understanding is just as speculative as any other, of course, but at least it shows that it is possible to reconcile the notion of eternal punishment with belief in a loving God. It is not necessary to embrace a doctrine of annihilationism in order to counter the objection that eternal punishment is pointless cruelty and incompatible with the love of God, and the weight of the Biblical evidence (such as it is) would seem to argue against it.

We must not try to push people into the Kingdom of Heaven by threatening them with the alternative of eternal torment, because to think like that is to falsify the Gospel of God's love, but at the same time neither must we underrate the seriousness of rejecting God or make light of the consequences that follow from that. Unbelievers are unlikely to be too worried by something they do not believe in, but believers can easily be lulled into a sense that preaching the Gospel is not the most urgent priority, because the ultimate fate of those who fail to respond to it will not be as bad as it sounds. To put it another way, the horrors of hell ought to be an encouragement to believers to persist in the preaching of eternal salvation to those who are lost, because we do not want them to suffer the consequences of unbelief.

Questions for discussion:

1. In what sense is hell a place? What does it mean to 'go down' to it?

2. Does eternal punishment necessarily involve eternal torment?

3. Why do people today find it so hard to believe in the existence of hell?

Key Bible Passages:

Ephesians 4:8-10; 1 Peter 3:18.

For further reading:

Blanchard, J. *Whatever happened to hell?* London: Evangelical Press, 1993.

Fudge, E. *Two views of hell.* Downers Grove, Ill.: IVP, 2000.

Powys, D. J. *Hell. A hard look at a hard question.* Carlisle: Paternoster, 1998.

4.   *The Resurrection of Christ*

*Christ did truly rise again from death, and took again his body,
with flesh, bones and all things appertaining to the perfection of
man's nature, wherewith he ascended into heaven, and there
sitteth, until he return to judge all men at the last day.*

Like the previous articles, this one is no more than a paraphrase of the
ancient creeds and adds nothing to them, although it spells out in
greater detail what the resurrection body of Christ was like.

Christ came back from the dead with the same body in which he
was crucified, which is an important point. Salvation is not the casting
off of what we have in order to receive something entirely new and
different. Rather it is the transformation of our present reality into
something which stands in direct continuity with it but which is made
perfect by being cleansed of all sin. In this article, the word 'perfection'
does not refer to sinlessness because Jesus was sinless already. It refers
instead to the fullness of his human nature. There have always been
people who have been tempted to regard matter as evil or inferior to the
spiritual side of our being, and so have been inclined to view the
resurrection as an exclusively spiritual affair. But Christians believe in
the redemption of matter as well as of spirit, and the resurrection affects
the body as much as the soul.

The term 'resurrection of the body', which is common in
English, dates from 1542, when Cranmer used it to translate the Latin
resurrectio carnis, which means 'resurrection of the flesh'. Here we
have a rare instance in which the translation is actually better than the
original, and the wording of this article suggests that it may have been
done intentionally, because mention of the flesh is accompanied by
reference to the bones and everything belonging to the human body.
Whether that is so or not, it is clear that the Reformers understood that
salvation touches every aspect of our being, and that no part of us will
be ignored, detached or left behind in the resurrection.

The ascension of Christ into heaven is one of the most
important of the commonly neglected doctrines relating to his life,
death and resurrection. It is amply attested in the New Testament,
where it forms the link between his earthly ministry and his heavenly
one, and marks the transition from one to the other. The words of
Christ on the cross: 'It is finished' (John 19:30) are often misinterpreted.

They are used by many to emphasise that his atoning sacrifice is completed by his death, which is true, but they unfortunately leave the impression that his work is over at that point, when in fact his work has continued in another form. When he ascended into heaven and sat down at the right hand of the Father, he took his sacrifice with him. In his heavenly state he uses it to plead for us before the Father's throne, and it is on that basis that we gain admittance to the Father's presence. It is nonsensical to suggest that this sacrifice can be repeated or 're-presented' by some priest here on earth who is empowered to bring Christ's body back to us by the supposed miracle of transubstantiation. That view, which was strong in the middle ages and is still the official teaching of the Roman Catholic Church, was rejected by the Reformers, and Anglican liturgies of holy communion have usually taken great care to exclude any such idea. But the reason for this is not that his sacrifice was a past event with no relevance to us now. On the contrary, it is an event that happened once in time and space but that has now been taken into eternity, where we too are 'seated... in the heavenly places in Christ Jesus' (Ephesians 2:6). The ascension is the sign that we have moved into another dimension of being and that our life is now hidden with Christ in God (Colossians 3:3), making it safe from attack by hostile forces that might cause us to lose our salvation (Romans 8:34-39).

The heavenly session of Christ is also the beginning of his kingly rule, which will continue until he returns again at the end of time. This is essential for us to understand, because it is the age of salvation history in which we are living. The supreme manifestation of Christ's kingly rule is the sending of his Holy Spirit at Pentecost. It is the work of the Holy Spirit to confirm the teaching of Christ in our hearts, to make his atoning sacrifice a real and life-transforming experience for us, to build up a body of believers, to equip us for the tasks of spiritual warfare and ministry and to prepare us for the return of the Lord in due course. The Kingdom of Christ has many manifestations on earth, but it remains at heart a spiritual reality that cannot be tied down or manipulated by material means. In particular, we cannot say that the visible, institutional church is the repository of the Kingdom, not that it is necessarily extended by religious activities associated with it. The visible church is a sign and a vehicle of the Kingdom which God uses to proclaim and establish his rule on earth, but it is not that Kingdom itself and its ministers have no power to limit the grace of God or to prevent it from being given to those outside its fellowship if God chooses to do so.

At the end of time, Christ will return to judge the living and the dead. The dead will be raised up, regardless of whether they are saved or not, and they will be judged. Those who have been chosen for salvation will then claim their place in heaven and the others will be sent to hell (Daniel 12:2; Matthew 25:29-30). The judgement will be of our works, which cannot earn us salvation but which cannot participate in it either without being cleansed. This is why there will be some whose works will be destroyed but who will nevertheless be saved, because they have been chosen by Christ to reign with him in heaven. What they did on earth is of no value and will be discarded, and in varying degrees that will be true of us all. If we have done something valuable as Christians we can be sure that God will honour it, but we can also know that we shall not be burdened with our failures – they will be destroyed in the judgement and we shall be given a fresh start in heaven.

How this picture of the end of time can be reconciled with the immediate transition from this world to the next that believers experience when they die is a mystery. It can only be understood to some extent by remembering that we are talking about two different dimensions of reality. In eternity there is no time, so concepts of past, present and future are inapplicable. In time and space however, these things take on meaning, and of course the 'end of time' is essentially a temporal concept. It may help to remember that, strictly speaking, there is no 'present' in time, even though we all think there is and use this notion as a way of dividing the past from the future. The temporal present is in fact a sign of eternity in our midst, as can be seen from the way God uses it to describe himself – I AM, not 'I was' or 'I shall be'. By thinking (as we invariably do) in the 'present' we are in fact bearing witness to the existence of a non-temporal reality, and it is in that reality that we find God – *today* is the day of salvation! (2 Corinthians 6:2).

Questions for discussion:

1. In what ways was the resurrection of Jesus like and unlike the general resurrection of all people at the end of time?

2. Can somebody who rejects the bodily resurrection of Christ be a Christian?

3. What is the significance of the ascension of Christ?

Key Bible Passages:

Matthew 28:1-17; Luke 24; John 20-21; 1 Corinthians 15:12-28.

For further reading:

Beasley-Murray, P. *The message of the resurrection.* Leicester: IVP, 2000.
Swinburne, Richard. *The resurrection of God incarnate.* Oxford: Clarendon, 2003.
Wright, N. Thomas. *The resurrection of the Son of God.* London: SPCK, 2003.

5. Of the Holy Ghost

The Holy Ghost, proceeding from the Father and the Son, is of one substance, majesty and glory with the Father and the Son, very and eternal God.

The article is taken from the Athanasian Creed and its triadic formula of substance, majesty and glory, reflects that origin. It was not in the 1553 version of the articles but was added in 1563, probably because it was felt that something needed to be said about the Holy Spirit in order to reflect the Trinitarian pattern of the creeds more exactly. Even so, it is noticeable that the doctrine is not developed at all, being less comprehensive even than the creeds themselves.

Modern English usage prefers the Latinate word 'Spirit' to the Germanic 'Ghost', presumably because a 'ghost' is usually thought of as a phantom and is therefore both spooky and unreal. However, it must be remembered that the word 'spirit' can also be used in that way and can even be extended to refer to alcohol, which is not true of 'ghost'! The modern preference for 'spirit' cannot be denied, but in purely linguistic terms it makes little sense.

The Holy Spirit is fully God in his substance, sharing the majesty and glory of the other two persons of the Trinity. In the Athanasian Creed, the majesty refers primarily to the divine lordship and the glory to the divine being, but the two terms overlap to such an extent that they are virtually synonymous expressions of the infinite power and sovereignty of God.

The real theological issue here is contained in the first part of the article, which expounds the so-called 'double procession' of the Holy Spirit, from the Father and from the Son. This doctrine is not found in the original version of the Nicene Creed, which mentions only that the Spirit proceeds from the Father (John 15:26), but the expression 'and from the Son', or in Latin, *Filioque*, was added in Spain, sometime in the sixth century. It has been traditionally thought that this occurred at the third council of Toledo in 589, when the ruling Visigoths of Spain abandoned their Arianism for orthodox Christianity, but this is not certain. However, it has sometimes been claimed that the addition was anti-Arian in intention, because there were apparently people who were arguing that the procession of the Spirit from the Father and not from the Son was evidence that the Father was God in a way that the Son was not.

Be that as it may, the addition to the creed was accepted by Charlemagne and included in the liturgy as celebrated in his empire, although Rome refused to recognise it until the early eleventh century. The Eastern churches have never accepted it and by the time it reached Rome they had begun to oppose it on theological grounds. The argument put forward by Photius, who was twice patriarch of Constantinople (858–867 and again 878–886), was that the Holy Spirit proceeds from the Father *alone*, because the Father is the 'fount of deity' from which the other persons of the Trinity derive their divinity. In saying this, Photius was putting his own gloss on the Nicene Creed of course, which had no more authorisation than the *Filioque* clause had, although it could claim support from respected theologians like Maximus the Confessor (d. 662) and John of Damascus (d. 749). The difference of opinion did not provoke any lasting schism between the Eastern and Western churches at that stage, but when political and other considerations came into the matter in the eleventh century, disagreement over the *Filioque* was recognised as a stumbling-block to church unity.

By that time, the doctrine had found an able defender in the West, in the person of Anselm of Canterbury (1033–1109), who lectured on it during his exile in Bari in 1098. Anselm knew of course that the doctrine had been developed long before, by Augustine of Hippo (354–430) in his great book on the Trinity (*De Trinitate*), though there is some evidence that it was already being taught before his time. As Augustine saw it, God is a Trinity of love, in which the Father is the one who loves, the Son is the beloved and the Holy Spirit is the bond of love which unites them. For this love to be perfect it must be equal to the Father and the Son, since otherwise the Father's love for the Son would be unrequited. This means that the Spirit who proceeds from the Father as his love for the Son must also proceed from the Son in his responsive love for the Father. This idea caught on in the Western church and found creedal expression as early as the sixth century, in the so-called Athanasian Creed, which was almost certainly composed without pressure from the Arians or in contrast to the theology of the Eastern churches, which was not yet fully articulated on this point.

What we are faced with here is not a controversy so much as two different models of the Trinity which are incompatible on this point. The Eastern model logically excludes the double procession because of its view of the Father as the only source of divinity, whereas the Western one requires it to balance the love of the Father and the Son for each other. Centuries of discussion and argument, some of it very acrimonious, have failed to find a mutually acceptable form of words, and it remains a major difficulty in ecumenical relations today. As far as the Western church was concerned however, the problem was resolved at the council of Florence in 1439, which declared that the Holy Spirit proceeds from the Father *through* the Son, a formula that allows for the primacy of the Father without abandoning the double procession. On that understanding, the papacy stopped trying to force the Eastern churches to include the *Filioque* in their version of the Nicene Creed, and in return the Eastern churches were expected to drop their insistence on the single procession of the Spirit from the Father to the exclusion of the Son. Unfortunately, passions were so high by then that this rather sensible compromise was rejected by the Eastern churches, and there the situation has remained.

The Anglican church is part of Western Christendom and therefore it accepts the double procession as enunciated at Florence in 1439. The theologians who included this article were not trying to prolong or reignite a quarrel with the Eastern churches, with whom they had no direct contact, so it should not be read as a statement designed primarily in opposition to them. It must also be remembered that the Eastern churches agree that the Holy Spirit is the Spirit of the Son (Galatians 4:6) and that he acts as the Son's envoy in his temporal mission on earth. The difference has to do with the origin of the Spirit's divinity, and only secondarily does it touch on the question of his relationship to the Son. It might be helpful to say that the Western church understands the relationship of the Son to the Holy Spirit as belonging to his divine nature – as God, he is the source of the Spirit just as much as the Father is, whereas the Eastern church tends to think that the Son's possession of the Holy Spirit is an act of the Father's grace. Though they have never defined their position, they tend to say that the Spirit proceeds from the Father and rests on the Son, rather in the way he does in the story of the baptism of Jesus, where the Trinity is first revealed (Matthew 3:16-17).

In recent years Anglicans have been tempted to delete the *Filioque* from the Nicene Creed as a gesture of ecumenical reconciliation, but although that is occasionally done, removing it completely has proved to be more difficult than it originally seemed. The main reason for this is the growth of the charismatic movement, some of whose spokesmen can speak about the work of the Holy Spirit in a way which says little about the Son and seems to be disconnected from his work. A doctrine which suggests that it might be possible to go to the Father in the Spirit without reference to the Son must therefore be resisted, because it removes the cross and the atoning work of Christ from the central experience of the believer. It is also the case that the doctrine of the work of the Holy Spirit has been elaborated in Western Christianity to such an extent since the Reformation that it is now virtually impossible to remove such a key idea from it. The work of the Spirit has always been seen as consequent on the work of the Son and closely tied to his relationship with the Father. Even if the Eastern churches do not disagree with that, their own theology has developed in a rather different direction, which must be recognised. Perhaps one day it will be possible to reconcile the two ancient traditions, and if so, the common formula will probably look very similar to the one adopted at Florence in 1439. But that has not happened yet, nor is it likely to in the foreseeable future. For the time being we must live with our different approaches to the mystery of the Holy Trinity and learn from them that our attempts to understand God will always fall short of the reality we seek to confess.

Questions for discussion:

1. What difference does it make to believe that the Holy Spirit proceeds from the Son as well as from the Father?

2. Does the Holy Spirit have a personal name of his own?

3. How important is the Holy Spirit in the experience of the believer?

Key Bible Passages:

John 14:16-26; John 15:26: John 16:7-14; Romans 8:1-16; Galatians 4:6.

For further reading:

Ferguson, Sinclair. *The Holy Spirit.* Leicester: IVP, 1996.
Jackman, D. *Spirit of truth.* Fearn: Christian Focus, 2006.
Vischer, L., ed. *Spirit of God, Spirit of Christ. Ecumenical reflections on the filioque controversy.* London: SPCK, 1981.

6. Of the Sufficiency of the Holy Scriptures for Salvation

Holy Scripture containeth all things necessary to salvation: so that whatsoever is not read therein, nor may be proved thereby, is not to be required of any man, that it should be believed as an article of the faith, or be thought requisite or necessary to salvation.

In the name of the Holy Scripture we do understand those canonical books of the Old and New Testament, of whose authority was never any doubt in the Church.

Of the names and number of the Canonical Books

Genesis
Exodus
Leviticus
Numbers
Deuteronomy
Joshua
Judges
Ruth
The first book of Samuel
The second book of Samuel
The first book of Kings
The second book of Kings
The first book of Chronicles
The second book of Chronicles
The first book of Esdras [Ezra]
The second book of Esdras [Nehemiah]
Esther
Job
Psalms
Proverbs
Ecclesiastes
Song of Solomon
4 Prophets the greater
12 Prophets the less

And the other books as Hierome [Jerome] saith, the Church doth read for example of life and instruction of manners, but yet doth it not apply them to establish any doctrine. Such are these following:

The third [first] book of Esdras
The fourth [second] book of Esdras
Tobias [Tobit]
Judith
The rest of the book of Esther
Wisdom
Jesus the son of Sirach [Ecclesiasticus]
Baruch
Song of the Three Children
Susanna
Bel and the Dragon
Prayer of Manasses
The first book of Maccabees
The second book of Maccabees

All the books of the New Testament, as they are commonly received, we do receive and account them canonical.

With this article we come at last to the theological issues that divided the church at the Reformation. Chief among these was the status and content of Holy Scripture, which was especially important because the Reformers made it the sole basis of their official doctrine. This belief, often known by the Latin words *sola Scriptura*, goes back at least as far as John Wycliffe (1328–1384), who argued that whatever could not be proved from the Bible (like transubstantiation or papal authority) should not be part of the church's official teaching.

Cranmer's approach to this was to start by saying that everything required for salvation was contained in the canonical Scriptures. He then went on to say that for that reason, nothing above and beyond them was to be demanded of anyone as an essential belief. This was a clear attack on the Roman doctrine of tradition, which the papacy believed could be used to supplement the teaching of Scripture when required. On that basis, a number of beliefs had crept into the church and become part of its official teaching, even though they had no basis in the Bible – purgatory and transubstantiation being obvious examples. More recently, the Roman church has added such things as papal infallibility (1870), the immaculate conception of Mary (1854) and her bodily assumption into heaven (1950), none of which has any solid basis in Scripture and some of which, like the immaculate conception of Mary, were actually denied by revered doctors of the church like Thomas Aquinas. Sometimes a particular belief or practice will be justified by an appeal to one of the apocryphal books, as happens with prayers for the dead, which is apparently based on 2 Maccabees 12.

Needless to say, Anglicans cannot accept such 'evidence' and so prayers for the dead have no legitimate place in our doctrine or worship.

Wycliffe also objected to the fact that the Bible was available only in Latin and he wanted it translated into the vernacular so that ordinary people could read and understand it. Whether he ever did that himself is uncertain, but his followers certainly produced two different versions in English, which are now given the name 'Wycliffite' or 'Lollard', after the name by which Wycliffe's disciples came to be known. Lollard Bibles circulated in England from the late fourteenth century until the Reformation, but only in manuscript. (The first printed edition did not appear until 1850, by which time it was of interest only to scholars and antiquarians.)

Lollardy was thought to be so dangerous that in 1407 the church made translating the Bible a heresy punishable by death, which is why William Tyndale was forced to flee the country in 1523 after he had proposed to do just that. The irony of course is that the Latin Bible was itself a translation, and the ban imposed in England did not exist in other European countries, where vernacular Bibles began to appear in the fifteenth century. The invention of printing coincided with a revival of scholarship that reintroduced the Hebrew and Greek originals of the Scriptures into European intellectual life. By 1500 it was becoming impossible to claim to be a Biblical scholar without knowing those languages and inevitably it was not long before people noticed that the familiar Latin text differed from them in many places. The natural assumption made at the time was that the Latin, which had been translated by Jerome (340–420) in the late fourth century, was corrupt, but that is unfair. Jerome, whom the article refers to as 'Hierome' (his Latin name was Hieronymus) was a gifted linguist and a careful scholar who sought out the best readings he could find and even took the trouble to learn Hebrew so that he could translate the Old Testament from the original language. The discovery of more ancient Greek manuscripts than those which were available in the sixteenth century has often vindicated him against his Renaissance critics, but that could not be known at the time. Following Jerome's own principle of going to the originals, Erasmus (1466–1536) and the Reformers after him sought out whatever manuscripts they could find and translated from them.

The New Testament was originally written in Greek, even though it was not the mother tongue of most of its authors (and certainly not of Jesus, who quite possibly did not know it at all) which made things relatively straightforward. The Old Testament however, circulated in both Greek and Hebrew versions (with a few portions in

Aramaic) and there were considerable differences between them. The search for original texts naturally persuaded the Reformers that the Hebrew was superior to the Greek, and here they could rely on Jerome for support. The most widely circulated Greek version was the so-called Septuagint, translated in Alexandria in the third century BC, supposedly by seventy (or seventy-two) scholars who worked separately but miraculously came up with identical translations! That cannot be right of course, but it is possible that the text was produced by a group of about seventy scholars who divided up the Hebrew text among them. More problematic was the fact that the Septuagint also contained a number of books that were not extant in Hebrew or Aramaic and which were therefore not part of the Hebrew Bible. What should be done about them?

Modern scholarship has shown that this is a very complex question that cannot be answered by a simple appeal to the Hebrew originals alone. For a start, the Hebrew Bible as we now have it was edited by the so-called Massoretes, a group of Jewish scholars who lived several centuries after the time of Jesus and who edited the text available to them, among other things supplying the vowel points which were needed for non-Hebrew speakers to be able to read the language fluently. It was sometimes alleged that the Massoretes had doctored their text in an anti-Christian direction, for example, by replacing the word 'virgin' in Isaiah 7:14 with 'young woman' so as to counter Christian claims that this was a prophecy of the virgin birth of Christ. Nobody could say whether there was any truth in this sort of accusation, because no variant forms of the Hebrew text were available. The Septuagint, on the other hand, was a pre-Christian translation that did have 'virgin' in this verse, so there was at least a possibility that it represented the true original text. This kind of argument was used by Augustine, Jerome's contemporary, to advocate the use of the Septuagint and not of the Hebrew as the church's Old Testament. Augustine, who did not know Hebrew and whose Greek was poor, was also aware that the New Testament writers had often used the Septuagint when quoting the Old Testament, which led him and others to believe that it was a divinely-inspired translation. Even Jerome retained the names and order of the Septuagint books when he made his Latin translation from the Hebrew, and our modern Bibles reflect this.

The question of how the Hebrew and the Septuagint were related was further complicated by the issue of the canon. The canon, as we now understand it, is the list of books regarded by the Jews (and later by the church) as authoritative and divinely inspired. In Jerome's day and even in the sixteenth century, it was universally believed that the first five books of the Old Testament, known collectively as the Pentateuch or Torah (the Hebrew name for them), had been written by Moses after the people of Israel escaped from Egypt. That gave them an authority that no other texts could match, and it is clear from the way the New Testament uses the Hebrew Bible that the Torah was its most basic and most important component. Next in order came the Prophets, a category which included not only the prophets as we understand them, but also the so-called 'Deuteronomic history' from Joshua to 2 Kings (excluding Ruth). Some of these books were still being edited when the Septuagint was translated, as we can see from the different versions of Jeremiah, but in principle it was agreed that the prophetic writings ceased to appear after about 400 BC. Finally, there was a third group of books, known collectively as the Writings, which included a disparate array of texts, of which by far the best-known and most often used was the book of Psalms. Whether this part of the Hebrew Bible had been 'closed' in the time of Jesus is not entirely clear. Books like Esther and Daniel, for example, were apparently still growing in size until shortly before Jesus was born, because their Greek versions are considerably longer than their Hebrew ones. There were also a number of other books in this category which are found in the Septuagint but whose exact status among the Jews is uncertain. All we can say for sure is that they were never quoted in the New Testament, which is perhaps surprising if the early church was using the Septuagint as its Bible.

Jerome's insistence on using only books found in the Hebrew canon, which was certainly closed by his time, finds some interesting support in the writings of the church fathers. Though they sometimes quoted from the other books, they never wrote commentaries on them, which is very revealing. Commentaries were intended to be study guides for preachers and teachers, and the fact that only books in the Hebrew canon were commented on shows that they alone were in regular use in the church. The debate between Augustine and Jerome was evidently more theoretical than practical, since whatever the canonical status of the non-Hebrew books was, they were not much used in practice.

Modern readers are often surprised to discover that the early church never bothered to define its canon in any formal way. This has led some scholars to claim that there was no such thing as a canon in ancient times, but that is a misreading of the evidence. It is clear that there was a core of books in what we now call the New Testament that was recognised as authoritative by virtually all the churches, and the few that were doubted by some (like Hebrews and Revelation) were recognised by the great majority. Even without an official definition, there was no doubt after the fourth century at the latest, that the twenty-seven books we now recognise as canonical, and no others, constituted the New Testament. Doubts which persisted, and in some cases were raised once again in the sixteenth century (and of course, since then) have not succeeded in overturning this judgment, which the entire church now accepts. There is of course a rich literature of pseudepigraphal writings, which are attributed to various apostles and other important figures in the early church, but which have always been regarded as spurious by most people. Some of them are fairly innocuous, but others present Jesus and his companions in ways that seem to go against what the four canonical Gospels tell us. Unfortunately, these texts (among them the *Gospel of Thomas* and the *Gospel of Judas*) have been used by unscrupulous film-makers and novelists to create fantasies of an alternative Jesus, which have proved to be very popular with an uninformed public. How much real damage this kind of activity does is hard to tell, but it forces the church to re-emphasise the unique legitimacy of the New Testament canon as a true record of the life and teaching of the historical Jesus.

What is important to recognise is that it was usage, not any official statement, that determined what the canon of Scripture should be. All over the Christian world, people discovered that there were certain books that fed them spiritually, and these became the staples of their preaching and teaching. To some extent, the choice was related to authorship, so that a letter written by one of the apostles was more likely to be included in the canon than one that was not. But even that was not an infallible rule, since we know that there were letters of Paul that have disappeared and some New Testament books (notably Luke-Acts) were not written by apostles. Whether anyone ever preached from one of the apocryphal or deuterocanonical books is impossible to say, but if they did, it was not a common practice and has left no trace in the commentary tradition. On the other hand, some books that were regarded as dubious or that were not universally accepted (Esther, 2 Peter) eventually overcame all objections and were incorporated in the Bible in spite of opposition to them, because they were seen to be life-giving in the everyday experience of the people of God.

Amazingly enough, the first official list of the canonical books of Scripture was not made until the fourth session of the council of Trent (8 April 1546), centuries after they had come into general use in the life of the church. As one might expect, the council accepted the

Augustinian position and included the entire Septuagint in the canon, though it went on to say that the only official version permitted in the church was the Latin translation (known to us as the Vulgate) made by Jerome. This was an extraordinary decision by any standard, and even the Roman Catholic Church soon realised that a revision of the Vulgate was necessary, though it took a generation to produce one and it was so poor that it had to be done again. The decree did, however, force the hand of the Reformers, who had to declare their position on the matter. As a result, in 1563 Matthew Parker drew up the list we have here, the first catalogue of canonical books known to have been authorised by any Protestant church. It is identical with that found in most English Bibles today, although a few names have been changed (indicated in square brackets above).

When it came to the extra books found in the Septuagint, Parker was unwilling to reject them completely and he relegated them to secondary status, as the above list indicates. Today they are sometimes printed between the Old and New Testaments and are generally known as the Apocrypha ('hidden books') which is the wrong name for them, since they are not hidden at all! They are better referred to as the 'deuterocanonical books', which they sometimes are in official statements, even though 'deuterocanonical' can hardly be called a household word and for most people needs as much explaining as 'apocrypha'.

The discovery of the Dead Sea Scrolls at Qumran in 1947 made pre-Massoretic texts of the Hebrew Bible available for the first time, and these have shown that there was greater variety in the Hebrew of Jesus' day than had previously been realised. In some cases, the Septuagint readings have been vindicated as authentic, at least to some degree, and this has revived interest in the Greek text. The deuterocanonical books are also recognised as valuable sources for the development of Jewish theology in the inter-testamental period, but most modern scholars, including Roman Catholics, agree that they should not be put on the same level as the Hebrew Bible. Somewhat surprisingly perhaps, the position first enunciated by Archbishop Parker and contested at the time by both Catholics and more extreme Protestants, now seems to be closest to what most experts are prepared to accept, regardless of their formal denominational allegiance. The apocryphal books are still occasionally read in Anglican churches, but this practice is marginal and the books concerned cannot be used to establish the church's doctrine.

Article 6 does not say anything about the divine inspiration of

Scripture or how it is to be interpreted, but the Anglican view on these matters is contained in the homily on Scripture, which Cranmer also wrote. In that sermon he outlines a comprehensive doctrine of how it is to be understood and interpreted. For him, the key to right understanding is a pure and humble heart. Not everything in the Bible is easy to understand, but its essential teaching is plain enough and the hard parts must be interpreted in the light of the clearer ones, a principle which goes right back to the early church. He does not go into the details of textual criticism, a discipline which scarcely existed in his day, but it is clear from what he does say that its purpose can only be to illuminate the harder parts of the text and that it will not discover anything that contradicts what is already plain. Ultimately Cranmer believed, like the other reformers, that only a person who was in tune with the Spirit of God, who had inspired the text in the first place, would ever be able to understand it properly. Naive as that may sound, it is a valid principle that remains true today in spite of all our advances in technique and technology. True interpretation is a spiritual gift, and there is still nothing more effective than a humble and contrite heart, linked to a lively and inquisitive mind, for understanding and applying the Word of God in daily life.

Cranmer's views obviously implied the need for translating the Scriptures into the vernacular, an effort which he promoted and which had already borne considerable fruit when he wrote this article. Here however, we must distinguish between translations that were official and translations that were not. William Tyndale's version, completed after his death by Miles Coverdale, was very good and widely read, but it was never official, (although Cranmer was prepared to use Coverdale's psalms in his prayer books), and faded out of use. The first official text was the Great Bible of 1538, also called Cranmer's Bible because from the second edition onwards it contained a preface written by the archbishop. It was reissued in 1568, with minor alterations, as the Bishops' Bible, which remained the church's official text until it was replaced by the Authorised (King James) Version in 1611. By then, another very good and popular version, the Geneva Bible of 1560, had appeared and was being widely read, though it was never officially approved in England. (Scotland was a different matter; it was official there from 1572 onwards.) The co-existence of two different texts was regarded as harmful to the unity of the church, and in 1604 King James I agreed to set up a commission to prepare a new translation which eventually displaced both the Bishops' and the Geneva Bible to become the classic English-language version we know today.

Questions for discussion:

1. What authority should the Bible have in the life of the church?

2. In what sense can we say that God is the author of the Bible?

3. If somebody discovered a new letter written by one of the apostles, would we have to put it in the New Testament?

Key Bible Passages:

Luke 24:25-47; Acts 17:1-12; 2 Timothy 3:13-17; Hebrews 4:12; 2 Peter 1:21.

For further reading:

Beckwith, Roger. *The Old Testament canon of the New Testament church.* London: SPCK, 1985.

Jensen, Peter. *The revelation of God.* Leicester: IVP, 2002.

Metzger, Bruce. *The canon of the New Testament: Its origin, development and significance.* Oxford: Clarendon, 1987.

Ward, Timothy. *Words of life: Scripture as the living and active Word of God.* Nottingham, IVP, 2009.

7.   The Old Testament

The Old Testament is not contrary to the New, for both in the Old and New Testament everlasting life is offered to mankind by Christ, who is the only Mediator between God and man, being both God and man. Wherefore they are not to be heard, which feign that the old Fathers did look only for transitory promises.

Although the law given from God by Moses, as touching ceremonies and rites, do not bind Christian men, nor the civil precepts thereof ought of necessity to be received in any commonwealth; yet notwithstanding, no Christian man whatsoever is free from the obedience of the commandments which are called moral.

The first part of this article comes from Thomas Cranmer's version (1553) with some slight rewording, and the second is from the 1563 revision, which is basically the first paragraph of Cranmer's nineteenth article. That article was dropped in 1563, except for the first paragraph which replaced the original article on the Old Testament. In 1571 that original article was restored to become the first paragraph of the one we now have. It should be noted that this article has no immediate precedent in any other Reformation statement of faith, although something similar can be found in the Second Helvetic Confession of 1566 (chap. 13). This is rather surprising, given its importance amid the controversies which the use of the Old Testament was arousing at the time, but it is a reminder of how important the interpretation of the Bible was to the English reformers.

How the church should make use of the Hebrew Bible is a question around which the entire history of Christianity can be written. The New Testament is essentially a commentary on the Old, insisting that the promises of law and the prophets had been fulfilled in Jesus Christ. This claim made Christianity a different religion from Judaism, even though they both used the same Scriptures, and it obliged the church to adopt an interpretation of them which would justify the claims made for Christ. Broadly speaking, there were three approaches to this, each of which manifested itself at different times. The first was to reject the Old Testament as an outmoded text whose authority had ceased with the coming of the New. This position was advocated in the early church by Marcion (d. c. 144) and although it was quickly rejected, something not unlike it has reappeared in modern times. It is not uncommon nowadays to hear that the Old Testament speaks about a God of wrath, as opposed to the New, which supposedly reveals a God of love instead. The Old Testament is presented as ethnocentric and semi-barbaric, with animal sacrifice and the mass murder of non-Israelites forming an essential part of its teaching. The controversial re-establishment of a Jewish state in Palestine has reinforced this outlook, since the displacement of the native population there by immigrant settlers can only be justified by an appeal to the ancient Hebrew Scriptures, which are thus made to appear to support a grave injustice that contravenes the true spirit of Christianity.

The second approach to the Old Testament is to allegorise it. The principle here is that the text gives a picture in earthly terms of what is essentially a spiritual and heavenly reality. Interpreters must therefore strip away the material overlay, look for the underlying principle and seek to apply it in the life of the church. Jerusalem (or Zion) becomes the city of God, whereas Babylon and Nineveh represent the forces of evil that are opposed to it. The wars of ancient Israel are reinterpreted as spiritual struggles and their wilderness journey from Egypt to the Promised Land becomes the pattern of the Christian life, which takes the believer from the bondage of sin (Egypt) to the gates of heaven (the Promised Land). The sacrifice and temple rituals of the Old Testament are recycled in the church by making elders (presbyters) priests and reinterpreting the Lord's Supper as a sacrifice for the propitiation of sin in the way that the Old Testament sacrifices were. This approach was common in the middle ages and can still be found today, even though most Christians officially reject it. Negro spirituals, for example, rely heavily on allegorical imagery and it may even be the right way to read certain texts, like the Song of Solomon, where the literal interpretation seems to be inadequate.

The third approach is to think in terms of the covenant history of God's people. This takes the literal meaning of the Old Testament seriously but at the same time accepts that it can no longer be applied in the way that it was before the coming of Christ. The principles it lays down have not changed, but the way in which they are worked out has. In theological language, there is now a new 'economy' or 'dispensation' of the covenant of grace that God originally made with Abraham. In this new dispensation the promises made to the ancestors of Israel and repeated in the sayings of the prophets down through the centuries have been fulfilled in the life and work of Jesus Christ. The temple sacrifices, for example, are no longer necessary because the sacrifice of Christ on the cross has done everything they were intended to do, and more. The ancient rites had to be constantly repeated because their efficacy was strictly limited. All they could really do was point to the need for sin to be atoned for. The inadequacy of the animal sacrifices around which they were built merely demonstrated their temporary nature and encouraged those who understood that to look for something permanent and effective that would make the traditional rites redundant. Even in Old Testament times, spiritually-minded people looked beyond what the article calls the 'transitory promises' of the law and waited patiently for the coming of Christ.

It is this way of interpreting the Old Testament that is endorsed in article 7. Without going into details, it tells us that the Old Testament is to be read as a preparation for the New. By understanding its promises we can better appreciate what Christ achieved. Furthermore, this way of interpreting the text is not a Christian invention. Believing Jews also read it in the same way, although they were still looking for the promises to be fulfilled in the future. When Christ appeared, faithful Israelites like Simeon and Anna (Luke 2:25-38) recognised him and became his followers – in their case, even before he said or did anything. Those Jews who refused to accept Jesus as the Messiah were blind to the true meaning of the Scriptures, which they read as if they had a veil over their faces and could not see properly (2 Corinthians 3:13-16; see also John 5:37-40).

This method of interpreting the Old Testament, or 'hermeneutic' as it is technically called, causes problems for modern students of the Bible because it clashes with the 'scientific' approach to the texts taken in the academic world. It is obvious that the Hebrew Bible was written before the coming of Christ and that there is an entire religious community still in existence that reads it without reference to him. Is this legitimate? An 'objective' scholarly approach tends to think that it is because it rejects the notion that a text – any text – can or must be understood in the light of events that occurred several centuries after it was written. According to this way of thinking, Isaiah (for example) cannot be interpreted as the prophet of a distant future that was unknown to him, but should be read instead as a commentator on current affairs. This might involve some form of 'prophecy' but only in the sense of predicting what contemporary figures could reasonably do in the foreseeable future. Thus, the verses which speak of Cyrus as the deliverer of Israel (Isaiah 44:28; 45:1) may have been written a few years before Cyrus decided to let the Jews go back to Palestine, but not a couple of centuries before Cyrus appeared on the scene as someone who would be able to act in that way. That in turn means that the verses in question cannot have been written by Isaiah, since the prophet we know by that name lived two hundred years before Cyrus did. Even less is it legitimate to read other passages in Isaiah as referring to Christ, since whoever wrote them could not possibly have known about someone who did not come into the world until centuries later.

What is at issue here is not just the interpretation of a few verses but the whole way in which we read the Old Testament and understand the relationship of Christianity to it and to Judaism. Is the Jewish interpretation of the Hebrew Bible valid? Did Christ fulfil prophecy or did his followers merely appropriate certain texts and use them to justify their own understanding of him? To put it bluntly, is the New Testament a revelation from the God of Israel or is it nothing more than Christian propaganda? Article 7 commits us to an interpretation of the Scriptures which sees them as prophecies which were not only fulfilled in Christ but which God's people in ancient Israel understood would be fulfilled in him, even if they could not predict the exact details or say precisely when the Messiah would appear. Seen in this way, the Christian interpretation of the Old Testament as the first dispensation of the eternal covenant between God and his people is not just valid but is the only legitimate one, which means that other ways of reading it, including the traditional Jewish one, are correspondingly false or inadequate.

The division of the law of Moses into ceremonial, civil and moral categories is not one that is explicitly laid out as such in the Biblical text, though it can certainly be analysed in that way. In ancient Israel all three elements were held together as parts of a single pattern of worship that embraced the entire community in every aspect of its life. Distinctions such as the above only became necessary when it was no longer possible to do this. The destruction of the temple and the exile of the people to Babylon removed the ceremonial and civil parts of the law from the sphere of practical application, but did not absolve the Israelites from keeping the moral precepts as best they could. The return from exile led to the restoration of the ceremonial law but its civil aspects were less easily revived, partly because the Jews remained under foreign domination and partly because circumstances had changed, making much of the law obsolete or inapplicable. This was essentially the position in the time of Jesus, and after the destruction of the second temple in AD 70 Jews were forced to revert to the conditions that had applied during the exile, where they have remained ever since. Even the establishment of the modern state of Israel has not led to a restoration of the Mosaic law in its fullness, partly because the temple has not been rebuilt and partly because modern life requires a different legal system for civil affairs. Some Jews do not accept this situation, of course, but even they have to face certain ethical dilemmas. For example, would it be right to reinstate animal sacrifice if the temple were ever to be rebuilt? There would be strenuous opposition to this from within the Jewish community itself, but it is hard to see how the ceremonial law of the Old Testament could be revived without it.

Christianity resolves this problem by transposing the law to the person and work of Christ. What he has fulfilled is valid in the context of that fulfilment and has therefore passed away in terms of everyday worship and practice. At the same time, what he reaffirmed continues to be enjoined on his followers, who cannot use 'the abolition of the law' as an excuse for evading their obligations in this respect. In practice, this means that the temple rituals have passed away because Christ has offered the one perfect and sufficient sacrifice that needs no repetition. The civil aspects of the law are no longer in force because the Christian church is not a state in the way that ancient Israel was, and modern states are free to adopt or adapt them as they see fit. The moral aspects of the law remain valid for us though, because they reflect the character of God and what he expects of his people. Christians have not been set free from the law in order to kill, steal or commit adultery! Admittedly, there are some gray areas, like the keeping of the Sabbath. Is that a ceremonial, a civil or a moral precept? It contains an element of the first, because the Sabbath is the day set aside for worship. It may also contain an element of the second, in that historically Christian countries recognise the Christian Sabbath (*i.e.* Sunday, not Saturday) as a public holiday. It may also have a moral aspect, in the sense that one day's rest in seven is good both for individuals and for societies as a whole, but it is hard to believe that working on a Sunday is morally equivalent to murder or defamation. Anglicans have never felt obliged to commit themselves to a strict Sunday observance for moral reasons, though some have done so on other grounds and it is clearly important to have a day on which it is possible to gather together for the worship of God.

In that sense it is probably best to see it as essentially a civil precept, since there is no compelling reason why Christians cannot worship God on another day of the week if circumstances so require (as they may do, for example, in some Muslim countries where Friday is the normal day of rest.) However, flexibility on this score does not mean that there is not a ceremonial and moral element in the command to observe the Sabbath, since it is still necessary for us to pause from our normal labours and spend time in worshipping God together. The importance of this is underlined by the fact that Sabbath observance is one of the Ten Commandments, which remain foundational to Christian beliefs. As with the other commandments, we may have to work it out in different ways but the underlying spiritual principle remains as valid now as it was when it was first issued.

Questions for discussion:

1. Should Christians pay as much attention to the Old Testament as to the New?

2. How should we interpret the Old Testament law in a Christian context?

3. Can Jews be saved without becoming Christians?

Key Bible Passages:

Matthew 5:17-37; Acts 7:1-53; Romans 9-11; Galatians 3:15-25; Hebrews 11.

For further reading:

Berding, K and J. Lunde, eds. *Three views on the New Testament use of the Old Testament,* Grand Rapids: Zondervan, 2008.

Routledge, Robin. *Old Testament theology, a thematic approach.* Nottingham: Apollos (IVP), 2008.

Schreiner, T. *The law and its fulfilment.* Grand Rapids: Baker, 1993.

Waltke, B. K. *An Old Testament theology: an exegetical, canonical and thematic approach.* Grand Rapids: Zondervan, 2007.

8.   The Three Creeds

The three Creeds, Nicene Creed, Athanasius's Creed, and that which is commonly called the Apostles' Creed, ought thoroughly to be received and believed, for they may be proved by most certain warrants of Holy Scripture.

Acceptance of the creeds of the ancient church was common to the main Reformation churches, but the reasons for this were different from the ones usually put forward by the Roman Catholic Church or sometimes advocated by ecumenical bodies today. The latter like to refer to the tradition of the church, and the more universal that tradition is, the more acceptable is the creed. On that basis, it is the Nicene Creed which is preferred above the others, because it is the only one of the three that is officially accepted in both the Western and the Eastern churches (without the *Filioque* clause, of course). The Apostles' Creed is also very widely accepted in the Western church and not objected to in the East, though it is not part of their tradition. The Athanasian Creed, on the other hand, is less widely used in the West and not at all in the East, where the false association with Athanasius is a factor that helps to discredit it.

Article 8 advocates accepting the creeds not for traditional reasons, but because they state the clear and unequivocal teaching of Holy Scripture. On that basis, all three of them are equally valid and to be retained in the church. In practice, the Apostles' Creed is used in the daily offices of Morning and Evening Prayer and the Nicene Creed at holy communion, an arrangement that goes back to the time of Charlemagne and was simply taken over unchanged by the Reformers. The Athanasian Creed is printed in the Prayer Book after Evening Prayer and is meant to be used on thirteen feast days in the year, chosen apparently because they were about four weeks apart from each other. In practice however, it is seldom if ever used today and is not usually found in modern liturgies, despite the wide range of choice which they offer in other areas. (An abbreviated form of it does however appear in *Common Worship*, which was authorised for use in the Church of England in 2000.) For most practical purposes it has faded away and even specialists are unlikely to be very familiar with it nowadays.

The production of doctrinal statements in the form of creeds, which the church was expected to confess, goes back to the earliest days of Christianity. Some people have claimed that Biblical passages like Philippians 2:5-11 are proto-creeds, but this is impossible to prove and much depends on how we define our terms. There is no doubt however that something like the creeds as we know them had appeared before AD 200 and that by the time Christianity was legalised in AD 313, most churches would have been familiar with the pattern of words, even if they did not possess a fixed, agreed text.

The Nicene Creed is so called because it was believed to have been the creed promulgated at the first council of Nicaea in 325, though we now know that this was not so. The council did produce a creed which looks something like our Nicene Creed, but the resemblance is accidental and it omits certain important things, like the article on the Holy Spirit. The creed we call 'Nicene' is more closely attached to the first council of Constantinople, held in 381, and many people believe that it was actually produced there at that time. Unfortunately, the decrees of the council contain no mention of it, so it may be that it was composed somewhat later and circulated as a digest of what the council taught. The first council of Ephesus, held in 431, legislated that no change was to be introduced into the creed of Nicaea, but it is not clear whether this referred to the creed of 325 or the one we now know as Nicene. The first unequivocal mention of our Nicene Creed comes from the council of Chalcedon in 451, since when it has been accepted as the standard of orthodoxy in virtually every church. Apart from the *Filioque* clause, which was added by the West in the sixth century and later, it has remained the same ever since.

The Athanasian Creed, also known as the *Quicunque vult* from the opening words of the Latin text, was probably produced in southern Gaul in the first half of the sixth century, and seems to be linked in some way to Caesarius, who was bishop of Arles from 502 to 542. It is not a creed in the same sense as the others, and has a complex style which shows that it was intended as a learning device for theological students more than for regular congregational use. It contains a very full statement of Trinitarian theology which reflects the Augustinian model, as its inclusion of the *Filioque* doctrine indicates. Its association with Athanasius (296–373), such as it is, is not historical but doctrinal. Athanasius was known for his fierce opposition to Arianism, which was still a real problem in Western Europe at the time the *Quicunque vult* was written, and it may well have been called 'Athanasian' in opposition to 'Arian' since the word 'orthodox' had not yet come into common use and the word 'catholic' would have been reserved for a creed that had received the official stamp of approval from an ecumenical council like that of Nicaea.

The Athanasian Creed was well known to the Reformers, who

relied on it for their understanding of the Trinity, but it met with serious objections in the eighteenth century. These centred on the so-called 'damnatory clauses' which are annexed to it like bookends at the beginning and the end of the text. These damnatory clauses read as follows:

> (Beginning): Whosoever will be saved, before all things it is necessary that he hold the Catholic Faith. Which faith, except everyone do keep whole and undefiled, without doubt he shall perish everlastingly.

> (End): This is the Catholic faith, which except a man believe faithfully, he cannot be saved.

The objections, as we may imagine, came mainly from theologians who had been influenced by the liberalism of the Enlightenment, who could not believe that a person would be condemned to hell for failing to agree with a fairly complex doctrinal statement. Put like that of course, they had a point, in the sense that nobody would believe that an illiterate peasant would forfeit his eternal salvation for failing to grasp the Athanasian Creed. But as is so often the case in these matters, this kind of argument misses the point. Knowing God is a total experience and a Christian who makes that claim is expected to recognise him when they meet him. Recognising another person is not something that can easily be put into words, but we must be able to sense when false claims are made about them and be able to say something that will focus our minds on the truth. Some people can do this better than others, but teachers in the church have a special duty to learn how God should be spoken of, because they are the ones who are expected to protect the flock of Christ against error. This is the true meaning of the damnatory clauses and the context in which they must be understood. Anyone whose beliefs contradict those of the Athanasian Creed does not know the God of the Bible and is therefore condemned to eternal damnation. This is because what the creed says faithfully reflects what the Scriptures teach and not because it has any inherent authority of its own. Even people who belong to churches that have no creeds are liable to sense heresy if someone stands up and preaches doctrines that contradict the Athanasian Creed, whether they are aware of this or not. In some cases, it is only when that happens that a church will see the need for a doctrinal statement and adopt one, which will probably contain clauses very similar to those found in the *Quicunque vult*. From an Anglican point of view, this is rather like reinventing the wheel – the doctrinal statement that such people feel obliged to make already exists in a highly developed and comprehensive form, so why not use it instead of spending time and energy trying to devise something similar? Even if we do not refer to it very often, its teaching remains fundamental to our faith and we must be grateful that the Reformers were prepared to include it in the Articles of Religion.

The Apostles' Creed is both the earliest and the latest of the three creeds of the ancient church. It does not go back to the apostles themselves, despite the medieval legend which said that they sat around and each produced a line of it under the inspiration of the Holy Spirit! The Reformers knew that this was false, and the article refers to the creed in a way which shows that they recognised that it was not authentic in that sense. On the other hand, forms of it appear in the Western church as early as AD 200 and something very much like it appears very frequently after that time. It is possible that it emerged from a baptismal formula that candidates for baptism were expected to learn and repeat before being baptised, but this is not certain. However, the frequency with which it appears shows that it must have been widely used for catechetical purposes, and so some association with baptism seems almost inevitable.

What is striking about it is that there was no set or official form of words. Several versions exist that differ in minor details, though the overall Trinitarian format is immediately recognisable. The text as we have it now first appears in the writings of Pirminius, who founded the monastery of Reichenau in 724. It was picked up by Charlemagne and included in his liturgies, which is how it became the officially accepted form. It is generally less detailed than the other creeds, but it does say that Christ *died,* and not merely that he *suffered and was buried,* as the Nicene Creed states. The reason for this clarification seems to have been that there were people who believed that Christ merely swooned on the cross and that he revived three days later, a view which was certainly not intended by the Nicene Creed but which could be read into it by literalists who would not accept that suffering necessarily included death.

Key Bible Passages:

1 Timothy 6:12-16; 2 Timothy 1:6-14; Jude 1-7.

For further reading:

Bray, G. L. *Creeds, Councils and Christ.* Leicester: IVP, 1984. Repr., Fearn: Mentor, 1997.

Kelly, J. N. D. *Early Christian creeds.* 3d ed. London: Continuum, 2006.

Kelly, J. N. D. *The Athanasian creed.* London: Adam and Charles Black, 1964.

9. Of Original, or Birth Sin

Original sin standeth not in the following of Adam, (as the Pelagians do vainly talk,) but it is the fault and corruption of the nature of every man, that naturally is ingendered of the offspring of Adam, whereby man is very far gone from original righteousness, and is of his own nature inclined to evil, so that the flesh lusteth always contrary to the spirit; and therefore in every person born into this world, it deserveth God's wrath and damnation. And this infection of nature doth remain, yea in them that are regenerated; whereby the lust of the flesh, called in Greek phronema sarkos, which some do expound the wisdom, some sensuality, some the affection, some the desire, of the flesh, is not subject to the Law of God. And although there is no condemnation for them that believe and are baptized, yet the Apostle doth confess that concupiscence and lust hath of itself the nature of sin.

After expounding the basic foundations of the Christian faith, the Articles move on to discuss the more specific question of salvation, different understandings of which lay at the heart of the Reformation. Modern readers may find it disconcerting to begin this discussion with the subject of original sin, which sounds so negative and off-putting, but it is the necessary starting point for our doctrine of salvation. A doctor cannot cure his patient without diagnosing the illness first, and the same is true in spiritual matters. Unless we understand and accept what is wrong with us we cannot be healed, and what is wrong begins with the problem of original sin. This was understood by all parties in the Reformation debates, as can be seen from the evidence of their statements of faith. The Augsburg Confession begins in exactly the same way, even putting the doctrine of original sin before the divinity of Christ (who came to pay the price for it). The Roman Catholic Church also issued a decree outlining its position on the matter as early as the fifth session of the council of Trent (17 June 1546), which shows that it too understood its fundamental importance.

The immediate reason for this emphasis on original sin was what everyone in the mid-sixteenth century perceived as a strange revival of Pelagianism. Pelagius was a British (*i.e.* Celtic, not Anglo-Saxon) monk who was teaching in Rome in the early fifth century. According to reports about him that reached Augustine in North Africa, he was saying that the fall of Adam and Eve into sin was not total. There still remained in human nature some capacity for recovery, a free will that, given the right training and favourable circumstances, could fight back against the invasive cancer of sin and with the help of God, overcome it. Unfortunately, almost everyone failed to do this, and like Adam and Eve, chose the pathway of rebellion against God and not that of voluntary submission to his will, with the result that, as the Apostle Paul said: 'All have sinned and fall short of the glory of God.' (Romans 3:23). Pelagius failed to understand that we do not sin in the way that Adam and Eve did (by a free choice of our will) but because we have inherited the consequences of their transgression. Nobody now has a choice in this, because we are all born as sinners, whether we like it or not. Sin is not a kind of cancer that spreads from one part of us to another, but which may not yet have consumed our entire body, leaving healthy cells somewhere that might conceivably be used to fight back against it. Sin is spiritual disobedience, and because of that it affects every part of our being. It is not possible to be only partly disobedient, because even if we disobey in only one thing (as Adam and Eve did) we have still broken the law of God.

Pelagius' doctrine, or something like it, was not at all uncommon at the time and by no means everyone understood why Augustine was so incensed by it. Even after he was condemned in the West, Pelagius was received in the East where his views were regarded as essentially orthodox, and his commentary on the Pauline epistles was so valuable that it was recycled under the names of Cassiodorus and Jerome, the true author remaining undetected until 1859. Augustine however, launched a major offensive against Pelagius, insisting that the fall of Adam was complete and that no human being had any natural innocence left in him. Only (and entirely) by the grace of God was it possible to be saved, which is why Jesus told Nicodemus that he had to be 'born again' (John 3:7). Unfortunately, Augustine then went on to say that this regeneration was available in baptism, and that everyone who was baptised was automatically cleansed from original sin. This made the sacrament especially important for infants, who could be purified from their inherited sinfulness by being baptised. In a world where infant mortality was very high, this was a great comfort to parents who lost a child, because they could be reassured that their loved ones were in heaven, since they had not committed any sin after baptism. Of course, those who grew up invariably did sin again, and then they had to return to the grace of God available through the sacraments of the church if they wished to be cleansed. Augustine and his followers saw all this as a work of divine grace, but the Reformers realised that in fact it was a kind of semi-Pelagianism, reintroducing the idea of co-operating with God for salvation by the back door. The baptised sinner, after all, was a born-again Christian in whom the Holy Spirit dwelt, and therefore he possessed the inner resources needed to fight back against the wiles of the devil. Further divine aid was certainly necessary (and available through the church) but there was no question of being born again a second time, since that had already been taken care of.

The Reformers rejected this concept of baptismal regeneration, even though they accepted that baptism was the sign of spiritual rebirth. Original sin could not be washed away and remained in the believer even after his regeneration. What was taken away was not sin, but the condemnation which sin entailed. A Christian is a sinner who can stand in the presence of God, not because he is no longer sinful, but because his sins have been paid for by the shed blood of Christ, who stands between us and the Father's justice and uses his sacrifice, which the Father has accepted, to plead on our behalf. To be born again therefore is not to be cleansed from sin by baptism, but to be united with Christ in his death and resurrection. This union enables us to fight back against the 'old Adam' which is still our fundamental human nature. We do not turn to God merely for help in eradicating the effects of the sins we commit after being baptised, but depend on him at every moment for the life and strength we need for this spiritual struggle against what the Bible calls 'the lusts of the flesh' that continue to affect us all. We are sinners to the day we die and go to be with Christ in heaven, not transformed beings theoretically capable of achieving sinless perfection if only we try hard enough.

At the time of the Reformation there were some people who rejected infant baptism because they believed that it could not be a true profession of faith. Like other Protestants, they believed in the permanence of original sin and did not believe that they were depriving their children of salvation by refusing to baptise them. But so strong was the perceived link between baptism and regeneration that these Anabaptists, as they were called, were regarded as being Pelagians because it was thought that they refused to baptise their children on the ground that their children did not need it. Not having committed actual sins, they were innocent in God's eyes and would go to heaven if they died, whether they were baptised or not. Indeed, baptism might even be dangerous for them, because if they claimed a faith which they did not have on the basis that they had received the sacrament, they might be accused of mocking the grace of God and losing the salvation promised to them, not gaining it!

Here it must be said that the Anabaptists were misunderstood. In the original article of 1553, Thomas Cranmer had mentioned them by name and identified them as latter-day Pelagians, but the revisers of 1563 took this out. They also removed a later reference to baptism by changing the English word 'baptised' to 'regenerated', which corresponds more closely to the Latin *renatis*, just before speaking about the *phronema sarkos* that remains in the believer after his conversion. Unfortunately, the revisers did not go on to correct the last paragraph of the English version of the article, which is a possible source of confusion to those who do not know Latin. The original text reads *renatis et credentibus*, which ought to have been translated as 'regenerated and believing', or as we would say today, 'born-again believers', but unfortunately says 'them that believe and are baptised' instead. This translation suggests that rebirth is to be equated with baptism, which the revisers of the Articles wanted to avoid, and it puts the order the wrong way round. It is not those who believe first and who are then baptised (as the Anabaptists would have agreed) but those who have been born again and then believe, which is the order actually observed in conversion. The article goes on to assure us that born-again believers have been set free from God's condemnation, but it also reminds us that far from living the life of heaven on earth, a Christian is a soldier engaged in spiritual warfare against the 'flesh', a term which also requires some explanation.

To understand all this we must begin with the concept of 'nature'. A superficial reading of this article would suggest that human nature is essentially sinful, and that is what many people believe. But what it actually says, and what the Bible teaches, is that human nature is corrupted and infected by sin. In other words, what God created as essentially good has become sinful because of the intrusion of an alien power of evil. Being a spiritual force, evil does not corrupt the physical body in the way that a cancer does (for example), but controls it by perverting its natural desires and turning our thoughts away from what is right. This corrupt nature is inherited from Adam and Eve and there is nothing we can do about it. Every human being is affected and therefore stands condemned in the sight of God. This may seem unfair, but we have to remember that we inherit everything we have and are from our parents. We cannot pick and choose, by keeping what is good and rejecting what is bad. Most people recognise that we are responsible for the sins of our ancestors (like slavery, for example) and have to do what we can to put them right, and we also know that if we misuse natural resources today, the consequences will be felt by generations yet unborn. They will have to live with depleted resources, polluted rivers and so on and it will not do them any good to complain that they are not personally responsible for having caused the problem. So it is with our inheritance of sin. We are not 'sinners' in an active sense until we are old enough to do something wrong, but we are sinful from birth because what the Apostle Paul calls the *phronema sarkos* (Romans 8:6) is alive and active in us from the moment we come into existence.

Article 9 borrows the Greek term here because although we could say 'the mind of the flesh' in English, as many translations in fact do, it is impossible to translate this phrase succinctly in a way that brings out its full meaning. The Greek language is famous for having many words (like *logos*, for example) which have a wide range of meanings that have to be held together. Linguists call this a broad 'semantic field' or 'semantic range'. This makes Greek (and Hebrew too, incidentally) a very expressive language, but attempts to render such words into English inevitably narrow this range of meaning, because the most obvious English equivalents seldom have the same semantic range. This can lead to misunderstanding, as we know from the common habit of translating *logos* as 'word'. So it is with *phronema sarkos*. The Greek is clear enough, but how are we going to express the range of meaning it contains in English?

The first thing we have to bear in mind is that the word *sarx* ('flesh') is a spiritual concept as well as a physical one. It can certainly refer to what we normally think of as the flesh, but it also designates a spiritual force that stands in opposition to God. It is called the 'flesh' because this spiritual force appeals to our bodily senses and tries to use them to turn us away from God's will for our lives. God does not want us to despise or ignore our bodies, but neither does he want us to be dominated by them to the extent that we forget all about the things we cannot see, but which are eternal. Physical flesh is inert and therefore has no *phronema* or mind of its own, but this is not true of the spiritual force that goes by the same name. As people who have fallen into sin because of the disobedience of Adam, our minds have been corrupted by the power of Satan, who is described in Scripture as 'the prince of this world'. Like the term 'flesh', 'world' does not mean the planetary globe we live on, but the mindset that is hostile to God and subject to the devil instead. It is because this mindset is attracted by things that are visible and temporal (like wealth and power) that it is called by such names. The *phronema sarkos* is all-pervasive and works in us whether we are specifically tempted by outside influences or not. For example, I may be encouraged to steal by seeing an opportunity to do so open up before my eyes, but whether that happens or not, there will always be an innate greed inside me that will materialise as stealing whenever it gets the chance to do so. This inner desire, which the article describes by using the synonymous terms 'concupiscence' and 'lust', does not disappear when we turn to Christ, but the presence of his Holy Spirit inside us gives us the strength to struggle against it. The Christian life is therefore one of constant spiritual warfare which does not end until we go to be with him in heaven. It is even likely to get worse as we grow older, not because we are further away from God but because his presence in us reveals even greater depths of sin that we have to combat. Paradoxical as it sounds, it is probably better to measure our spiritual progress by the degree of our awareness of sin rather than by our willingness to swear allegiance to Christ, since it is the former that reveals just how much we really understand the latter.

In this connection, it must also be said that Christians can easily fall into the trap of a false asceticism, that denies the realities of this life in a vain search for some super-spiritual 'holiness', but this too is an expression of the *phronema sarkos*. Self-denial is not an end in itself but a means by which it may be possible to glorify God – if that is what God wants us to do. The key to the Christian life, as can be seen from the sin of Adam, is not self-denial but obedience. In eating the fruit of the tree of the knowledge of good and evil, Adam and Eve were not being particularly gluttonous. They were not out to satisfy their hunger, and still less did they want to stuff themselves with the good things of this world. What they were doing was disobeying the command of God, and it is that which constitutes the essence of the *phronema sarkos*. It cannot be overcome by external or mechanical means, whether these are sacraments or ascetic practices. Only a radical transformation of the will from disobedience to obedience is capable of bringing about the necessary change, and that can only be done by changing the mind of the flesh into the mind of the Spirit of God.

Questions for discussion:

1. Was Eve responsible for Adam's sin?

2. Why do we all have to suffer because of Adam's sin?

3. Is sin a normal part of human nature or a corruption of it?

Key Bible Passages:

Genesis 3:1-19; Romans 3:9-18, 5:12-21; 1 Corinthians 15:21-22.

For further reading:

Blocher, H. *Original sin: illuminating the riddle.* Nottingham: Apollos, 1997.

Lundgaard, K. *The enemy within.* Phillipsburg: Presbyterian and Reformed, 1998.

Shuster, M. *The fall and sin; what we have become as sinners.* Grand Rapids: Eerdmans, 2004.

10. Of Free Will

The condition of man after the fall of Adam is such that he cannot turn and prepare himself by his own natural strength and good works to faith and calling upon God; wherefore we have no power to do good works pleasant and acceptable to God, without the grace of God by Christ preventing us, that we may have a good will, and working with us, when we have that good will.

The first part of this article was added in 1563, but the rest (after 'wherefore') was in the forty-two articles of 1553. The question of free will was tackled by the Augsburg Confession (18) along similar lines but using different language.

The denial of free will is intrinsic to the Reformation, as Martin Luther demonstrated when he wrote his famous treatise on *The bondage of the will*, in response to Erasmus, who thought that human beings can decide for themselves whether they will obey God or not. The notion that we have free will in this matter is one of the most deeply held prejudices that we come across, all the more remarkable because it often goes hand in hand with various forms of determinism (Marxism, Freudian psychology) and fatalism. Christian teaching is neither libertarian nor fatalistic, but derives from a different set of principles altogether.

First of all, we believe that the world is ordered by a sovereign and providential God who is in control of everything that happens. We are specifically told that there is no power in heaven or on earth than can separate us from his love (Romans 8:38-39) which means that everything that happens to us works together for our good, because we love him as he loves us. Love is not a bondage but a commitment; it is a liberating and not a limiting force in our lives.

When Adam and Eve disobeyed God they rejected his love and his providential care for them, preferring to go their own way – only to discover that they were trapped in a world ruled by Satan. This is bondage, and every human being is caught up in it because we have all inherited the consequences of our first parents' sin. We are 'free' in the way that fish in an aquarium are free. We can move around within limits, but cannot escape from the confines in which we have been placed. The fish may not realise this, but the outside observer sees it all too clearly.

There is only one escape from our prison, and that is divine rescue. God can lift us out of our limitations, but we cannot do anything to help ourselves. We may be capable of great achievements within the limitations placed on us – remember that it is not impossible for prisoners to get university degrees, for example, and some achieve amazing things. But however brilliant and gifted they may prove to be, they are still in prison and cannot get out unless they are released. This is the state of fallen man, apart from the grace of God and there is nothing we can do to change it.

The only way that we can make any favourable impression on God is if we are set free to serve him as we ought to, and that is made possible by his free gift of salvation in and through Jesus Christ. We have not asked for this gift and have done nothing to deserve it – it is a gift, after all, and not a reward for services rendered. We are incapable of wanting it, or even of understanding what it is, until we receive it, which is why the article says that God's grace in Christ 'prevents' us, 'prevent' being used here in the older sense of 'precede'. When God gets to work in our lives he liberates our will and gives it a right understanding of what is good, as well as a desire to do it. Only when that happens is it possible to discover what true freedom is.

The truth of this can perhaps best be illustrated from something which parallels it in secular life. Alcoholics Anonymous is a well-known organisation that tries to solve people's drinking problems. However, they are quite clear that they can do nothing to help anyone unless and until the person concerned gets to the point where he recognises that he has a problem and that he cannot solve it in his own strength. Sadly, this often does not happen until the alcoholic has hit rock bottom, but in a curious way, the farther he falls the easier it is to rise again, because then his surrender to the treatment is total. Only when the patient has what the article calls here a 'good will' can he co-operate with the recovery programme and achieve lasting results.

This is a secular analogy of course, and like all analogies it is not exact, but it gives an idea of how God works in a sinner's life, and why it is necessary to tackle the problem in this 'total surrender' way. Is a recovering alcoholic free? There are some people who would say that he is not, that he has sold himself to a new tyranny which may be doing him good but at the price of taking away his free will. Such people do not seem to mind if he prefers to drink himself to death, because that is his choice! But is it? An alcoholic does not choose his condition, any more than a sinner does. Doing what comes naturally to him is not freedom, but a slavery to self-destruction so powerful that only the most

69

radical treatment can change it. The libertarian philosopher may say what he likes, but the recovering alcoholic, like the redeemed sinner, understands that he has been delivered from a bondage greater than his power to resist. Neither wants to return to his former state, and both rejoice in the freedom to build a new life, which they have acquired for the first time. What appears to some outsiders as an irrational dependence is experienced by those involved as the love of God at work in their lives. To those who know that, it does not matter what the scoffers think – they have been set free to exercise their good will in the way that God originally intended, and they have no desire to go back to anything less than that.

When it comes to salvation, the New Testament is very clear that we cannot pick and choose. Jesus told his disciples that no-one can come to him unless the Father draws him (John 6:44), and he reminded them that he had chosen them, not the other way round (John 15:16). Saul of Tarsus was chosen by God as the apostle to the Gentiles even though that was the last thing he wanted, and in his letter to the Romans he discourses at some length on the conflict between his will and his actual behaviour, which are contrary to one another and prevent him from doing what would be necessary for him to achieve his own salvation (Romans 7:15-19). Only God can set us free from this, and does so as and when he pleases (Romans 9:19-29). The prayer of the Christian is summed up in the collect for the ninth Sunday after Trinity in the Book of Common Prayer:

> Grant to us, Lord, we beseech thee, the spirit to think and do always such things as be rightful; that we, who cannot do anything that is good without thee, may be thee be enabled to live according to thy will; through Jesus Christ our Lord. Amen.

Questions for discussion:

1. What happened to Adam's will when he fell? Could he choose to go back again?

2. How much choice do we really have in our lives?

3. How does God's grace change the way we think and behave?

Key Bible Passages:

Romans 7:14-25; Galatians 3:10-23; Ephesians 4:17-32.

For further reading:

Anglin, W. S. *Free will and the Christian faith.* Oxford: Clarendon, 1990.

Cowburn, J. *Free will, predestination and determinism.* Milwaukee: Marquette University Press, 2008.

Peterson, R. A. *Election and free will: God's gracious choice and our responsibility.* Phillipsburg: Presbyterian and Reformed, 2007.

Sproul, R. C. *Willing to believe: the controversy over free will.* Grand Rapids: Baker, 1997.

II.   *Of the Justification of Man*

> *We are accounted righteous before God only for the merit of our Lord and Saviour Jesus Christ by faith, and not for our own works or deservings. Wherefore, that we are justified by faith only is a most wholesome doctrine, and very full of comfort, as more largely is expressed in the Homily of Justification.*

This article was twice reworked from its original form, most of which is now preserved in the second sentence. The first part was introduced in 1563, with some elements of the original tacked on, but the rest was restored in 1571 to give us the text that we have now.

It is clear that a subject as vast and as controversial as justification by faith alone cannot be reduced to a few lines, and the article recognises this by referring the reader to the homily on justification, by which it means the third homily, *On salvation*, which appears in the *First book of homilies* that was put out in 1547. The article itself is no more than a digest of that, but it is sufficient to show that the Church of England was firmly on the Reformed side in the great debate that was then raging between the Protestants and Rome. Apart from the homily just mentioned, the Protestant position on this subject, which Martin Luther regarded as the fundamental question of Christian theology ('the article of a standing or falling church') can be found in the Augsburg Confession (4) and in the ten articles of 1536 (5). The Roman counter-position is expounded at some length in the decree of the sixth session of the council of Trent (13 January 1547). It was not consciously anti-Anglican, since the Anglican doctrine expressed in this article (and in the relevant homily) had not yet been formulated, but this hardly matters since Thomas Cranmer clearly opted for the views that it condemned.

The main issue in dispute at the time was whether a person is justified by faith *alone*, or whether works also play a part in it. The problem arose because there was no real distinction made between justification and sanctification in the medieval church. Sanctification was a process of growth, and the more sanctified you were, the more justified you would also be. Only those who were fully sanctified could be sure of going straight to heaven – they were the 'saints'. Everybody else, and they were the vast majority, would be only partly sanctified at death and therefore not fully justified either, they would have to go through a further period of cleansing in 'purgatory' in order to improve their sanctification, so that they could be admitted into heaven as fully justified believers.

Martin Luther cut through all this with his famous remark that a Christian is *simul iustus et peccator* – justified but still a sinner at the same time. We stand in the presence of God not because of anything we have done but by virtue of what Jesus Christ has done for us. This is a great relief, because we know that what he has done is adequate to save us, whereas we can never be sure that we have done enough to deserve anything from God other than condemnation and punishment. Even the best people are sinners, and one of the marks of true saintliness is the recognition of just how bad we really are (see Ephesians 3:8). If salvation depended on our works, the holiest people would be the ones least assured of having obtained it! That is a nonsensical position, of course, but it helps us to see why justification by faith alone is such an important doctrine. Without it we would never know if we were saved or not, and our relationship with God would be rooted in fear rather than in faith, hope and love.

When talking about justification, we have to face the fact that we have a linguistic difficulty that needs to be recognised. In English we have two sets of words for this concept, one of which comes from Latin (just, justice, justification) and the other from Old English (right, righteous, righteousness) but we use them somewhat differently. The Latin words tend to refer to something external to ourselves, so that we think of 'justice' as fairness to people in general, whereas the Old English equivalents tend to be used more of something internal. We would normally expect a righteous judge to be just, but we can imagine that an unrighteous one might still administer justice because his personal state would not necessarily affect his professional conduct.

This difference in usage creates problems for us that do not arise in the Biblical languages, which do not have such a distinction. For example, is a justified person necessarily 'righteous'? Jesus told the thief on the cross that he would be in paradise that same day, so presumably the thief was justified by faith alone, but would anybody call him 'righteous'? Probably not, because we tend to think of righteousness in terms of morality and behaviour – a righteous person would not have been put to death for stealing. In other words, our concept of righteousness still retains much of the medieval notion of sanctification, which means that it acts as a back door for the reintroduction of a belief in justification by works without appearing to do so. Because of this confusion, it would not be surprising to hear someone say that he is justified in spite of the fact that he is not righteous – a contradiction in terms in any other language, but perfectly understandable in English!

Righteousness is not a thing or a quality that we possess, but a status that we enjoy because we have been accepted by God in Christ. Arguments about whether the Biblical phrase 'the righteousness of God' (*e.g.* in Romans 1:17) means something that God is in himself, something that he has done for us or something that he has given us therefore usually miss the point, because they are thinking in terms of some quality inherent in our character. As a believer in Christ I do not become more like God, even if I learn to act in a way that is pleasing to him. If that happens, it is not I who am responsible, but Christ who lives in me and who is the only hope I have of reaching the eternal glory of God (Galatians 2:20-21). In other words, I am righteous because he has claimed me for his own and made it possible for me to stand in the presence of God because he has paid the price for my sins. In myself, I have not changed at all and am just as much a sinner as I ever was. Yet at the same time I am also righteous, because I have been justified by Jesus Christ who has united me to himself and who pleads with his Father on my behalf. I know I am going to heaven because I trust in his ability to get me there – this is why I am justified *by faith*. Nothing else is needed, and any works I might have to offer in addition would be an embarrassment because their inadequacy would be painfully obvious. That is why I am justified by faith *alone*, and why this doctrine is so vitally important for Christian life and experience. Without it, we would be in a state of constant anxiety, forever trying to please God but never quite certain that we have succeeded. To be justified by faith alone is to be set free from that anxiety and have the confidence that we have fellowship with God even though we have not deserved it. This is why the article says that justification by faith is 'a most wholesome doctrine and very full of comfort', because we no longer have to worry about whether we are accepted by God or not.

Nowadays some people claim that the righteousness of God refers primarily to membership in the covenant community of God's people, something which was achieved by the law in the Old Testament and is now brought about by the church as the body of Christ. This understanding is controversial among scholars and theologians, and would have been incomprehensible to the sixteenth-century Reformers. If belonging to the church in a sacramental sense were all that was needed, there would never have been a Reformation at all, since everyone in Europe at that time (apart from the Jews, of course) fulfilled the necessary criteria. The debate about justification occurred precisely because this communitarian view was not held by either side. For Roman Catholics, the church was a means to an end, which would be justification, whereas for Protestants it was a witness to a justification already granted by faith alone. Either way, it applied to individuals rather than to groups and modern theories to the contrary notwithstanding, this approach still seems to be the one that is most faithful to the meaning of the Biblical text.

Questions for discussion:

1. Does believing in Christ make us better people?

2. Can sinful people be righteous at the same time or do they have to change first?

3. Why is it comforting to know that we cannot do anything to save ourselves?

Key Bible Passages:

Romans 1:16-19; Romans 4; Galatians 2:15-21; Colossians 1:21-23.

For further reading:

Fesko, J. V. *Justification: understanding the classic Reformed doctrine.* Phillipsburg: Presbyterian and Reformed, 2007.

McCormack, Bruce. *Justification in perspective: historical developments and contemporary challenges.* Edinburgh: Rutherford House, 2006.

Piper, J. *The future of justification.* Nottingham: IVP, 2008.

12. *Of Good Works*

Albeit that good works, which are the fruits of faith, and follow after justification, cannot put away our sins, and endure the severity of God's judgement; yet are they pleasing and acceptable to God in Christ, and do spring out necessarily of a true and lively faith, in so much that by them a lively faith may be as evidently known as a tree discerned by the fruit.

So confused was medieval thinking on the subject of salvation by works that the early Protestants were accused of being licentious, because they claimed that we are saved without doing anything good. It was even said that they claimed that it was actually better for us not to live a moral life so as to avoid leaving the impression that we might be trying to earn our salvation. This caricature of Protestant teaching was vehemently repudiated by the Augsburg Confession (20) but it remains surprisingly common even now, despite the fact that the evidence would seem to point in the opposite direction. Few people would accuse Protestants of being morally lax in practice; if anything, they are usually reproached for the opposite failing of excessive 'puritanism' in such matters. The Protestant work ethic may have been the imaginary construction of the economist Max Weber, but that there is some truth in it can hardly be doubted. The Protestant countries of northern Europe (and North America) are self-evidently more developed than the Catholic ones to the south, and it is hard to believe that religion does not play at least some part in this. Why are Protestants so industrious, and so full of good works, if they are not supposed to be doing any?

Part of the confusion here comes from a misunderstanding of what a 'good work' is. In medieval theology, good works were things done in order to earn favour (merit) in the sight of God. Some of these were morally positive, and therefore 'good' in the normal sense of the term, but others were simply obligations laid on penitent sinners. Making a pilgrimage, for example, was a good work, as was saying the rosary, fasting or anything else that a priest might expect a sinner to do as proof that he was truly sorry for his sins. The Reformers saw through the hypocrisy and pointlessness of this sort of thing, and rejected practices which had no meaning other than trying to curry favour with God. Perhaps they went too far in some cases, virtually abolishing fasting, for example, even though it is a practice recommended in the New Testament, but their motive for doing so is understandable in the circumstances.

If however, we understand 'good works' to mean moral actions or activities designed to further the purposes of God for his people, then the Reformers took a completely different approach. Nobody could lie, cheat or steal and claim to be a good Christian, because the Christian life is one that is lived in the power and Spirit of God, who does not tolerate such behaviour. In this respect, there were only two things that concerned them. The first was the danger that people might rely on such good works as proof of their faith and therefore claim them as some sort of entitlement to God's blessing. Even the best of human works fall short of the glory of God, and the Bible tells us that however much we do, at the end of the day we are still unprofitable servants in need of divine grace (Luke 17:10). The other danger was the exact opposite, that people would fail in their efforts and be so disheartened by this that they would lose the joy of their salvation and even imagine that they had lost their salvation itself. Their pastoral efforts were therefore directed at countering these two problems so that the true place of good works in the Christian life would be understood and honoured.

Christian behaviour springs naturally out of Christian experience, just as good fruit grows naturally on a well-pruned tree. If that does not happen, then the authenticity of the Christian experience must be called into question. People who profess Christian faith but continue to lead immoral lives are lying and it is the duty of the church to put them right if that is the case. On the other hand, the good works expected of a Christian are not specified in such detail as to make them immediately recognisable in all circumstances. The Ten Commandments lay down general principles that must be observed, but the details may vary from person to person and from place to place. Jesus demonstrated this in his own life. It was important to worship God in the right way, but observing the Sabbath was not supposed to become a burden that prevented genuine acts of charity and Jesus became a notorious 'Sabbath-breaker' for that reason. The ultimate motivation for doing good, and therefore also the ultimate criterion for deciding what a good work is, comes from the law of love written by the Holy Spirit on the heart of the believer and not from some external code of conduct.

In normal circumstances of course, the internal and the external will coincide to a large extent, but there are exceptional cases, and it is then that the true motivation is revealed. If a believer fails to do what is right and justifies this by appealing to some legalistic criterion, he is not fulfilling the law of Christ, even if he is staying on the right side of the civil law. For example, if I refuse to cross the street to help someone who has fallen down and cannot get up, and justify this by saying that the light was red and I could not cross, I have failed in my duty. Of course things can be much more complicated than that and there are always hard cases that are difficult to decide, but the principle is clear. Love must come before legalism, even if it leads to suffering because of it. That is what Jesus did and that is what he expects of his followers also.

Questions for discussion:

    1. What are 'good works'?

    2. What kind of life should a Christian lead?

    3. Does God reward us for doing good?

Key Bible Passages:

Romans 12:1-21; Ephesians 2:8-10; James 2:17-26.

For further reading:

Gundry, S. N. *Five views on sanctification.* Grand Rapids: Zondervan, 1987.
Hughes, P. E. *Faith and works. Cranmer and Hooker on justification.* Wilton, Conn.: Morehouse-Barlow, 1982.
Oden, T., ed. *The good works reader.* Grand Rapids: Eerdmans, 2007.

13. *Of Works before Justification*

Works done before the grace of Christ, and the inspiration of his Spirit, are not pleasant to God, forasmuch as they spring not of faith in Jesus Christ, neither do they make men meet to receive grace, or (as the School authors say) deserve grace of congruity; yea rather, for that they are not done as God hath willed and commanded them to be done, we doubt not but they have the nature of sin.

This article seems strange to many people today. On the one hand, we can see the logic in saying that if good works do not earn us salvation, there is no reason to suppose that we can do them in order to curry favour with God since we have nothing to gain by doing so. But at the same time, it is hard for us to think that good works can somehow be sinful. Surely, we think, unbelievers who act like Christians ought to be given credit for doing the right thing?

That is certainly the line that was taken by the medieval theologians who developed the theology taught in the schools of the thirteenth to the sixteenth centuries. They maintained that good works done by unbelievers were sufficiently close to those done by Christians that they received a blessing from God (though not salvation) because of that similarity, or 'congruity' as they called it. That makes sense if we believe that we are saved by our works, but it goes against the logic of the Gospel. Jesus told the Jews that he had come, not to save the righteous, but to bring sinners to repentance (Matthew 9:13). This was not because he thought that there were righteous people around who did not need him, but because he rejected the very idea that anyone could be righteous on his own merits. The young man who came to him asking what he needed to do to inherit eternal life told Jesus that he had kept all the commandments since childhood, but Jesus pointed out that even that was not enough – he had to abandon everything and follow him if he wanted to get to heaven (Mark 10:17-22).

This is the key. The Christian life is not a succession of good deeds that is essentially no different from any other form of morality. It is a life of obedience to God. Good deeds done outside that context may be perfectly acceptable in the eyes of the world, but they are done because the person doing them has decided to behave in that way, not because God has commanded him to do them. They may be well-intentioned and beneficial to the recipients, but they are not the result of a saving relationship with God and it is for that reason that they have no value in his eyes. For example, if someone had rescued Jesus from Herod and Pilate and spirited him away so that he was not crucified, he would have been doing a 'good deed'. At one point even Peter suggested that if anyone tried to lay hands on Jesus, he would come to his aid in exactly that way. But far from being grateful to him for his kind thoughts, Jesus rounded on him with the words: 'Get behind me, Satan', adding for good measure that Peter was thinking in human terms and not in divine ones (Matthew 16:21-23).

Today there are many people who believe that as long as they lead a good life and do no harm to anyone else, they will be on the right side if and when they are brought to judgment. Such people may not be trying very hard to earn their salvation, but they have concluded that if there is a God, he is a nice man who will see their good intentions and reward them accordingly. What they do not realize is that their whole approach is deeply rooted in selfishness and pride. They are the ones who have decided what is good (and good enough) in God's eyes; the thought that they might have to listen to the Lord and be instructed by him in the ways of goodness has never crossed their minds. At best, their morality is enlightened self-interest, and the suspicion must be that if their circumstances were to change, their moral awareness would change along with them. Doing 'a good deed for the day' is in fact a way of justifying sin, because once the good deed is done, that (self-imposed) obligation can be ticked off and we can get on with whatever else we want to do. Sacrifice and repentance are nowhere in sight, having been drowned out by self-congratulation. Good works are neither meritorious nor sinful in themselves, but in an unbeliever, they 'partake of the nature of sin' because they are ultimately rooted in pride, which is the first and greatest of sins. The Christian who does good works because of his faith nevertheless turns to God in repentance, because he realizes that after having done all he can, he is still an unprofitable servant. The unbeliever on the other hand, does what he thinks he can manage without undue strain or sacrifice, and then pats himself on the back for having succeeded so well. That is the difference between the good works of a believer and those of an unbeliever. The good works of a believer have value because they come in the right place – after conversion. The good works of an unbeliever, on the other hand, are worthless, because they come in the wrong place – before conversion. Once we look at the matter from that angle, we can see that far from there being any similarity or 'congruity' between the two situations, they are totally different and opposite to one another in every fundamental respect.

> *Questions for discussion:*
>
> 1. Can a non-Christian be a good person?
>
> 2. Why are the good words done by non-Christians regarded as sinful?
>
> 3. Does our motivation for doing good count for more than the good we actually do?

Key Bible Passages:

Psalm 51; Romans 6:1-23; Ephesians 2:1-3, 11-12.

For further reading:

Shore, J. *I'm OK, you're not: the message we're sending unbelievers and why we should stop.* Colorado Springs, NavPress, 2007.

Vaughan, C. R. *The gifts of the Holy Spirit to unbelievers and believers* Edinburgh: Banner of Truth Trust, 1975.

14. *Of Works of Supererogation*

> *Voluntary works besides, over and above God's commandments, which they call works of supererogation, cannot be taught without arrogancy and impiety; for by them men do declare that they do not only render unto God as much as they are bound to do, but that they do more for his sake, than of bounden duty is required; whereas Christ saith plainly: 'When ye have done all that are commanded to you, say: "We are unprofitable servants."'*

The quotation of Jesus' words in Luke 17:10 shows that we are dealing in this article with the noxious effects of medieval merit theology. When people have done something wrong and then try to put matters right, it is not uncommon for them to add a little extra, in order to show that they really mean it when they say that they are sorry. For example, if I forget my mother's birthday I may decide to buy her the flowers I would have got anyway *and* throw in a box of chocolates, in the hope that she will say: 'You shouldn't have, dear' and forget all about my original thoughtlessness. Going the extra mile, as this is sometimes called (see Matthew 5:41) is not a bad thing in itself, but we should not think of it as putting the other person (or God) in a position of having to forgive us because of our extra exertions.

In the merit theology of the middle ages, it was often thought that such works of supererogation, as acts above and beyond the call of duty were called, could be used as credits to set off against other misdemeanours elsewhere, even those committed by other people. For example, by doing a bit more than is strictly necessary, I might be able to reduce the time one of my loved ones was spending in purgatory, by transferring my superfluous merit to him. Of course this all makes sense in the context of salvation by works, but once we start believing in justification by faith alone, such behaviour loses its meaning. It is no more than an attempt to buy favour with God, which is not only impossible but blasphemous. What God does for us, he does out of the goodness of his heart and not because we have twisted his arm or ingratiated ourselves with him by doing more than we were originally asked to do. This way of thinking may be common in human affairs but it is blasphemous in the sight of God, because it detracts from the sheer mercy and unmerited grace of our salvation in Christ.

Christian people never have any cause to be proud of what they do, or satisfied that it is enough to keep God happy. At the same time, we have no need to fear that we have failed in our duty and are therefore likely to be punished or rejected by him. Here, perhaps more than anywhere else, we can see clearly just how different the basis of our faith relationship with God is from any notion of salvation by works. God loves us and saves us in spite of ourselves, a truth which is at the very heart of the Gospel and is the foundation of our assurance of salvation.

Questions for discussion:

1. Is it possible to do more than God requires of us?

2. Is it right to have goals in the Christian life and try to live up to them?

3. Why does Jesus call us unprofitable servants even when we have done our best?

Key Bible Passages:

Luke 17:7-10; Galatians 2:17-21; Ephesians 3:7-13; Philippians 1:19-26.

For further reading:

Flescher, A. M. *Heroes, saints and ordinary morality.* Washington, D.C.: Georgetown University Press, 2003.

Heyd, David. *Supererogation: its status in ethical theory.* Cambridge: CUP, 1982.

15. Of Christ alone without Sin

Christ in the truth of our nature, was made like unto us in all things, sin only except, from which he was clearly void, both in his flesh and in his spirit. He came to be the lamb without spot, who, by the sacrifice of himself once made, should take away the sins of the world; and sin, as St John saith, was not in him. But all we the rest, although baptized and born again in Christ, yet offend in many things, and if we say we have no sin, we deceive ourselves and the truth is not in us.

This article does not appear to be very controversial but it conceals a number of issues that have surfaced in debate at different times in the history of the church. The first of these concerns the precise nature of Christ's humanity. Granted that he is one person in two natures, how does this work in practice? Does his divine nature operate on his humanity in such a way as to overrule its inherent limitations and defects? In other words, is Christ sinless because his divine nature transfers its holiness to his humanity? If that is the case, must we also say that the human Jesus was omniscient for example, because the omniscience of his divinity would also have been transferred to his human mind? Or was it possible for the divine nature to transfer some of its properties to the humanity of Jesus but not all of them?

The answer to these questions and others like them is that the two natures of Christ are distinct and remain entirely separate from one another, because it is the person which unites them and not some fusion of the natures. Christ is therefore sinless *as a human being* and not because he was also divine.

But how could this be when there are no other sinless human beings? If his humanity was genuine and he got it from his mother, would he not also have inherited her sinfulness? One possible answer to this question is to say that Mary was also sinless, either because she had been cleansed at the moment of Jesus' conception in her womb (a common view in the middle ages) or because she was herself born sinless (the doctrine of her 'immaculate conception' promulgated by the Roman Catholic Church in 1854). Needless to say, this view has no Biblical evidence to support it and is rejected by all Protestants, including Anglicans. Mary was a sinner in need of a Saviour just as much as anyone else, and the sinlessness of her son has nothing to do with her.

The answer to this question can only be that sin is not inherent in human nature. Adam and Eve were not created that way and when they fell from grace their human nature did not change. It is true that they died as a result of their sin, but this was because the protection given to them in the Garden of Eden was taken away. They had always been mortal beings, unlike angels who, when they sinned, did not die but became demons and in that sense are still alive. Jesus was sinless because as a human being, he was perfectly obedient to the will of his Father. We may think that because he was also the Son of God, obedience to his Father's will came 'naturally' to him, but the Bible tells us that he still had to work it out in his human life, through the sufferings and death that he was called to endure (Hebrews 5:8). Even in the Garden of Gethsemane, the night before his crucifixion, this was the struggle that he faced: 'Not my will, but your will be done' (Mark 14:36). Jesus would not have been a normal human being if he had had a death wish, and so it was necessary for him to submit his natural human desire to live to the will of his Father that he should die for the sins of the world. It was not easy for him to do that, and the Bible tells us that he sweated blood in the course of his struggle to submit to his Father's will. But submit he did, and therefore he remained sinless even as he 'became sin for us' on the cross (2 Corinthians 5:21).

Paradoxical though it may sound, his sinlessness was a precondition for his 'becoming sin'. In ancient Israel, only a spotless lamb was suitable for sacrifice, because if there was some defect in it, killing it might be justified. The death of the lamb had nothing to do with its own inadequacy, but was a propitiatory sacrifice for the sins of the people. So it was with Jesus also. He did not sacrifice himself because there was something wrong with him which deserved death, but entirely for our sake (Hebrews 4:14-5:10).

It was therefore because Jesus had no sin in him that he could and did take away our sin (1 John 3:5). But what exactly does 'taking away our sin' mean? Can we say that we have been cleansed from sin in such a way as to become perfect? Here the answer must be no, and the article quotes 1 John 1:8 to reinforce this point. Our sins are taken away, not in the sense that we become sinless in the way that Jesus was, but in the sense that they no longer stand as a barrier blocking our access to God. We go on being sinners and therefore we go on sinning. Even if we can learn not to commit particular sins deliberately, every action of ours has something sinful about it because of our inherent sinfulness. We can recognise it and struggle against it, but we cannot get rid of it as long as the 'old Adam' continues to shape and control our human nature.

The continuance of sin in those who have been saved is an important factor in determining the way in which believers today have to understand the life of the earthly Jesus. There are many who think that we are called to imitate Christ, if not by becoming carpenters and itinerant preachers, then at least by doing the miracles he did and making prophetic statements which can claim the same divine authority as the ones he made. 'What would Jesus do?' seems like an innocent question to ask, but it is impossible to answer literally and does not reflect the teaching of the New Testament. As Christians we are not called to do what Jesus did (or what we might think he would do if he were in our shoes) but to do what he tells us to do – to obey his commands, not to copy his actions (unless, of course, that is what he tells us to do!) We must resist the temptation to turn Jesus into the first Christian, or as some translations of Hebrews 12:2 put it, the 'pioneer' of our faith. A Christian is a sinner saved by grace, which Jesus was not. His life was lived in a different context and had a different purpose from anything that our life could ever have. He is not a man who discovered a new relationship with God that he is now sharing with us, but our Saviour and Lord, and we must respect that essential difference. What he was capable of is not possible for us because we are still sinners, and must continue to depend on him for the grace we need to live the life that he wants us to live.

To claim to be able to copy the actions of the historical Jesus (or guess what he would do if he were alive today and do the same) is to claim to be in a state of sinless perfection, which is a lie. There have certainly been those who have made such a claim, and there is an entire tradition of the so-called 'second blessing' which purports to be a perfecting of those who have been saved by grace but who have not yet ceased from sinning. The truth is that there is no such blessing and no such perfection. To the end of our days we remain as we were when we were first converted – sinners in need of grace. The only way we can grow to be more like Jesus is to become more aware of how unlike him we really are and therefore submit more completely to his rule in our lives. 'I have been crucified with Christ,' said the Apostle Paul. 'It is no longer I who live, but Christ who lives in me. And the life I now live in the flesh I live by faith in the Son of God who loved me and gave himself for me.' (Galatians 2:20).

Furthermore, just as Jesus did not eradicate the sinfulness of those who believe in him, so too his death 'for the sins of the whole world' does not apply to those whom he has not called and chosen for salvation. In principle, of course, his death is *sufficient* to take away their sins, since nobody can sin in a way that goes beyond Christ's ability to forgive, but it is not *intended* for them, any more than the death of the lamb in ancient Israel was intended to pay for the sins of non-Israelites. Christ's atoning work must be seen in its context, which is that of covenantal election and predestination. If it is removed from that and made to apply to everyone without distinction, the result must be a doctrine of universal salvation (universalism), since it is impossible to believe that human beings have the power to thwart or nullify the grace of God. If he has died for us, then we have been saved whether we want to be or not, as Saul of Tarsus discovered on the road to Damascus (Acts 9:1-8). The choice is his, not ours, and the true disciple must always acknowledge that fact (John 15:16).

Questions for discussion:

1. If Jesus was sinless, why did the people of Nazareth not think there was something strange about him?

2. Was Jesus sinless in his human nature or only because he was also God?

3. When Jesus 'became sin for us' on the cross, did he become a sinner too?

Key Bible Passages:

Romans 5:12-21, 7:7-25; 2 Corinthians 5:21; Galatians 3:10-14; Hebrews 4:14-5:10; 1 John 1:5-10.

For further reading:

Warfield, B. B. *Studies in perfectionism.* Phillipsburg: Presbyterian and Reformed, 1958.

16. Of Sin after Baptism

Not every deadly sin willingly committed after baptism is sin against the Holy Ghost, and unpardonable. Wherefore the grant of repentance is not to be denied to such as fall into sin after baptism. After we have received the Holy Ghost, we may depart from grace given and fall into sin, and by the grace of God we may arise again and amend our lives. And therefore they are to be condemned, which say they can no more sin as long as they live here, or deny the place of forgiveness to such as truly repent.

The context and background to this article takes us back to a controversy in the early church that was associated with the name of Donatus, a presbyter of the church in North Africa. In the year 303 the Emperor Diocletian launched a massive persecution against Christians, who were multiplying dangerously fast in the Roman Empire. To save themselves, many Christians recanted and went back to paganism, at least on the surface, but when the danger subsided many of them changed their minds. After Christianity was legalised in 313, they sought readmission to the church, which did not know what to do with them. On the one hand, they appeared to be repentant sinners, but on the other hand, many people had lost family members and friends who had gone to their deaths rather than renounce Christ, and those people not unnaturally felt that the weaker ones should not be let off so lightly.

The official line was to readmit those who repented, provided that they gave adequate assurances that they were sincere, but although this was the humane solution (and probably the only practical one in the circumstances) it was not good enough for some people in North Africa, where church discipline had in any case always been stricter than elsewhere. These people, of whom Donatus was one of the leaders, believed that a baptised person was cleansed of original sin and therefore made perfect. If he sinned again, he lost his salvation because there was no second chance. Biblical support for this view could be found in Hebrews 6:4-5 which seems to refer to post-baptismal sin, and Jesus himself had spoken about the blasphemy against the Holy Spirit which could not be forgiven (Matthew 12:31). This was interpreted by the Donatists as sin committed after baptism, which was in turn regarded as the Holy Spirit's work of regeneration in the life of the believer. The original reason for Jesus' remark, which was the opposition of the Pharisees to miracles performed by him, played no part in this equation.

The issues involved here are often charged with emotion, which makes it especially difficult to distinguish what the principles are and try to apply them correctly in practice. It is easy to question the sincerity of those who repent, especially if what they are repenting of has done considerable harm. Would anyone have believed Adolf Hitler, for example, if he had said sorry at the end of the war instead of killing himself? Could he have been restored to the fellowship of the church? Theoretically, the answer to this must be yes, but it is hard to imagine anyone accepting that in practice. That is an extreme example, of course, but it illustrates the point that although we believe in principle that forgiveness is possible for even the worst of sinners, and agree that it is not for us to decide who is and who is not entitled to receive it, we find it hard to put those beliefs into practice when the sins in question go beyond the norms that we would ordinarily encounter.

It is also true that there are people who make a profession of faith and join the church for a time, but then fall away. Are such people true believers who have relapsed into their former life for a time but who will eventually return to the fold? Or are they people who never really knew the truth, and when something happened to make them aware of that, they turned away and will not be coming back? Is it possible for a believer to lose his eternal salvation, and if it is, what assurance of salvation can we possibly have? I do not know what tomorrow will bring, and can I really say that I shall still be a child of God whatever happens to me? We see these kinds of things happening all the time, but often it is impossible for us to judge what is really going on in particular cases. Whether a backslider is a believer who is temporarily blinded or an unbeliever who has finally seen the light and departed from the sheepfold is often beyond our ability to discern. All we can say for sure is that true believers cannot fall away eternally, because there is nothing in heaven or on earth that can separate us from the love of God (Romans 8:38-39). It is a promise that we cling to when those dear to us fall away but sometimes we shall not know the truth until the books are opened at the last judgment. Here perhaps more than anywhere, our faith is tried to the limit and we have no option but to believe and trust in the promises of God.

Receiving repentant sinners back into the church can also be much harder in practice than it is in theory. In some cases, the civil law takes matters out of our hands. For example, if a sex offender is barred from working with young children for the rest of his life, the church cannot ignore that, and the question of whether he should be allowed to become a Sunday school teacher does not arise. But of course most cases are not that cut and dried. Very common is the problem of the minister who has divorced and remarried. Should such a person be allowed to continue in his ministry? There is no simple answer to that question, since so much depends on circumstances, but churches have to have some kind of policy which will not set a bad precedent for the future. It is probably wiser to err on the side of caution and risk excluding some people who have genuinely repented, rather than go the other way and risk opening the gates to those who are insincere and may turn out to be repeat offenders. But not everyone will agree with that assessment and differences of judgment leading to differences of practice are almost inevitable. Here too, at the end of the day we can only walk by faith and trust the Lord for guidance, being prepared to change our minds (and our policies) as we are taught by our mistakes.

Questions for discussion:

1. Why do Christians still sin if they have the Holy Spirit dwelling in their hearts?

2. Is it possible to stop committing certain kinds of sin?

3. How can we tell if someone has truly repented of sin?

Key Bible Passages:

Luke 15:11-32; 2 Corinthians 2:5-11; 1 John 2:1-17.

For further reading:

Bash, A. *Forgiveness and Christian ethics.* Cambridge: CUP, 2007.

Henderson, M. *No enemy to conquer; forgiveness in an unforgiving world.* Waco, Tex.: Baylor University Press, 2009.

Null, J. A. *Thomas Cranmer's doctrine of repentance.* Oxford: OUP, 2006.

17.   Of Predestination and Election

Predestination to life is the everlasting purpose of God, whereby (before the foundations of the world were laid) he hath constantly decreed by his counsel secret to us, to deliver from curse and damnation those whom he hath chosen in Christ out of mankind, and to bring them by Christ to everlasting salvation, as vessels made to honour. Wherefore they which be endued with so excellent a benefit of God be called according to God's purpose by his Spirit working in due season;

they through grace obey the calling;

they be justified freely;

they be made sons of God by adoption;

they be made like the image of his only begotten Son Jesus Christ;

they walk religiously in good works and at length by God's mercy,

they attain to everlasting felicity.

As the godly consideration of predestination, and our election in Christ, is full of sweet, pleasant and unspeakable comfort to godly persons,

and such as feel in themselves the working of the Spirit of Christ,

mortifying the works of the flesh and their earthly members,

and drawing up their mind to high and heavenly things,

as well because it doth greatly establish and confirm their faith of eternal salvation to be enjoyed through Christ,

as because it doth fervently kindle their love towards God;

so for curious and carnal persons, lacking the Spirit of Christ, to have continually before their eyes the sentence of God's predestination, is a most dangerous downfall, whereby the Devil doth thrust them either into desperation, or into wretchlessness of most unclean living, no less perilous than desperation.

Furthermore, we must receive God's promises in such wise as they be generally set forth to us in Holy Scripture; and in our doings, that will of God is to be followed which we have, expressly declared to us in the Word of God.

The subject of predestination is one of the most emotive (and least understood) in Christian theology, and in some circles mere mention of the word is enough to provoke hostility. Along with election (which is essentially the same thing, seen from a slightly different perspective) predestination has been denounced by a wide range of people, who see it either as a form of determinism that takes responsibility away from individuals for their actions, or as a hindrance to evangelism. What is the point of preaching the Gospel, they ask, if the number of the saved is already fixed in the mind of God and unalterable? At times this doctrine has even been seen as justifying a sense of ethnic or racial superiority, when one nation (the Jews, the British, the Afrikaners, the Americans) are thought to be God's chosen people and the rest are dismissed, in Rudyard Kipling's words, as 'lesser breeds without the law'. That the doctrine has been misunderstood and misused cannot be doubted, but the fact that something has been abused does not mean that it must be discarded, and the task of the theologian is to understand and communicate to others why predestination matters and why it must be kept close to the heart of our Christian profession.

Election and predestination are both Biblical concepts, but they were not much developed in Christian theology until the time of Augustine (354–430). For him, they were part and parcel of the doctrine of God's grace, and it was in the course of his struggles against the Pelagians that he worked them out most fully. No other Christian teaching is as 'Augustinian' in feel as this one is, and its fortunes in later history are very much tied up with the degree to which subsequent generations have appreciated and appropriated the Augustinian heritage.

The Western church was always 'Augustinian' in theory, but during the middle ages it was not always so committed to his teaching in practice, and the doctrines of election and predestination were often more honoured in the breach than in the observance. The Reformation changed all that. Martin Luther was an Augustinian monk, which meant that he knew more about the great bishop of Hippo's theology than most people in his day did. He also became a professor of Holy Scripture at a time when the Bible was assuming a new prominence in the church and in intellectual life generally. It is not possible to read the Bible without being struck by the doctrine of election, since that was the entire basis of Israel's existence. Abraham's descendants had little going for them in worldly terms. They were few in number compared to the surrounding nations, and they were enslaved in Egypt for several centuries. Even after they escaped from that, it took them several more hundred years to establish a viable independent state, which did not last long. The nation split in two, exhausted itself by constant internecine warfare and eventually succumbed to foreign empires. A century of independence shortly before Jesus was born turned out to be no more than an interlude, followed by two millennia of exile and persecution which culminated in genocide. Yet the amazing thing is that whilst the Pharaohs, the Babylonians, the Assyrians, the Persians, the Hellenistic kings, the Romans, the Spanish Habsburgs and the German Nazis have all disappeared, the Jews are still with us. What is more, for a small nation, they have been extraordinarily productive and successful, and even today it is possible to meet people who are convinced that there is a 'Jewish plot' to take over the world.

That the Jews have survived against all the odds is indisputable, but what is their secret? The Bible is clear about this – they are still with us because they are God's chosen people and he will not let them disappear, however sorely they are tried by various enemies at different times in their history. Even after the coming of Christ, the Jewish people have a special place in the plan of God which will be revealed when they are converted at the end of time (Romans 11:25-29). It may be true that Jewish national consciousness can sometimes be ethnocentric to the point of racism, as Jesus pointed out by making favourable references to Samaritans and Gentiles who put Israelites to shame by their faith (Matthew 8:10). Even today, Judaism is the only major religion where inheritance is more important than belief or conversion. This is clear from the modern state of Israel, which is officially Jewish without being a country full of people who worship every Sabbath in the synagogue – far from it! Yet however far they may have strayed from the ideal, all Jews know that there is something special about them whether they like it or not, and that ultimately this distinctiveness is bound up with the covenant that God made with Abraham. What exactly Paul meant when he said that in the end 'all Israel will be saved' is not entirely clear, but the general thrust of the text surely indicates that the blindness which now prevents the Jewish nation from turning to Christ will be removed and the faithful remnant of historic Israel will be grafted into the tree of life once more.

Israel's calling by God has been extended to the Christian church thanks to the person and work of Jesus. God has not gone back on his promises or permanently abandoned his Old Testament people, but he has opened the bounds of the chosen nation to allow non-Jews, or Gentiles as we call them, to share in the blessings of their election. We are like branches which have been grafted into the Jewish tree, children of Abraham by faith rather than by physical descent. The coming of this new dispensation has had some curious, but important effects. One of them is that the focus has shifted from the community to the individual. The Apostle Paul points this out in Romans 2-4, where he makes the astonishing claim that not all Jews are true children of Abraham. It is not enough to have his blood running in your veins, or to be circumcised and placed under the law of Moses. The true Israelite must also believe the promises of God and recognise that they have been fulfilled in Christ. Gentiles who come to the same awareness are not attached to the physical nation of Israel by being circumcised and put under the law, but they are united with Jewish believers in the body of Christ, which is the church.

Like Israel, the visible church is a mixed body of believers and unbelievers, but unlike Israel it recognises this and therefore thinks of election and predestination in primarily individual terms. A Christian is not chosen and predestined by virtue of belonging to the church (still less because he has been born in a superficially 'Christian' country), but because God has picked him out and set his seal on him. Baptism manifests this, but it must not be confused with the reality of election. The most that baptism can do is bear witness of the calling of God to repentance and faith; it cannot produce those things in the heart of the recipient merely by being administered to him. In a very real sense, election is the doctrine most deeply opposed to sacramentalism, because it states that a person is chosen by God in a way that is unique and mysterious to him, and not processed into the kingdom of heaven by means that are controlled and administered by other human beings.

Unbelievers have no idea about any of this and they cannot understand or accept it. Deprived as they are of the indwelling presence of the Holy Spirit, their minds remain in darkness and they are liable to draw all the wrong conclusions when the doctrine is preached to them. By far the most damaging of these misunderstandings is the conviction that they are already condemned and unable to do anything about it. The trouble with this is that it is a half-truth. They *are* condemned because of their unbelief, but it is not true that there is nothing they can do about it. If they have heard the Gospel (and they would not be perturbed by this idea otherwise) they can always repent and be saved. The fact that they do not is their responsibility and it is that which guarantees their eternal condemnation, not the unwillingness or inability of God to rescue them. They are like people who have been told that they have a terminal illness and decide to blow all they have on a last round of enjoyment before they are snuffed out. The thought that there might be something better waiting for them simply does not cross their minds and they end up co-operating in their own destruction rather than doing what they can to resist it.

Christian preachers have to be sensitive to this and not provoke unnecessary speculation which will only do harm. We know that those who are not chosen for eternal salvation are condemned, and the Bible is sufficiently clear about this that we are fully entitled to speak of reprobation, or 'double predestination' as it is sometimes called (2 Corinthians 4:3; 1 Peter 2:8; 2 Peter 2:12; Jude 4; Revelation 17:8). But the article reminds us that we must be careful about the way in which we apply it to particular cases. For example, what are we supposed to say about the fate of those whom we know have never heard the Gospel? Such people have obviously not put their faith in Christ, at least not in the way that we understand it, but whether that means that they are all doomed to spend eternity in hell is something we cannot say for certain. The Apostle Paul told the Athenians that God has overlooked the time of ignorance (Acts 17:30), but what this means is unclear. We know from what he says in Romans 1:18-2:16 that pagans have turned away from God and although they will not be judged by a law they have never heard of, they are unlikely to escape condemnation either, because the law written in their hearts tells them that they have done wrong at some point. Our duty as Christians is not to speculate about such things but to preach the Gospel so that those who hear it will have a chance to repent and believe. Similarly, in the case of predestination, our job is to hold out to people the wonderful benefits that follow from receiving Christ as Lord and Saviour and not to concentrate on examining the terrible fate of those who do not know him. The benefits of the Christian life are guaranteed because they are predestined, and we must preach them without fear, but we must do so in a way that invites people to receive them. Whatever we do, we must avoid giving people the impression that there is no hope for them because they have been rejected already. Anyone who thinks that is liable to relapse into a life of debauchery brought on by a sense of hopelessness, which is the very opposite of the Christian Gospel. The doctrine of predestination is a comfort for believers, who can be assured that they are saved. Whatever may go wrong in our lives, or whatever burdens we may have to bear, God's purpose for us cannot be thwarted because he is in control. On the other hand, predestination is not meant to be used as a way of condemning others either explicitly or implicitly. Our job is to sow the seed of the Gospel wherever we can and not to choose or reject the ground it falls on in advance (Matthew 13:3-8).

At the time of the Reformation, there was relatively little disagreement among the churches about the principles of this doctrine, though the emphasis placed on it varied enormously. In 1551 Martin Bucer gave a series of lectures in Cambridge in which he expounded Ephesians, one of the classic texts of predestinarian teaching. In the course of those lectures he acknowledged that there are risks in preaching the doctrine of election but insisted that we must not be put off by them. Instead, we ought to preach it boldly and clearly, not in order to condemn the reprobate but to encourage the people of God in their vocation. It is possible that Archbishop Cranmer, who wrote this article only a year or so later, was following Bucer's advice when he did so. It certainly corresponds very well to what Bucer had in mind and to this day it remains one of the classic and most balanced statements of the doctrine.

First of all, election and predestination are part of the eternal plan of God for our redemption. Our salvation was not an afterthought, a kind of plan B that occurred to him only after his initial work of creation had failed. God knew all along that his creatures would turn away from him, but he determined right from the beginning that he would rescue and restore some of them in and through the work of his Son Jesus Christ.

This eternal plan is worked out in practice by the Holy Spirit, whom Cranmer describes as 'working in due season'. This means that the time and the means of revealing God's will to his elect varies from person to person; no two conversions are exactly alike. Some, like that of Saul of Tarsus, are sudden and dramatic. Others, like that of C. S. Lewis, are slow and painful, leaving the convert surprised by the joy that comes from believing. Some are a mixture of the two, like that of Martin Luther, whose spiritual journey was both gradual and dramatic, while others are almost imperceptible, like that of Calvin, who seems to have gone to bed a nominal Catholic and woken up a convinced Protestant sometime in 1533 or 1534, but we know little more than that. It does not matter *how* the Spirit works; what counts is *that* he does so. What follows next is a series of steps known as the 'order of salvation' (*ordo salutis*), which Cranmer outlines as follows:

1. The elect hear God's calling and obey it by the grace given to them (Romans 8:28).

2. The elect are then justified by the free gift of God (Romans 3:24).

3. The elect are next made children of God by adoption (Romans 8:15).

4. The elect are then transformed into the image of Jesus Christ (Ephesians 1:4).

5. The elect live a life of good works dedicated to the service of God (Ephesians 2:10).

6. The elect finally obtain everlasting happiness by the mercy of God. (Romans 8:38-39).

These are the principles, but they are not illustrated or spelt out in detail. For example, we are told that the elect hear God's call and obey it, but not what form that call actually takes. The reason for this is that it is different in different cases. Usually it involves conviction of sin, followed by repentance, but not always. The conversion of Saul of Tarsus cannot really be interpreted like that. Jesus asked him why he was struggling against God and Saul fell down as if he were dead, but we are not told that he confessed his sins or repented of them at that point. Of course he did later on – indeed, his entire life can be seen as a kind of ongoing repentance for having persecuted the church, but at the time all he did was hear God's voice and obey. The consequences came later.

Justification follows our encounter with God. It is the result of our conversion and not its cause, something that many people fail to understand. God calls us to himself first and then he justifies us by pointing us to the shed blood of his Son. It is easy for people to be moved by the sufferings of Jesus, but that is not the same thing as being justified by his atoning sacrifice. It is only as we meet him that we start to understand what he has done for us, and we cannot benefit from that until we are put in the right relationship with him. By its nature, justification has to be an individual experience, even if it is symbolised by the sacraments of the church. Baptism stands in relation to justification rather in the way that a wedding ring stands in relation to a marriage. The two things go together and the one reflects and reinforces the other, but just as wearing a ring cannot by itself produce a relationship, so being baptised in water and incorporated into the church does not automatically produce justification.

Adoption follows on from justification and is one of the most important points that we must observe. It is because I have been adopted by God as his child that I have become an heir of salvation and entitled to receive all the benefits and privileges which that status implies. I am not a child of God by nature (as the Son is) and therefore cannot claim these benefits as of right, but God has reached out to me in love and given them to me in spite of the fact that I am not entitled to them by anything that I have done. Adoption is literally election in practice – it is what happens when the doctrine comes home to my experience.

To be transformed into the image of Christ is to be given his mind and his will. This is made clear in 1 Corinthians 2:14-16. It was all too obvious to Paul that the Corinthians were still the same sinful people they had been before their conversion and that the consequences of that event for their subsequent behaviour had not fully sunk in. The message of his letters to them can be summed up as follows: 'You have been given a new status, so live up to it.' We often see something like this when people receive a promotion that forces them to change their outlook on life. A classic example of it is when a student becomes a teacher. It often takes time for him to adjust to his new role, especially if he is only slightly older than the students he is teaching, but adjust he must, because that is what is expected of him in that position. Similarly, when a member of the congregation becomes a minister, he cannot go on thinking and acting in exactly the same way as before, even if he does not feel any different inside. The Corinthian Christians were still citizens of Corinth and active participants in the city's affairs, but because of their new faith they now had a different relationship to those things, and Paul expected that difference to show up in the way they lived their lives. They had the mind of Christ and had to act in accordance with it.

The Christian life is one of good works dedicated to God, and the final reward is everlasting bliss in heaven. It is not by any means always a smooth progression from one state to the next, and some Christians are called to undergo terrible hardship and suffering on their way to glory. It is not for us to choose, as Jesus told his disciples after his resurrection (John 21:20-23); our task is to obey and to follow along the pathway he has prepared for us (Ephesians 2:10).

The benefits of our election are great, and again Cranmer sets them out as basic principles:

1. The Holy Spirit mortifies the works of our flesh (Romans 8:13).

2. The Holy Spirit turns our minds to higher things (Romans 8:5).

3. The Holy Spirit establishes and confirms our faith in eternal salvation (Romans 8:16).

4. The Holy Spirit kindles our love for God (Romans 8:11).

Each of these things is set out as a hierarchy of steps leading towards a deeper knowledge and experience of the Lord. First, we see how he gets to work on our old life, making us understand why it is wrong and showing us how we must adjust it in order to please him. Next, he replaces our desires for earthly things with a deeper desire for heavenly ones. So much of what we do depends on the way we think, and for that reason this second step is perhaps the most important one of them all. We are not merely rescued from our past; we are turned towards something different and better for the future. What that is becomes clear in the third stage, when we are strengthened in our hope of eternal salvation. As we feel God at work in us, so we become convinced that he really does care about us, and start to trust him more for whatever lies ahead. We begin to see a purpose in it all, and as we get to that point, the reverses and disappointments along the way cease to disturb us. We know that however long and hard the road may be, the end is in sight, and that end is a life of eternal joy and peace. It is also a life in which our love for God will be complete and all-embracing. Heaven is not a retirement home where we can relax and catch up with old friends, but a complete absorption in and by the love of God in Christ. It is the wedding feast of the Lamb that will carry on forever as Christ unites his bride, the church of the redeemed to himself. That is what election is all about, and it is to that end that we have been predestined. The Spirit and the bride say: 'Come'. And those who hear reply: 'Amen. Come, Lord Jesus.' (Revelation 22:17, 20).

Questions for discussion:

1. If God knows in advance who will be saved, is there any need to evangelise them?

2. Can we know whether another person has been chosen by God?

3. Are we able to give any reason why God chooses some and not others?

Key Bible Passages:

Isaiah 43:1-7; Matthew 13:3-8; Romans 9:1-29; Ephesians 1:1-10; 2 Peter 1:3-11.

For further reading:

Jewett, P. K. *Election and predestination.* Grand Rapids: Eerdmans, 1985.

Peterson, R. A. *Election and free will: God's gracious choice and our responsibility.* Phillipsburg: Presbyterian and reformed, 2007.

Schriener, T. R. and B. Ware, eds. *Still sovereign: contemporary perspectives on election, foreknowledge and grace.* Grand Rapids: Baker, 2000.

Storms, C. S. *Chosen for life: the case for divine election.* Wheaton, Ill.: Crossway, 2007.

Wallace, D. D. *Puritans and predestination: grace in English Protestant theology 1525-1695.* Chapel Hill, N.C.: University of North Carolina Press, 1982.

18.   *Of obtaining eternal Salvation, only by the Name of Christ*

> *They also are to be had accursed that presume to say that every man shall be saved by the law or sect which he professeth, so that he be diligent to frame his life according to that law, and the light of nature. For Holy Scripture doth set out unto us only the name of Jesus Christ, whereby men must be saved.*

This article is unusual, not so much in what it says (although it is the only article which pronounces an anathema on anyone) as in the fact that it is one of the few articles which has without a doubt become even more relevant to us today than it was in the sixteenth century. At that time there was no Christian church which suggested that it was possible for a person to come to God in any way other than through the Lord Jesus Christ (John 14:6) and those who followed other religions were universally condemned for being in error. The exclusive claims of Christianity go right back to the earliest preaching of the Gospel, as this article reminds us with its quotation of Acts 4:12. The notion that it does not matter what you believe as long as you are sincere was completely alien to Christians of any persuasion and would have been rejected by Catholics even more vehemently (if that were possible) than by Protestants. But as often happens in times of controversy, there were some people who tried to restore peace by relativising the issues at stake. Why fight over religious principles, they said, if everyone was heading in the same direction anyway? The niceties of doctrine are surely less important than a spirit of love, joy, peace and fellowship. If Jews and Muslims are decent people, what can possibly be wrong with them? How can we claim that we are better than they are or that we shall be saved but they will not?

It will now be clear why this line of argument is more prevalent today than it was in the sixteenth century. At that time, people had very few (if any) non-Christian neighbours, especially in England, which did not even have any Jews. (They had been expelled in 1290 and were not readmitted until 1656.) But what was largely theoretical then has become common now and is an important social issue. No public figure in any Western country today would dare to suggest that Christianity is better than other religions, because that would look like racism and discrimination. Even when Muslim extremists terrorise the countries they live in and condemn to death anyone who disagrees with their religion, our so-called 'Christian' spokesmen hardly ever say anything against them. Occasionally, it is true, some brave reporter will point out that life in Saudi Arabia, India or South-east Asia is less than utopian, and will suggest that local religious teachings and practices are a large part of the problem. But almost invariably, the prevalence of this unwelcome religiosity is presented in terms of social and economic underdevelopment. The assumption is that, given time, those places will evolve into secular liberal democracies along Western lines and there will be no difference between their way of thinking and ours. It is even said that Islam is still only in its fifteenth century, which is supposed to mean that, by analogy with Christianity, a reformation should occur within the next hundred years or so and remove the current medieval darkness.

In historically Christian countries there is now no danger that the churches will launch a campaign against non-Christians of a kind that would make the state nervous of civil disturbance. With the possible exception of the Russian Orthodox Church, which harbours some very chauvinistic elements, no Christian church today is interested in practising religious repression. On the other hand, it is our duty as Christians to preach the Gospel to every creature, and we cannot do that without giving offence to others, whether they practise another religion or not. This has nothing to do with us or our methods; it is inherent in the Gospel itself. It gave offence in Jesus' day, when he was virtually the only one who proclaimed it and could not have threatened anyone very seriously, so how much more will it appear as a threat to people today?

A further complication here is that although we must tell the adherents of other religions that they are worshipping false gods, (or in the case of Jews, worshipping the true God in the wrong way,) it is seldom people of those faiths who get most upset by this. After all, they think the same about us and often see no reason why we should not be just as honest about our claims as they are about theirs. No, the most determined opposition often comes from people with a nominally Christian background – the secular humanists of our society and those in the church who agree with them. Here we have to be blunt and say that some of the worst enemies of the Gospel are members, and often clergy, of the Church of England, who not only preach a message far removed from the unique and exclusive claims of Christ, but also take every opportunity to criticise and condemn those who insist on proclaiming the truth. These are the people who are most likely to claim that all religions and philosophies are ultimately the same and that we should seek dialogue and understanding with people of other faiths rather than try to convert them to ours.

The trouble with this apparently attractive idea is that it is impossible to share our faith without sharing the claims that it makes. Jesus said that he is the way, the truth and the life, and that no-one can come to the Father except through him (John 14:6). Are we supposed to say that he was wrong? If we do, then we cease to be Christians and can no longer claim to speak for the church with any integrity. But if we uphold the teaching of Christ, what dialogue is possible with those who cannot accept his exclusiveness? We do not have to be unpleasant to them or persecute them, of course, but we do have to try to persuade them that we are right and that they are wrong. Christians are not morally superior to anyone else – we are sinners saved by grace, after all – but we do know the truth, and the truth has set us free. To fail to say this, and to accept other beliefs as equivalent to ours, is to deny the truth and leave those who have not accepted it in bondage. If we love them as Christ loves them and believe that he has died for them, we cannot do this. We cannot sit back and assume that the world is full of 'anonymous Christians' who will be saved because they are faithful to their own erroneous beliefs. On the contrary, we must share with them the secret of eternal life through faith in the one Saviour and Lord of mankind, and expect that those who have been chosen for salvation will respond to the message as God has promised us that they will. People who do not understand this and who object to preaching the Gospel message are actually trying to prevent the word of eternal life from reaching those for whom it is intended. They may mean well, but as this article reminds us, they are cursed in the sight of God because their apparent tolerance is misguided. Christians cannot remain silent as millions perish for want of hearing and receiving the Word of God and it is our duty to take the Gospel to them, in the hope that God has already chosen those whom we are sent to call to receive salvation.

Questions for discussion:

1. Can people who have never heard of Christ be saved?

2. Can Christians learn anything from other religions?

3. Is it ever right for Christians to participate in inter-faith worship?

Key Bible Passages:

John 14:1-13; Acts 17:16-34; 1 Timothy 2:1-7; Romans 2:12-16.

For further reading:

Baker, David W., ed. *Biblical faith and other religions: an Evangelical assessment.* Grand Rapids: Kregel, 2004.

Morgan, C. W. and R. A. Peterson. *Faith comes by hearing: a response to inclusivism.* Nottingham: IVP, 2008.

Muck, T. C. *Christianity encountering world religions: the practice of mission in the twenty-first century.* Grand Rapids: Baker, 2009.

19. Of the Church

The visible Church of Christ is a congregation of faithful men in which the pure Word of God is preached and the sacraments be duly ministered according to Christ's ordinance in all those things that of necessity are requisite to the same.

As the Church of Jerusalem, Alexandria and Antioch have erred, so also the Church of Rome hath erred, not only in their living and manner of ceremonies, but also in matters of faith.

The doctrine of the church is one of the most important bones of contention to have emerged at the time of the Reformation, because it touches not only on the visible institution which goes by that name and the authority which it claims, but also on the invisible company of the elect and their relationship to the visible church.

Before the Reformation, questions concerning the nature of the church were seldom raised by anyone. There was a general sense that there was only one body of Christ in the world and that it extended to every tribe and nation where the Gospel had been preached. It was understood that over time some churches had lost contact with the main body of the church and got out of step with it as a result. That was the case of the Celtic church in the British Isles, which was eventually reconciled to the rest of the Christian world, though not without some difficulty. Some churches had fallen into error, but in those cases the orthodox had normally appointed other bishops to take the place of the schismatic or heretical ones. That had happened in the Eastern Mediterranean, where the majority of Christians had become Monophysites after the council of Chalcedon. As they broke communion with Rome and Constantinople, the latter church (being the nearer of the two) sent other bishops to maintain an orthodox presence in the east, however small and insignificant that might have been. Later on, when the Western (Roman) church and the Eastern churches owing allegiance to Constantinople split apart, a similar procedure was followed by the former, with the result that to this day there are so-called 'Latin' patriarchs and bishops of places like Constantinople, Antioch and Alexandria.

It would be wrong to pretend that these divisions were not deep and sincerely felt. The schism between East and West in particular continues to rankle, and there is no chance of any reconciliation between them as long as Rome insists on appointing its own bishops to traditionally Eastern sees. The snag is that in the course of time, a community of Roman loyalists has grown up in many eastern countries, including Greece, and they want to keep their traditions, which in some cases are now many centuries old. There is no easy solution to this problem, but it would be fair to say that in the sixteenth century it was localised and somewhat parochial as far as most Western Christians were concerned. To them there was but one church, whose head on earth was the bishop of Rome.

It was this idea that the Protestants objected to and which forced them to develop a doctrine of the church that could counter the claims of the papacy. One of the most persuasive arguments put by Roman Catholic polemicists, both then and now, is that the Roman church has been around since New Testament times whereas the Protestant churches are relatively new creations. To express it another way, how is it possible for Protestants to put so much store by the Apostle Paul's letter to the Romans while at the same time rejecting the authority of the head of the church to which it was written?

The first answer given to this was to claim that Rome, like the ancient churches of the East before it, had erred. This article does not say how, but Article 23 elaborates on the theme to some extent and it is possible to fill it out from what is said elsewhere in the Articles. The nub of the matter was that Rome (and the other ancient churches) had erred, not only in matters of practice and ceremonial, but also on points of doctrine. Obviously, the Roman church could not (and still cannot) accept this, although it must be remembered that a full-blown doctrine of papal infallibility did not emerge until 1870. But even in the sixteenth century, Rome maintained that its church was 'indefectible', that is to say, that it had been preserved from error throughout its history, and papal apologists used this argument to demonstrate its superiority not only over Protestants but also over the churches of the East which had not been so fortunate.

The main reason that the Reformers rejected the Roman claim was that the church did not base its teaching on Scripture alone. The principles laid down in article 6 were not accepted by the papacy, which believed (and still believes) that it has the power to impose beliefs on the church whether they are found in Scripture or not. Here there is a fundamental difference of approach to the sources of Christian doctrine that cannot be overcome by simple dialogue. Either Scripture's teaching is sufficient for salvation or it is not – no middle way or compromise solution is possible. Anglicans say that it is, and Rome says that it is not, which from the Anglican standpoint means that Rome has fallen into error in a matter of faith.

When it comes to the positive question of what constitutes a church, the article is deceptively clear. A church is a body of faithful people in which the pure Word of God is preached and the sacraments are properly administered. That sounds straightforward, but it is not quite as simple as it looks.

First of all, the term 'faithful men' refers to people who are doctrinally orthodox, not just to people who are loyal members of the institutional church. We are not dealing here with a club full of dedicated supporters, but with a fellowship of those who share the same fundamental beliefs. Anglicans know only too well that the church includes any number of people who do not meet this criterion, and Thomas Cranmer knew it too. He had to deal with many in the church of his day who were ignorant of (or unsympathetic to) the doctrines he was setting out in these Articles, and it cannot have surprised him too much when barely a year later the Church of England meekly submitted to Rome once more. Faithful men have never been all that easy to find!

The word 'congregation' is also difficult. To us it suggests a parish church, but although some people argue for this interpretation, it is doubtful whether Cranmer intended it in that sense. His concurrent mention of the great patriarchates of the ancient world suggests that he thought more in terms of national or regional churches, which were 'congregations' in a wider sense, and it is even possible that he was speaking of the universal church as a single 'congregation' formed of believers from around the world. It would certainly be stretching things to suppose that this article would justify someone separating from a parish church if the minister or people in it were unorthodox, although that is what often happens in practice today.

The preaching of the 'pure Word of God' and the right administration of the sacraments is another difficulty that we have to face. For Cranmer, this was at least partly a question of ordination. As we discover in Article 24, no-one who was not lawfully called and appointed had any hope of doing either, and a parish which allows non-ordained members, however gifted they may be, to preach and celebrate the sacraments is not acting like a true church. (It should perhaps be said here that those who argue for 'lay presidency' at the Lord's Table are advocating that lay people should be licensed to preside at holy communion, which is really a form of ordination by another name.) Of course, proper ordination was not the only criterion. The ministry of the Word and sacrament also had to be faithful to the meaning and purpose of those things. It was not possible for a man to preach the pure Word of God if he had no idea what it was, and that demanded a proper theological education. Likewise, the sacraments had to be administered within the context of the church's life and discipline. Indiscriminate baptism and private communion were both abuses that had to be checked, because in the first instance there was no attempt to investigate the sincerity of those seeking baptism (almost always for their children in the sixteenth century) and in the second there was no fellowship in the body of Christ. In sum, the criteria laid down here for discerning the true church of Christ were to be applied by giving prospective ministers a solid theological grounding and by avoiding practices that obscured the nature of the Gospel, particularly in the administration of the sacraments.

The formularies of the church (the Articles, the Prayer Book and the Ordinal) were all designed to further these ends and when matters are viewed from that angle, it can be said that the Church of England and the other Anglican churches that follow its lead, are within the definition of the church set out here. In theory at least, nobody is forced to believe or to do anything that goes against the teaching contained in these formularies, although it would be a brave soul who would suggest that there is nothing in the church today that is contrary to them. The point is that as long as those things are optional they can be regarded as aberrations and ignored by the 'faithful men' who make up the true church of Christ.

One of the problems facing Anglicans today is whether the current option of ignoring or avoiding the beliefs and practices of others in the Communion will remain viable for much longer. A good example of the difficulties is provided by the ordination of women, which traditionalists argue cannot be justified from Scripture and goes against the general tenor of its teaching about women's ministry, even if the exact issue is not directly addressed in the New Testament. Technically, the church recognises that there are 'two integrities' on the subject, which is a polite way of saying that there is a disagreement that will not go away and must be accommodated by allowing both sides to live according to their own convictions. In reality however, it is now all but impossible for someone who rejects the ordination of women to be consecrated as a diocesan bishop and the supporters of women's ordination are loud in their demands that those who are against it should be obliged to submit or to leave the church. They frequently reject any compromise on the subject, because to them the issue is a matter of justice and has therefore become a fundamental article of faith. For opponents, on the other hand, the pure Word of God is not being preached when women are allowed to be ordained, and of course women cannot properly administer the sacraments either, at least not in normal circumstances. Here the church is faced with a demand that in the eyes of many compromises its faithfulness to the teaching of the Bible but which threatens to impose itself as obligatory. If that happens, claim the traditionalists, the Church of England and the other Anglican churches will also have erred in the way that the churches of the East and of Rome have erred, and their claim to be true churches will no longer be tenable.

Questions for discussion:

1. Can a local congregation of believers be a church by itself?

2. How important is correct doctrine for the life of the church?

3. How much agreement should there be between different congregations in order for them to have fellowship (communion) with each other?

Key Bible Passages:

1 Corinthians 5; Galatians 2:1-14; Ephesians 2:19-22; 1 Peter 2:9-10; 2 Peter 2:1-9; Jude 1-25; Revelation 2-3.

For further reading:

Avis, P. *The identity of Anglicanism: essentials of Anglican ecclesiology.* London: T. and T. Clark, 2007.

Bradshaw, T. *The olive branch: an evangelical Anglican doctrine of the church.* Carlisle: Paternoster, 1992.

Clowney, E. P. *The church.* Leicester: IVP, 1995.

Locke, K. A. *The church in Anglican theology: an historical, theological and ecumenical exploration.* Farnham: Ashgate, 2009.

Watson, D. *I believe in the church.* London: Hodder and Stoughton, 1978.

Woodhouse, H. F. *The doctrine of the church in Anglican theology, 1547-1603.* London: SPCK, 1954.

20. *Of the Authority of the Church*

The Church hath power to decree rites and ceremonies, and authority in controversies of faith; and yet it is not lawful for the Church to ordain anything that is contrary to God's Word written, neither may it so expound one place of Scripture that it is repugnant to another. Wherefore, although the Church be a witness and a keeper of Holy Writ; yet as it ought not to decree anything against the same, so besides the same ought it not to enforce anything to be believed for necessity of salvation.

This article elaborates further the meaning of the previous one, and the two ought to be read together. On the one hand it is clear that the church can and must establish rites and ceremonies for the ordering of its public worship. There is a strand of Protestantism that insists that the New Testament is the only guide for this, and that nothing should take place in a church service that does not have specific New Testament warrant or precedent. Unfortunately for people who think this way, the New Testament is not a directory for Christian worship and it is impossible to reconstruct exactly what any ancient congregation did. We do not know how often the early Christians met for worship, nor at what time of day they gathered, nor how long their services lasted nor what they consisted of. We know that they sang psalms, hymns and spiritual songs, but apart from the first of these, we cannot say much about them and have no idea how central they were to the overall pattern of worship. We also know that they broke bread together in remembrance of Christ's death, but we do not know what ceremonies accompanied this or who presided over them. The testimony of 1 Corinthians 12 and 14 suggests that there was room for congregational initiative in what we would now call a time of 'open prayer' but we know little more than that. The *Didache*, a very early Christian writing which may date from apostolic times, indicates that people were expected to memorise the Lord's Prayer and make regular use of it in their private devotions, but whether the church itself followed any sort of participatory liturgy is not known.

Given this situation, churches today have no choice but to 'add' to the New Testament if they are to function at all, since even the giving out of notices is not a known Biblical practice! It is also necessary to make doctrinal statements from time to time, so as to clarify points that have been misunderstood or underemphasised. Historically, the church has been slow and cautious in this area, and that must surely be the right approach. But sometimes things have to be said in order to make certain practices clear. A good example today is the need to insist that marriage is meant to be a lifelong, heterosexual and monogamous relationship between two responsible adults. Thomas Cranmer would have been shocked to be told that such a definition was necessary, because he and all his contemporaries were agreed on the subject. Even a generation ago, anyone who proposed that a definition of marriage was needed would probably have been dismissed as a time-waster, if nothing else, because there was no serious disagreement about it. But this is not true anymore! Obviously the church has not just recently discovered its doctrine of marriage, a doctrine which it has held consistently since New Testament times, but it has been forced to articulate it in the face of opposition to its basic principles. Some small and very conservative denominations can rely on the consensus of their membership in such matters, but Anglican churches have to make a formal statement, which may be treated as authoritative even if it is not elevated to the status of the creeds or the Articles of Religion.

Having said that, there are clear limits to what the church is and is not entitled to do. In particular, it has no authority:

1. To enact or ordain anything that goes against the teaching of the Bible.

2. To interpret one part of Scripture in a way that contradicts other parts.

3. To decree anything that goes beyond the bounds of Scripture or to make it necessary for eternal salvation.

The ordination of women, to which we made reference in our discussion of Article 19, serves as a good example for testing these criteria. Does it go against the teaching of the Bible? The New Testament did not have a concept of ordination in the modern sense, but it is clear that people were appointed as overseers in the different churches and that they were invariably men. Furthermore, we know that this was not an accident, or an accommodation with prevailing social norms. In 1 Timothy 2:10-15 the Apostle makes it clear that women are not to teach or have authority over men because it was Eve who was deceived first (and who led her husband into disobedience, though this is implied rather than expressly stated in the text.) Supporters of women's ordination often quote Galatians 3:28 ('there is neither male nor female, for you are all one in Christ Jesus') and use it to cancel out the other prohibition, ignoring the fact that in Galatians Paul was speaking about salvation, not ministry in the church, and that to interpret the text in that way is to set one part of the New Testament over against another.

To those who would say that this is just an example of male chauvinism on the part of some post-Pauline author and therefore it should not be taken seriously, it must be objected that to come to that conclusion is to deny the canonical authority of the text, which has been universally recognised since ancient times. Furthermore, it is quite plain that what Paul is saying here is factually correct as far as the Genesis account is concerned, and that far from being an example of male chauvinism, the blame for sin rests on Adam, not on Eve, when the issue arises in other parts of the New Testament (Romans 5:12). A consistent reading of the Biblical text must therefore exclude any notion that the author harboured a prejudice against women that is unworthy of a Christian, let alone of an apostle. To make the acceptance of women's ordination a necessary criterion for anyone who wishes to minister publicly in a church is to go beyond the bounds of Scripture and elevate to the level of the essential something that in itself has nothing to do with the purpose for which the ministry was instituted, which is to proclaim and maintain the Gospel of eternal salvation in Christ. One way or another, all three of the principles laid down in this article are violated by this kind of procedure and those who do such things have exceeded the authority given to them by the Word of God.

Questions for discussion:

1. How much does the Bible tell us about how a church should be organised?

2. What principles should be used to determine the best form of worship in a particular church?

3. How should the church handle things that are not mentioned in the Bible (like global warming, cloning, nuclear warfare, etc.)?

Key Bible Passages:

Matthew 15:1-9; 1 Corinthians 12, 14; 2 Timothy 3:1-17; Revelation 22.

For further reading:

Arthur, G. *Law, liberty and church: authority and justice in the major churches in England.* Aldershot: Ashgate, 2006.

Doe, N. *An Anglican covenant: theological and legal considerations for a global debate.* Norwich: Canterbury Press, 2008.

Doe, N. *Canon law in the Anglican communion: a worldwide perspective.* Oxford: OUP, 1998.

21. Of the Authority of General Councils

General councils may not be gathered together without the commandment and will of princes. And when they be gathered together, (forasmuch as they shall be an assembly of men, whereof all be not governed with the Spirit and Word of God,) they may err, and sometimes have erred, even in things pertaining unto God. Wherefore things ordained by them as necessary to salvation have neither strength nor authority, unless it may be declared that they be taken out of Holy Scripture.

By 'general councils' of the church must be understood the so-called 'ecumenical councils' that were called together following the legalisation of Christianity in the early fourth century. At that time, most Christians lived inside the Roman Empire, and so it was natural for them to think in terms of an 'imperial' council of the church, which is what 'ecumenical' originally implied. When Augustus Caesar decreed his famous tax census, recorded by Luke (2:1), the decree went out 'to the whole world (*oecumene*)' which of course could only have meant the whole empire. After the legalisation of Christianity in the fourth century, the backing of the emperor for a general council was considered necessary because the bishops summoned to it would need a safe conduct to travel and also because the decrees of the council would have to be ratified (and probably implemented) by the state. This did not give the emperor the right to tell the church what to do, but it put certain limits on its actions. For example, a church council might impose the death penalty on heretics, but this could not be carried out unless the secular ruler was prepared to do it, since no state could allow an organisation outside its control to make the law. The medieval period saw long running battles between the papacy and the secular rulers of the time over this, and Thomas Cranmer was writing in the aftermath of a dispute between Pope Paul III (1534–1549) and the Emperor Charles V over the convening of a council to deal with the Protestant crisis. Eventually there was a compromise – the pope summoned the council, but it met on imperial territory (at Trent) where its proceedings could be supervised by the emperor, and after it ended there were some countries, notably France, which refused to ratify its decisions.

In the sense that the church cannot legislate against the laws of the state, the principle is still operative today. Even in countries where there is a clear separation of church and state, the church cannot go against the laws of that state or set itself up as a rival society with laws of its own. For example, in countries where civil matrimony is obligatory, the church cannot marry people who are not acceptable to the state. In those places, a church wedding is essentially no more than the blessing of a marriage that has already taken place and has no legal force. That does not apply in England or in most common-law countries, but the same issue does arise in the case of civil divorce. The church makes no provision for ecclesiastical divorce, but it accepts civil divorce and remarriage in a civil ceremony as valid, at least for civil purposes and occasionally for ecclesiastical ones as well. In practice, this means that it can (and sometimes does) decree that divorced people who have been remarried in a civil ceremony cannot be ordained during the lifetime of a previous partner, but it does not excommunicate them on the ground that they are 'living in sin'.

Having said that, it must also be said that the role of secular rulers in relation to the church has changed dramatically since the sixteenth century and is no longer what it was. Even in countries where the overwhelming majority of the citizenry belongs to the state church, the state itself is basically secular and unsuited to exercising the kind of power that was granted to Christian kings in centuries gone by. No secular ruler today would presume to call a general council of the church, and it is an open question as to whether such a gathering is now possible. Bringing every Christian community together would be a formidable task at the best of times, and a representative gathering of all the churches in the world would be much too large to manage properly. The Roman Catholic Church would not attend (at least not officially) unless the pope were the president of the gathering, and if he were, a number of other churches, Orthodox as well as Protestant, would fail to turn up. No-one can predict the future of course, but as things stand at the moment, a general council of the church in the sense intended by this article is almost certainly no longer feasible.

In the history of secularisation that has taken place in Europe since the time of the Reformation, England is an anomaly to some extent, because remnants of the medieval order of things have survived to the present day. It is often thought that it was the Reformation that created the close links between church and state in England, amounting at times to state control of the church, that we are familiar with today, but this is not so. In the period from 1377 to 1529, for example, there were eighty-six provincial councils called by the archbishop of Canterbury, only six of which were not summoned by a royal writ. Five of those took place between 1378 and 1434, after which there was only one (in 1510). The northern province of York was somewhat freer, in that of the seventy-nine councils known to have been called in the same period, no fewer than ten were summoned without a royal writ, and five of those took place after 1434, the last one being in 1515. The Reformation merely regularised this situation, and from 1545 the provincial councils of England, known as convocations, met in tandem with parliament. This practice was ended by statute in 1966, in preparation for the establishment of the present General Synod, which met for the first time in 1970 and is now elected on a fixed five-year basis, though still by leave of parliament which must approve its legislation before it can become law.

Nowadays of course, relatively few members of parliament are active churchgoers, many are openly non-Anglican and even non-Christian, and parliamentary approval of church legislation is usually a formality, unless some legal right or protection is involved. That can happen, as the difficulties over the churchwarden's measure of 2000 demonstrated. The members of the ecclesiastical committee of parliament were not convinced that the rights of churchwardens were being sufficiently protected, and they kept sending the measure back until it was amended to meet their concerns. Some church leaders were upset by this and regarded it as unwarranted state interference in the church, but they might have reflected that if the grounds for refusing the measure had some basis in civil rights protection law, it could have been challenged in the courts and thrown out. Parliament may have forestalled this by its caution, for which we may be grateful.

The article also states that general councils have occasionally erred, though it does not give specific examples of this. What it does say is that their decisions must be subject to proof from Holy Scripture, which is the sole criterion for determining Christian doctrine. In practice, the Anglican Communion accepts the decisions of the first six ecumenical councils (Nicaea I in 325, Constantinople I in 381, Ephesus I in 431, Chalcedon in 451, Constantinople II in 553 and Constantinople III in 680–1), at least as far as matters of Christian doctrine are concerned. It has greater difficulty with the seventh ecumenical council (Nicaea II in 787), because that council authorised the veneration of images which the Anglican church has repudiated. Later so-called 'ecumenical' councils were in reality councils of the Western church only and Anglicans have always felt free to pick and choose from among their decisions, accepting some and rejecting others. For example, the imposition of clerical celibacy by Lateran I (1123) has been rejected, but the definition of the double procession of the Holy Spirit at Florence

(1439) has not. The criterion has always been conformity to the teaching of Scripture, which (at least by implication) is taken to be inerrant in a way that no church council can ever be. The practical effects of this can be debated with respect to the acceptance or rejection of particular conciliar pronouncements, but the principle remains valid and the church has generally implemented it with a reasonable degree of success.

Questions for discussion:

    1. Who should summon and who should attend a 'general council' of the church today?

    2. What limits are there to the authority of church councils?

    3. What should we do if we disagree with a decision taken by a church council?

Key Bible Passages:

Ezra 4-6; Acts 5:27-41; 15:1-35.

For further reading:

Avis, P. *Beyond the reformation? Authority, primacy and unity in the conciliar tradition.* London: T. and T. Clark, 2006.

Kemp, E. W. *Counsel and consent. Aspects of the government of the church as exemplified in the history of the English provincial synods.* London: SPCK, 1961.

Tanner, N., ed. *Decrees of the ecumenical councils.* London: Sheed and Ward, 1990.

Of Purgatory

> *The Romish doctrine concerning purgatory, pardons, worshipping and adoration as well of images as of relics, and also invocation of saints, is a fond thing vainly invented, and grounded upon no warranty of Scripture, but rather repugnant to the Word of God.*

The title of this article is somewhat misleading, because although it mentions purgatory in passing, it is really more about a series of beliefs and practices which the medieval church had adopted and which the Reformers repudiated. Broadly speaking, they can be divided into two categories. The first, which includes purgatory and pardons, has to do with the concept of merit that had come to define the way of salvation in medieval theology. According to that way of thinking, Jesus had paid the price for every sin in the world, past, present and future, and when he ascended up to heaven, he took that payment with him. Because of this, there is an inheritance of divine grace, based on the merit attributed to Christ's sacrifice, waiting for us at the right hand of the Father, which we are entitled to draw on through the offices of the church, and principally by participating in the sacraments. For every sin that we commit, a certain amount of grace is required as payment for it, and it is as we confess to a priest, perform the penance which he assigns to us and receive his absolution that we have access to it.

Sin being what it is, it is extremely unlikely that we shall ever confess every one of our transgressions and even more unlikely that we shall ever be able to perform enough acts of penance to make up for them. As a result, the probability is that we shall die and be unable to go to heaven because of our outstanding debt of sins. This is where purgatory comes in. Unlike hell, it is not a place of condemnation but a place of rehabilitation. Souls who go there will eventually be saved, once they have done all the penance necessary to clear their account with God. This may take millions of years, but in the end the sinner will get to glory. Furthermore, the process can be speeded up by the intercession of concerned friends and relatives who are still on earth. By making special sacrifices, either in the form of penances or of some extraordinary act (like going on a pilgrimage) we can reduce the purgatorial sentence imposed on others, as well as on ourselves. This reduction, which the article refers to as a 'pardon', is more usually called an 'indulgence', and as time went on, the church even permitted them to be sold to whoever could afford them. It was this abuse that sparked off the Reformation and led Martin Luther to call the whole system of merit into question.

In modern times scholars, including Roman Catholics, have established beyond any doubt that the doctrine of purgatory was a medieval invention. It did not exist before the twelfth century, and is unknown in the Eastern churches. Even Rome tends to play it down nowadays, though of course it remains the official teaching of the church. Every Protestant church has rejected it, and in the case of the Church of England, it was repudiated as early as the Ten Articles of 1536. Three years later, Henry VIII tried to reverse the progress of reform and insisted on retaining (or reinstating) such doctrines as transubstantiation and clerical celibacy that were being called into question, but he never tried to revive a belief in purgatory, which shows just how untenable it was even in the sixteenth century.

The second category rejected in this article relates to the veneration of saints and their relics. This is also tied to a merit theology, but is only tangentially related to the notion of purgatory. In the New Testament all Christians are called saints because they have been chosen by Christ and sanctified by the shedding of his blood (Ephesians 1:1; Jude 1). There is no question of their moral superiority to others. Indeed, it is possible to argue that Paul wrote his letters to the saints in various places precisely because they were *not* living up to the standards he expected of them! Even so, they were still saints, and it was for that reason that Paul felt obliged to rebuke them.

In medieval times however, the notion of sainthood changed. Once a merit theology developed, a saint came to be interpreted as someone who had done well enough on earth to go straight to heaven when he or she died. Once there, these saints had access to the ear of God and so now they are able to intercede with him on our behalf. At the top of the list is the Virgin Mary, who is something of a super-saint with even greater access to God than the others have and who is even said (in some accounts) to share in her Son's work of mediation! A glance at history and geography will soon show that saints of this kind used to be much more common than they are now, and that the lands of ancient Christianity are vastly over-represented in the list of those who have been officially canonised. Virtually every known bishop and martyr from the early church is included among them, as are a large number of otherwise unknown figures from the early middle ages. Anglo-Saxon women were particular favourites, as names like Etheldreda, Sexburga, Werburga, Ebba, Hilda and Frideswide readily attest. Were these people any better than outstanding Christians today? Probably not, but after their deaths a cult of veneration grew up around them and their relics (bones, teeth, hair, etc.) were preserved in prominent shrines open to the public, who were encouraged to go there and to ask the saints in question to pray for them.

That this system could be (and was) abused is clear. St Denis, for example, never existed, in spite of the large cathedral near Paris dedicated to him. He was nothing other than the pagan God Bacchus (Dionysus in Greek) who was baptised and recycled for Christian use. It is the same with many ancient European churches, where the crypt often reveals the existence of a pagan shrine over which the church was later built. A famous example of this was the Parthenon in Athens, originally a temple of the goddess Athena that was later converted into a church and dedicated (naturally) to the Virgin Mary.

Given this situation, it would seem obvious that the official church would move rapidly to condemn this kind of thing and purge its worship of such pagan accretions. Yet it did not do so, and even today, both the Roman Catholic and the Eastern Orthodox churches give a prominence to the veneration of saints and their relics which scandalises Protestant Christians. The main reason for this seems to be the power of popular devotion, which keeps ancient shrines in being, and even creates new ones – Lourdes and Fátima, for example, which are now famous and popular places of pilgrimage, are modern inventions that did not exist at the time of the Reformation.

Here Anglicans have compromised with tradition and allowed the designation of 'saint' to be retained in the church calendar for people mentioned in the New Testament. It is also allowed in place names and church dedications, though often the latter are obscured, especially in villages where the parish church is known primarily by the name of the village rather than by the saint it was originally dedicated to. Anglicans also make provision for commemorating great Christians of the past, though this is usually a low-key affair and barely noticed by most people. On the other hand, Anglicans do not create new saints, do not erect shrines to the memory of great Christians and do not encourage anything that might be called veneration in the medieval sense of the term. We take our requests straight to God, praying to the Father through the Son in the Holy Spirit. Those who have gone to glory are at rest in the heavenly places – we do not pray to them. Still less do we pray for those who have died, although there are some people in the Anglican world who want to revive this practice. What for? The dead belong to God and whatever has happened to them, they have passed out of our reach. Whether they are in heaven or in hell, their eternal destiny has been decided, and there is nothing for us to pray for, one way or another. If the intention of praying for the dead is to comfort the bereaved, there are other (and far better) ways of doing that. We do not need to revive an unbiblical and ungodly form of devotion, which this article and the whole Anglican tradition have clearly and justifiably repudiated.

Questions for discussion:

1. What relationship do Christians on earth have with believers who have died?

2. Do we go straight to heaven when we die or is there an intermediate state before the final judgment?

3. What makes a person a 'saint'?

Key Bible Passages:

Luke 23:32-43; 1 Corinthians 15:12-58; Philippians 1:19-26; 1 Thessalonians 4:13-18.

For further reading:

Fenn, R. K. *The persistence of purgatory.* Cambridge: CUP, 1995.

Le Goff, J. *The birth of purgatory.* Chicago: University of Chicago Press, 1984. Repr., Aldershot: Scolar Press, 1990.

Wright, N. T. *For all the saints? Remembering the Christian departed.* London: SPCK, 2003.

23. *Of ministering in the Congregation*

It is not lawful for any man to take upon him the office of public preaching, or ministering the sacraments in the congregation, before he be lawfully called and sent to execute the same. And those we ought to judge lawfully called and sent, which be chosen and called to this work by men who have public authority given unto them in the congregation, to call and send ministers into the Lord's vineyard.

The question of who should be allowed to minister in the church is one that goes right back to the time of Jesus, who chose twelve disciples and appointed them to be the leaders of the church. Even then, Judas betrayed Jesus and had to be replaced by what seems to us to be the rather curious practice of casting lots. The justification for that seems to have been that there were two equally good candidates but only one place available, and so tossing a coin (as we would do today) must have seemed the fairest way to make the selection. There may also be a justification for it based on Proverbs 16:33, although this is not mentioned in the account of the affair (Acts 1:23-26). Later on the risen Christ intervened to summon the Apostle Paul, a point which the latter did not hesitate to make when he was forced to disagree with Peter and the church at Jerusalem (Galatians 1:1-17). Nevertheless, everybody, including Paul, recognised that this was an exceptional circumstance and it was not repeated. He and his fellow apostles chose and appointed men like Timothy and Titus, who in turn were commissioned to appoint elders in the churches they were sent to visit and organise.

Whether this top-down approach was universal in the early church though must be doubted. There is no indication that the apostles appointed the elders who ruled the churches of Corinth, Ephesus and so on, who seem to have been elected by the congregation. Nor is there any indication that one of these elders enjoyed a special position which set him above the rest in what was effectively a different order of ministry. The words 'bishop' and 'elder' could be used interchangeably in the first few centuries and the monarchical episcopate as we now know it did not become universal until the third century. Even then, bishops continued to be elected by their congregations for many centuries, not least at Rome, where papal elections could often turn into riots as the supporters of opposing candidates battled it out in the streets. Eventually it was necessary to restrict the election to a body of senior church officials appointed for that purpose, who we now know as the cardinals. Elsewhere, similar restrictions were put in place, so that today it is rare for a church leader to be chosen by direct election. In the Church of England, and broadly speaking in the Anglican Communion as a whole, a complex system has evolved which is far from perfect but which certainly makes it impossible for any individual to impose himself on the church without the consent of others.

Anglican bishops are still elected, though the procedures vary from place to place. Usually a candidate is chosen by the diocesan synod and then the choice must be ratified by the other bishops of the province, though again, there are many variations on this. In the Church of England, bishops are appointed by the state and the election (by the cathedral chapter) is a formality. Until fairly recently, the prime minister gave bishoprics to whoever he wanted, but in recent times this has been subjected to a procedure in which the church and the diocese are both represented. In practice, given the mixed nature of the church, this means that most bishops are middle of the road, compromise candidates who will be unlikely to offend any significant constituency in their diocese. In some ways that is a good thing, but it has the effect of making it hard to appoint men of outstanding ability and definite conviction who will be able to give real leadership to the church.

The clergy are appointed by a number of different methods. At some point in the process the bishop will be involved, and in parts of the Anglican Communion the decision is his from the beginning. But in many places parishes have acquired or retained the right to act independently of the bishop, who is left with little choice but to sanction the candidate chosen by whoever acts on their behalf. In England it was once common for the patron of a church (who might be almost anyone) to appoint the incumbent regardless of the congregation's wishes, and a glance at the boards in churches that record the names of previous clergy will sometimes show how the post was kept in the patron's family for generations. Modern reforms have virtually eliminated this practice and given congregations a much greater say in the appointment of their ministers, though the patron and the bishop are still involved and the latter (in particular) can wield a lot of influence. Parishes often have to put up with someone whom they would not have chosen, but whom they have been asked to accept, perhaps because the bishop has to find a place for the candidate to serve and his options may be limited.

Of course, only properly ordained clergy can be candidates for appointment to a parish, and it is here that the greatest control is exercised. In theory, a bishop can ordain anyone he likes, but this happens very rarely and usually only in exceptional cases (as, for example, when an older person is received into the church from another denomination). In practice, there is a selection procedure which varies from place to place but which almost always involves assessment by more than one person. Maturity, emotional stability and financial solvency all play a part in determining suitability, though it has to be said that some other, and equally important, factors tend to be ignored. For example, until recently it was almost unknown for a married candidate's spouse to be interviewed, her opinion being considered to be a private matter between the couple concerned. A number of disastrous clergy divorces which might have been avoided had the church taken the spouse's views into consideration from the start, has forced a reassessment of this policy, but it is still unsatisfactory. An unmarried clergyman is expected to ask his bishop's permission before getting married, but it is hard to imagine such permission being refused, even if the intended bride is divorced or a non-Christian. Most important of all, doctrinal orthodoxy is not seriously tested in most places, with the result that the clergy are an extremely heterogeneous body with a range of beliefs (and unbelief) scarcely imaginable in most other churches. Lamentably, it has to be said that Anglicans have done a poor job of implementing the intentions of this article, and the church has suffered as a result.

Ministerial training has long been recognised as essential for ordination, and the Reformers made great efforts to ensure that in future those who served in the church's ministry would have a university degree in theology. This took some time to realise in practice, but by the end of the seventeenth century it was the norm. At the time of the Evangelical revival, for example, there were men who wanted to be ordained but who did not have the required university degree and so were refused, or at least subjected to great difficulties. An example of this was John Newton, the author of *Amazing Grace*, who in spite of his obvious gifts and calling from God was forced to wait many years before he was ordained and allowed to become the incumbent of a parish church.

The secularization of the universities, the expansion of the church, the increasing number of mature candidates for ministry and the realisation that there is more to ministry than intellectual accomplishment all combined to change the pattern of training in the course of the nineteenth and twentieth centuries. Theological colleges were established, mainly by private interests, to provide a pastoral and later a theological grounding that university faculties were unable to give. More recently, part-time courses have been set up to cater for the needs of those who cannot undertake full-time residential training for one reason or another. Here it has to be said that cost has been a major factor in limiting the options open to ministerial candidates and now only a minority (at least in England) receives anything like an adequate training before being ordained.

The ecumenical movement of modern times has done a great deal to break down the barriers that once existed between clergy of different churches, though the theoretical difficulties usually remain. Anglicans like to insist on the need for episcopal ordination, which has made it difficult for them to acknowledge the validity of Presbyterian or Methodist orders of ministry, even though it was once not uncommon for ministers of other Protestant churches to be accepted by the Church of England without such reordination. The question of the 'validity' of orders is also two-edged – what Anglicans deny to other Protestants, Roman Catholics and Eastern Orthodox deny to them! In an episcopal church it is reasonable to maintain that a minister should be ordained and licensed by a bishop, since that is what bishops are for, but when episcopacy is detached from the life of the church and elevated into an essential principle in its own right, problems are bound to arise. A Presbyterian minister, for example, is certainly 'lawfully ordained' within his own church, and often has been subjected to a much more rigorous process of examination than his Anglican brethren have. To deny such a person recognition is absurd, and goes against the spirit of the article, which does not specify that 'lawful' must be interpreted as 'episcopal' and does not even mention bishops at all. Bishops are fine in their place, but they too are servants of the church, sent to minister in what is, after all, the Lord's vineyard and not theirs (Matthew 20:1-16). In that vineyard, all the labourers are fundamentally equal, and it ought to be recognised (as it generally is by scholars) that the claims made for the 'historic episcopate' are neither as ancient nor as compelling as they are sometimes made out to be.

This article probably was not intended to deal with the many forms of lay ministry that we have today, if only because they did not exist in the sixteenth century, but there is nothing in the wording to exclude them and the same principles apply. Perhaps the best way to look at this is to go back to the Middle Ages, when there were a number of recognised ministries that were not regarded as 'holy orders'. The distinction then was that those in 'holy orders' (bishops, priests and deacons) were not allowed to marry, whereas the others (subdeacons, readers, janitors, acolytes, parish clerks) were. Today that is irrelevant, but there is plenty of room for ministers who lack formal theological training or whose scope is more restricted ('local ordained ministry' for example.) Such people may be 'laymen' in the technical sense of the term, because they are not in 'holy orders' but their status and accountability as ministers is essentially the same as that of those who are. The important thing is that they should be responsible to the church for what they do, and that the church should see to it that only suitable people are entrusted with ministerial tasks in a congregation.

Questions for discussion:

1. What kind of training should a minister of the church have?

2. How should ministers be chosen?

3. How should the differences between men and women be expressed in the church's ministry?

Key Bible Passages:

Matthew 28:16-20; Acts 1:21-26; Romans 12:3-8; 2 Corinthians 10; 1 Timothy 2:8-3:13; Titus 1:5-16; 1 Peter 5:1-4.

For further reading:

Beckwith, R. T. *Elders in every city: The origin and role of the ordained ministry.* Carlisle: Paternoster Press, 2003.

Browning, W. R. F. *A handbook of the ministry: a guide to ordination in the Anglican Communion.* London: Mowbray, 1985.

Torry, M. and J. Heskins, *Ordained local ministry: a new shape for ministry in the Church of England.* London: Canterbury Press, 2006.

24. Of speaking in the Congregation in such a Tongue as the People understandeth

It is a thing plainly repugnant to the Word of God and the custom of the primitive Church to have public prayer in the Church, or to minister the sacraments in a tongue not understanded of the people.

What language shall I borrow
To thank thee dearest friend,
For this thy dying sorrow,
Thy pity without end?

These well-known lines from the passion hymn 'O sacred head once wounded' were not intended to reflect the language used in public worship, but they do remind us of how sensitive and difficult an issue it can be. Is there a human language that is more adequate or appropriate than others for praising God? The Apostle Paul told the Corinthian church that it did not matter whether he spoke in the tongues of men or of angels, if he lacked love, but he did not forbid speaking in tongues, and even encouraged it to a limited extent (1 Corinthians 12-14). What can we say about this?

Here, perhaps more than anywhere, historical perspective is essential. Jesus and his disciples spoke Aramaic as their everyday language, but worshipped God in Hebrew, a related but distinct Semitic tongue. This caused no problems and was not even mentioned in the New Testament, where Aramaic is regularly referred to as 'Hebrew'! This would be like calling Dutch 'German', or Portuguese 'Spanish' today. One can see why there might be a confusion of this kind because the languages are similar and closely related, but they are more than just variant forms of a common tongue, as British and American English are. Like it or not, Christians have the highest authority for *not* worshipping in the mother tongue, though of course understanding the language being used is a different matter.

The early church used Greek for most purposes and the New Testament is written in that language, though modern research has shown that it was not exactly the spoken vernacular of the day. Biblical Greek, following the model of the Septuagint translation of the Hebrew Bible, is full of Semitisms, turns of phrase which are not natural to Greek-speakers but can easily be understood once one assumes a

Hebrew or Aramaic substratum. The first generation of Christians knew when they were listening to the Bible because it has a special ring to it, which no doubt gave it a 'religious' feel to them. As time went on, other languages were also used in worship. Latin first appeared in the late second century, and was later followed by Coptic in Egypt and Syriac in the Middle East. These developments represented the increasing indigenization of Christianity in the Mediterranean world, though Greek retained its importance as a *lingua franca* for a long time. In the East, it is fair to say, translation was undertaken as a matter of policy when Christianity spread to non-Greek speaking peoples, but it seems that it also had something to do with whether the peoples concerned had an organised civil society of their own or not. Thus we find that it did not take long to produce versions of the Bible in Armenian, Georgian and Ge'ez (the ancient language of Ethiopia), but languages like Lycaonian or Phrygian, both of which were spoken in Asia Minor, lost out because they had no state or historic literary culture to support them. The legacy of these efforts can be seen today in the ancient churches of the East, which continue to use these liturgical languages in their worship, even though they are for the most part no longer spoken. Even when a language still exists, like Greek or Armenian, it is sufficiently different from the ancient ecclesiastical variety as to make the latter a foreign language to most of the worshippers, though admittedly long familiarity and a basic underlying similarity help to reduce the impact of the strangeness the ancient forms would otherwise have.

Initially at least, the same practice was followed in the West. The North African church used Latin, which was the official language of the state, even though many of its members were Berber-speaking. This was also true in Spain, Gaul and Britain, regardless of what the local tribes might have spoken. There was no Basque Bible, for instance, nor was anything produced in a Celtic language as long as the Roman Empire remained in existence. The fall of Rome in the fifth century began a long process of linguistic change. On the one hand, local languages gradually died out in most places, but the Latin that replaced them was increasingly altered. Nobody can say for sure when it ceased to be a spoken language because the process of change was gradual and undocumented, but the date usually chosen to mark its passing is 812, the year in which Charlemagne ordered preachers to use the *lingua rustica*, or country speech, in their sermons, and not the high-flown Latin of the official liturgy and Bible.

When Christian evangelists reached the non-Roman peoples of

Northern Europe, it was clear that the latter did not speak Latin in any form, and some effort was made to translate things into the local tongues. There is a Gothic Bible from the fourth century, and parts of the Scriptures were made available in Old Irish and in Old English, though these versions had limited support or success. One of the difficulties is that there was no standard language into which a translation could be easily made. The Anglo-Saxons could communicate with their fellow Germanic tribesmen across what is now Germany and Scandinavia, but they had to adjust to local variations in speech as they went along. Had they produced a Bible in an English dialect, for example, it might have seemed almost as strange as Latin to someone in Sweden or Switzerland. On the other hand, Greek missionaries to the Slavs, of whom the most famous were the brothers Cyril and Methodius, did translate the Scriptures into the Slavic dialect of their native Macedonia, and it was accepted throughout the Slavic world, where it is still used as the liturgical language of the Russian Orthodox Church. But it is quite clearly not Russian, even though it can be learned without too much difficulty by Russians who put their mind to it.

In the West, Latin remained a living language within the church structures, which enabled priests and monks to travel from Iceland to Sicily and from Portugal to Finland without needing a translator. Martin Luther was read all over Europe because he wrote in Latin, and the same was true of the other Reformers. The Articles of Religion were composed in that language, with an (unofficial) English translation appended, and it was not until 1733 that English became the official language of the Church of England. Even then, theology lectures at Oxford and Cambridge were given in Latin until the early nineteenth century, as was also the case in other European countries. For those who needed a language of international communication, Latin served a useful purpose and for that reason, it remained the everyday language of the Roman Catholic Church until the 1960s. Even Thomas Cranmer was not against using Latin in worship, as long as people understood it. That was the important thing, not the use of the mother tongue, and to this day there is provision for the use of Latin in special circumstances (as in the ancient universities, for example.) It may have been in order to make this point clearer that the wording of the original article (*lingua populo ignota*, 'a tongue unknown to the people') was altered in 1563 to *lingua populo non intellecta* ('a tongue not understood of the people'). Latin would not have been an 'unknown tongue' to sixteenth-century Englishmen who would have recognised it when they heard it, but most of them did not understand it, which was the point that the article was trying to make.

In sixteenth-century England the only way to communicate with the mass of the population was through the medium of English, which by then had become a reasonably standardised literary language. But even so, the task of translating the Bible and other religious texts was by no means a straightforward one. English lacked theological vocabulary because it had never been used in that context, and the Reformers set about inventing it. Some of these coinages were brilliant and have stood the test of time, like 'atonement' for 'reconciliation' and 'Gospel' for 'Evangel'. Others were partly successful, like 'Passover', which survived as the translation of *pesach* or *pascha* in the Old Testament, but not for *pascha* in the New, with the result that we now use a pagan word ('Easter') for the greatest Christian celebration of them all and the link with the Old Testament Passover has been effectively broken. In some cases, translations merely caused confusion. A good example of this is the word 'priest', which is probably a conflation of the Latin *praepositus* ('provost') and *presbyter*, the (originally Greek) word for 'elder'. The Latin word *sacerdos* (Greek *hiereus*) had no English equivalent, so the English word 'priest' was used to denote a person who offered sacrifice. In the Bible it is applied to Old Testament priests, to pagan priests, to Jesus our great high priest and to believers in general, who constitute a 'royal priesthood' but it is *never* used of a Christian minister. Yet because the word appears in the Prayer Book in the sense of *presbyter*, it continues to be employed by Anglicans, who can justify this usage on etymological grounds. They are right of course, but in a way it is rather like trying to insist that the word 'silly' means 'blessed', because that is what it used to mean (compare German *selig*) and why should we change merely because everybody else now thinks it means something different?

Whether the English of the Prayer Book and of the Authorised Version of the Bible was really the language of the people is open to dispute because the translators sought to create a religious register for the English language that it had previously lacked. People had to understand what they were doing when they worshipped God, but they also had to approach him in a spirit of reverence, and this was as much a matter of style and choice of words as anything else. Consider, for example, Mark 14:68, where it says that after Peter denied Jesus, the 'cock crew' (AV) or in a modern translation, 'the rooster crowed' (ESV). However, a student of mine once translated this from the Latin (*et tunc gallus cantavit*) as 'and then the chicken sang'. Is this wrong? In a sense, no, but it had the whole class laughing, which is not what the text intends! We can perhaps understand the problem the Reformers faced if we consider our modern sexual vocabulary, where Latin terminology is still preferred in polite discourse to the native English words. It is not that the latter do not exist, nor that they are not understood. The problem is that they are felt to be vulgar and inappropriate, which is a social and not a linguistic judgment. It was this feeling that the Reformers were up against when dealing with religious vocabulary, and which made their task of translation so delicate.

There was also the problem that something is always lost or altered in translation. The lines of the hymn quoted at the beginning of this section are moving and beautiful, but they are not in the original Latin, which is attributed either to Bernard of Clairvaux (d. 1147) or to Arnulf of Louvain (d. *c.* 1248). Nor are they to be found in Paul Gerhardt's famous rendering of it, *O Haupt voll Blut und Wunden,* which has been the immediate inspiration of most English translations. But it sounded good to James Alexander, who put it into his version of 1830 and it has now become a classic phrase in English, with no justification other than his poetic imagination. What if something like this were to happen with the Scriptures? It does, of course, from time to time, and eradicating the mistake can be very difficult. A classic example of it is found in the salutation of the angels to the shepherds outside Bethlehem. What they said was: 'Peace on earth to men of good will' but most English-speaking people think it was: 'Peace on earth, good will to men', a translation error which has attained almost canonical status because of its association with Christmas, the 'season of good will'.

Today the language question touches us in three distinct ways. First of all, there is the issue of how modern our worship should sound. Anglo-Saxon and Chaucerian English are too distant from us now to be readily understood, but Tudor English is more problematic. It sounds odd and some words have changed their meaning, but on the whole we can figure it out most of the time. Does it really need to be updated, and if so, to what extent? Oddly enough, this issue now tends to divide those who go to church from those who do not. Churchgoers are familiar with various modern versions of the Bible and the liturgy, whereas non-churchgoers tend to know only the traditional forms. So which one do we use in order to communicate to those outside the church?

The second way in which it touches us is in the charismatic renewal. Speaking in tongues has been revived in the last century, after having lain dormant (more or less) for several hundred years. Some of it is probably inauthentic, but leaving that aside, it may be seen as a reaction to the loss of traditionally 'religious' language in public worship. Many people feel that they ought to address God in a special way, and tongues are a possible outlet for this kind of devotion. The Apostle Paul did not forbid speaking in tongues, but he insisted on interpretation and told the Corinthian church that he would rather be understood than be seen to be spiritually gifted (1 Corinthians 14:1-11).

The third way in which it touches us is in the desire to translate the Bible into every language currently spoken in the world. This is a noble aim and it is still far from being fully accomplished. The mother tongue speaks to people more deeply than an acquired language can ever do, so the effort would seem to be justified. Yet, as we have already seen, it was not the practice of the early church to do that and today almost everyone in the world can find a Bible written in a language they can understand. Is it really worth spending enormous amounts of time and money chasing down the remainder? Without in any way wishing to denigrate the sincere efforts of those who do so, we must consider what has tended to happen with this sort of thing. At the time of the Reformation, the Bible was translated into English, but fairly soon it was also being translated into Welsh and Irish (as well as Scottish Gaelic in Scotland) because these languages were also widely spoken by people who did not know English. Cornish was overlooked, perhaps because it was already dying out, and so was Manx. But in the mid-eighteenth century the bishops of Sodor and Man made a huge effort to translate the Bible into Manx, which was finally accomplished in 1772. Fifty years later, however, it was no longer needed, because those who would have used it had either died out or preferred to use English. It is quite likely that the same thing will happen with minority languages today, as education spreads and people choose to use a major language instead of their local dialect. Linguists may object to this, but ordinary people who want a job think differently and the number of languages in the world is shrinking fast. Sad though it may be, the truth is that many of the Bibles being translated today will be monuments to a vanished past in a hundred years' time and not the foundation of a flourishing literary and religious culture. At the end of the day, it is what people understand that counts most, not what they might regard as a little-used and half-forgotten 'mother tongue'.

> *Questions for discussion:*
>
> 1. Is the use of 'religious-sounding' language a help or a hindrance in public worship?
>
> 2. Should hymns be modernised if it means rewriting them?
>
> 3. Should each language-group in the world have its own church?

Key Bible Passages:

Acts 2:1-12, 8:26-39; 1 Corinthians 14.

For further reading:

Brook, S. *The language of the Book of Common Prayer.* London: Andre Deutsch, 1965.

Hitchcock, H. H. *Politics of prayer. feminist language and the worship of God.* San Francisco: Ignatius Press, 1992.

Jasper, D. and R. C. D. Jasper. *Language and the worship of the church.* Basingstoke: Macmillan, 1990.

Targoff, R. *Common prayer: the language of public devotion in early modern England.* Chicago: University of Chicago Press, 2001.

Of the Sacraments

Sacraments ordained of Christ be not only badges or tokens of Christian men's profession, but rather they be certain sure witnesses, and effectual signs of grace, and God's good will towards us, by the which he doth work invisibly in us, and doth not only quicken, but also strengthen and confirm our faith in him.

There are two sacraments ordained of Christ our Lord in the Gospel, that is to say, baptism and the supper of the Lord.

Those five, commonly called sacraments, that is to say, confirmation, penance, orders, matrimony and extreme unction, are not to be counted for sacraments of the Gospel, being such as have grown partly of the corrupt following of the Apostles, partly are states of life allowed in the Scriptures; but yet have not like nature of sacraments with baptism and the Lord's supper, for that they have not any visible sign or ceremony ordained of God.

The sacraments were not ordained of Christ to be gazed upon or to be carried about; but that we should duly use them. And in such only as worthily receive the same, they have a wholesome effect or operation; but they that receive them unworthily, purchase to themselves damnation, as St Paul saith.

Thomas Cranmer originally conceived of this article as four separate ones, but when they appeared in 1553 they had already been combined into one. In 1563, the revisers retained only the last paragraph, making it the first, and added the second and the third. The second is essentially the same as the first paragraph of the original article, though the wording is slightly different. Finally in 1571, parts of the original second and third paragraphs were restored in what is now the last paragraph of the article. The end result is a text which in content mostly goes back to Cranmer but whose shape has been altered.

What exactly is a sacrament? The concept is not present in the Bible, though the rites that are now brought together under this term are certainly to be found there. Baptism and the Lord's Supper (to go no further) are New Testament ceremonies, but neither is called a 'sacrament' and there is no explicit connection between them either in the Bible or in the early church. Today, on the other hand, the notion of 'sacrament' is so powerful that what applies to one of them can be almost automatically transferred to the other, one example being the recent spread of the practice of infant communion, which is justified on the ground that it is the natural corollary of infant baptism. Suffice it to say that this link has not been obvious in the past, as the practice of confirmation shows. There may be good reasons for giving communion to infants as well as to adults, but this should be justified by something more than an appeal to the umbrella term 'sacrament', which is only dubiously Biblical. After all, following this logic it would also be possible to extend the penalty of unworthy reception to baptism and claim that those who have been only nominally baptised have purchased eternal damnation instead of salvation, but so far nobody seems to have drawn that conclusion!

The word 'sacrament' was first used in a Christian sense by Tertullian, sometime around AD 200, with reference to baptism. In Latin, *sacramentum* means an oath, and Tertullian thought of baptism as the equivalent of a Roman soldier's swearing allegiance to the emperor. His reasoning was that since a Christian is called to be a soldier of Christ, baptism can be understood as an oath of allegiance to him. This way of thinking was unknown in the Eastern churches, which did not have an equivalent term until the fourth century, when Cyril of Jerusalem used the word *mysterion* to define the rite of baptism. This word comes from the New Testament, but there it has a different meaning, referring to the message of the Gospel rather than to a ceremony of the church. In later centuries, the terms *sacramentum* and *mysterion* were merged into a single theological concept, but they have very different origins and are a reminder to us that the doctrine we are discussing is not really very ancient.

It is customary to define a sacrament as 'the outward and visible sign of an inward and spiritual grace', a phrase used by the Catechism drawn up in 1559 and included in the Book of Common Prayer, and this has led to controversy about the precise relationship between the two. Catholics of all shades generally insist that the administration of the outward sign is a guarantee that the inward grace is present in the recipient, whereas Protestants generally disagree with this, insisting that a sacrament is effective only if the recipient has faith. In this controversy, as article 25 makes clear, Anglicans take a moderately Protestant view and everything the articles and Prayer Book say about the sacraments must be understood in that light.

The Anglican doctrine is only moderately Protestant because, as the article makes plain, sacraments are not simply to be regarded as 'badges or tokens' of faith. This is the view traditionally ascribed to

Huldrych Zwingli and taken to its logical conclusion by the Swiss Anabaptists, who believed that no sacrament should be administered to anyone who had not already made a profession of faith. To them, as to many people today, baptism and the Lord's supper are things Christians do to demonstrate their faith, but they play no active part in strengthening or confirming that faith. It is at this point that Anglicans, in common with both the traditional Lutheran and Reformed churches, take a different view. Without denying the Anabaptist position, Anglicans add the following:

1. The sacraments are certain and sure witnesses.

2. The sacraments are effectual means of God's grace.

The first of these points underlines the objectivity of the faith we profess as believers. Every individual has his or her own understanding and experience of that faith, and it may increase or weaken as time goes on. Most people have dry periods in their lives when their faith means little or nothing to them, and all of us are assailed by doubt at different times. We may question our faith or wonder whether we have any at all and be subjected to bouts of anxiety or depression. We may even abandon the church for a time, feeling that it has nothing to offer us and is not interested in our problems. It is to meet such situations that the sacraments have been given. They are there to remind us that our faith is rooted not in how we feel at any given moment, nor in what we understand about God and the way he works, but in what he has revealed to us about himself and about what he has done on our behalf, whether we believe it or not. In their different ways, baptism and the Lord's supper tell us about the sacrifice and death of Jesus Christ, who made atonement for our sins and brought us his cleansing power and new life. That fact is rooted in historical events and does not change, however many people reject it or turn away from it. Even if I do not want it or understand it, it is there waiting for me and will never go away or lose its saving power.

This brings us naturally to the second affirmation, which is that the sacraments are effectual means of grace. This is very hard for many people to understand, because it seems to suggest that they possess some kind of magical power that can give us faith simply by being administered to us, rather as a medicine can give us health simply by taking it. That view is not uncommon, especially in traditional Catholic circles, and Protestants, aware of the widespread nominalism that results from an indiscriminate administration of the sacraments, naturally recoil from this. Here the answer must be that the sacraments are spiritual food for those who are spiritual. There is no sense in trying to feed a corpse, because a corpse cannot receive the food offered to it. Similarly, there is nothing to be gained by administering the sacraments to spiritually dead people, because they cannot receive them either. Food sustains and supports life but does not create it – in spiritual terms, only the Holy Spirit can do that. The Apostle Paul makes this abundantly clear in Ephesians 2:1-10, a passage of Scripture that describes the passage from spiritual death to life in detail. It is when that transition has occurred that the sacraments find their place.

First of all, they 'quicken' us. This sounds very much like giving life to the dead, but it is not quite the same thing. What we are talking about here is the spiritual equivalent of resuscitation, when life is present in the body but needs to be stirred. If we set this in the context of election, it means that there are people in the world who have been chosen by God for salvation and therefore have the potential for eternal life lying dormant in them already. The sacraments are a way of reaching out to such people and stirring that dormant life into action. Secondly, the sacraments strengthen us by drawing us back to first principles and reminding us that we must be continually fed spiritually on the body and blood of Christ, which were offered on the cross in payment for our sins and are now presented by the Son to the Father in heaven for our justification. Every time we reaffirm this we submit ourselves again to the power of his saving grace and are thereby strengthened by denying ourselves and relying more completely on him. Finally, the sacraments confirm our faith by reminding us that it is a total experience. Baptism speaks of dying and rising again to a new life; there can be no going back to the old ways, which are now dead and buried with Christ. The Lord's Supper reminds us that not only are we united in fellowship with him and with all who believe in him, but that his sacrifice and death penetrate to the inmost core of our being, reaching the hidden parts that we cannot see but which we know are fundamental to our survival. Those who are spiritual grow in their faith as they feed on these things in their spirits, and in this way the sacraments play a vital part in making us healthy and mature Christians.

The notion that there are seven sacraments was an invention of Peter Lombard, who popularised it in his *Sentences*, and it has never had any currency in the Eastern churches. Even in the West, it was never canonised by a church council, although the habit of thinking that there were seven of them became so widespread that the council of Trent spoke of them as such without formally defining their number.

From the medieval point of view, the most important thing about the sacraments is their objectivity. In the eyes of the Scholastic theologians whose views were canonised by the council of Trent, a believer's faith may go up and down and is hard to analyse, but if a person has received a sacrament he has received the grace of God, whether there is much evidence of that grace at work or not. In their own way therefore, the sacraments were an assurance of salvation, though they had to be received throughout one's life and access to them could be denied if the church so decided.

Another important image that shaped the doctrine of the sacraments was the idea that sin is a kind of spiritual disease and the sacraments are the medicine needed to combat it. This view was especially prominent in explanations of the Lord's Supper, in which the bread and wine were regarded as the 'drugs of immortality'. It sounds strange today, but medieval people believed that if they received the sacraments often enough, they would be healed of their spiritual weaknesses and made ready for the kingdom of heaven.

From this it will be obvious that the efficacy of the sacraments depended on a particular view of the relationship between spirit and matter. Water, bread and wine could not by themselves make any difference to an individual's spiritual state. Somehow the power of God had to enter into them if that was going to happen, and it was that belief that led eventually to the doctrine of transubstantiation. The full-blown medieval understanding of this was not officially proclaimed until the fourth Lateran Council in 1215, but elements of it can be found as far back as Tertullian, who believed that the Holy Spirit entered the water of baptism and used it as a means to work through the pores of the human body to get to the soul that needed spiritual cleansing. Later generations recoiled from so crude a view, but the principle remained the same. Sacraments did their work because of what they were, not because of who administered them or what the recipient thought about them. In this respect, the medicinal analogy is an apt one and helps us to appreciate what was at stake in the Reformation debates.

In crafting the article, the revisers of 1563 put Cranmer's original conclusion first, possibly because they were sensitive to these debates and the conclusions of the council of Trent, which had devoted sessions 7-14 to the subject (3 March 1547 to 25 November 1551), and returned to it again in sessions 21-24 (16 July 1562 to 11 November 1563). The last two of these, devoted respectively to holy orders and to matrimony, were held after the 1563 revision of the articles had been produced, but of course they were well known by the time the final revision was made in 1571 and did not affect the substance of the teaching given here.

As we now have it, article 25 starts out by rejecting the idea that the sacraments are purely symbolic. This view is usually regarded today as having been the teaching of Huldrych Zwingli (1484-1531), though that appears to be an oversimplification. Nevertheless, there were certainly many people in the so-called 'radical reformation' represented by different kinds of Anabaptists, who thought that way. In response to this, and largely following the line laid down by John Calvin in his *Institutes* (IV, 14), Thomas Cranmer insisted that the sacraments can be relied on as true witnesses and meaningful signs of God's grace towards us. They are not in and of themselves acts of divine grace, but rather they point towards an invisible action of God inside us. What they represent teaches us what our faith is all about and when we understand and accept that, then that faith is strengthened and confirmed in us. The context, of course, is that of election. Only those who are worthy recipients benefit from participating in the sacraments, and to be a worthy recipient means being called and chosen by God, since none of us can claim to be worthy in ourselves. If a sacrament is administered to someone who is not one of the elect, its effects will be the opposite of those intended. This is stated in what is now the concluding sentence of the article, which makes explicit reference to the words of the Apostle Paul in the New Testament, where he says that those who eat and drink unworthily do so to their own damnation, because they have failed to discern the body of Christ (1 Corinthians 11:27-30).

Of the seven sacraments recognised by Peter Lombard, only two can claim the authority of the Gospel – baptism and the Lord's Supper. The other five are rites and practices which may be valid in themselves but which do not have the same character. Baptism and the Lord's Supper are alike in two respects. First of all, they are both witnesses to the Gospel of the death of Christ as the atonement for sin. It is this focus on the Gospel that gives them their unity and it is only in that context that they can be understood. Secondly, their administration, including the visible sign(s) accompanying them, has been ordained by God. Baptism already existed before the coming of Christ, but it is portrayed in the New Testament as a rite that prefigured his coming, and it is noticeable that when Jesus came to be baptised himself, John the Baptist spoke of him as the Lamb of God who takes away the sins of the world – a direct reference to the atonement at the very beginning of Jesus' ministry (John 1:29). The Lord's Supper is more obviously linked to the death of Christ, having been instituted by Jesus on the night of his betrayal when he and his disciples met to keep the Passover.

An important aspect of this is that because the Gospel is essentially a message of salvation that must be proclaimed, the sacraments are an extension of the ministry of the Word and not something distinct from it. The administration of the sacraments is the preaching of the Word by other means, bringing home to people the meaning and application of the message. Because of this, the sacrament of baptism should never be administered without proper teaching beforehand, nor should the Lord's Supper be celebrated without an exposition of the Bible preceding it. Those who think of the sermon as a preliminary to the celebration of the sacrament have put the cart before the horse. Participation in the sacrament should be a response to the hearing of the Word, without which it is meaningless.

The other five rites do not share the same focus and if they are also regarded as sacraments, the only effect will be to obscure the centrality of the Gospel for Christian life and experience. As developed in medieval theology, three of these five were intended for all Christians, whereas the other two were reserved for some and were mutually exclusive. The three intended for all were confirmation, penance and extreme unction.

Confirmation has often been described as a sacrament in search of a theology, which neatly summarises its ambiguous status. On the one hand, when infant baptism is practised, some form of acknowledgement of it is expected of the recipient when he or she reaches the age of maturity. In this sense, it might be compared with something like citizenship and/or the right to vote. Some countries allow the children of parents who have more than one nationality to keep both until they reach the age of eighteen (usually), at which point they must decide for one or the other. Obligations undertaken by parents for their children must be confirmed by those children when they come of age or else they may run the risk of forfeiting them. That is perfectly understandable and valid, but does it make confirmation a sacrament in its own right? Many have said that it does not, that confirmation is really just the completion of baptism. Unfortunately, that argument leaves the impression that baptism is incomplete and therefore not really a sacrament either. When an adult is baptised it is not certain whether he must then be confirmed or not. Logic would suggest not, but practice varies, not least because baptism is administered by a minister of the local congregation, whereas confirmation is the preserve of the bishop. Presumably, if the bishop baptises the adult convert, confirmation is unnecessary, but if that is so, what benefit can it possibly convey in other circumstances? As its name suggests, it merely confirms something that has already been given and is not an extra blessing in itself.

Penance is more difficult and it is interesting to note that for some time after the beginning of the Reformation it continued to be regarded as a sacrament (in the Ten Articles of 1536, for instance) because it seemed to be a New Testament practice closely tied to the preaching of the Gospel. Gradually however, this view was abandoned as people came to realise that in fact it was a corruption of what the New Testament really meant. The trouble arose from the way in which the Latin word *paenitentia* (Greek *metanoia*) was understood. Did this mean the recognition of innate sinfulness and a willingness to submit to the redemptive power of God (repentance), or was it mainly an outward act performed as evidence of regret and in partial payment of some transgression (penance)? Ideally of course, these two things would go together, but the notion that the act of contrition was somehow the outward and visible sign of the supposed inward and spiritual turning away from sin was not viable. Inevitably it reduced sinfulness to a series of acts and did not recognise it for the incurable condition that it really was. All the regret in the world was insufficient to deal with the true depths of human sinfulness, as Martin Luther discovered when he tried to earn God's favour in that way. The Reformers rejected penance because it could not do justice to repentance, which was an essential ingredient of the Christian life.

Extreme unction was the anointing of the sick prescribed in James 5:14-15. What exactly James had in mind is not easy to say, but it was certainly not a rite of passage at the moment of death, which is what extreme unction had become by the sixteenth century. It is possible that it had developed in that direction as a substitute for deathbed baptism, which was practised in the early church by those who believed that a person who sinned after being baptised would necessarily lose his salvation. If the rite was deferred to the moment of death, there would be no time left to sin (so the argument ran) and therefore no danger of losing the salvation that baptism brought. As the church came round to the view that it was possible to be forgiven after baptism, there was a psychological gap at the moment of death, and extreme unction seems to have stepped in to cover it.

The two sacraments that were reserved for only some members of the church were holy orders and holy matrimony. The first of these was restricted to bishops, priests and deacons, though there were five other 'minor' orders in the church as well. A person in holy orders had received a special grace from God, enabling him to lead a higher kind of spiritual life, and in particular to practise celibacy. There was no ground for this in the New Testament of course, and it was not difficult for the Reformers to reject this notion, but lay people found it more difficult. Even today there persists the idea that the ordained clergyman is somehow special, and there are elements in the church which actively encourage this idea. The priest is elevated above the congregation, given the title 'father' and regarded as a representative of Christ. The resulting clericalism is a grotesque distortion of the truth that the clergy, although set aside to perform certain duties and functions within the church, are still only members of the people of God and intrinsically no better than anyone else.

Holy matrimony was reserved for the laity and regarded as the normal alternative to receiving orders in the church. It is obviously not an exclusively Christian phenomenon, since matrimony exists in one form or another in almost every society. The New Testament church recognised it of course, but did not perform it, because at that time it was a purely secular affair, governed by the laws and customs of the state. Only after the Roman Empire broke down did the church step into the vacuum and start making arrangements for matrimony, and then it took the opportunity to impose Christian principles on traditional practice. The most important of these were the principle of mutual consent and the principle of lifelong commitment. Mutual consent meant that no two people could be married if they did not agree to it. In other words, parents could not marry off their children against the latter's will. The practical effect of this, when it was applied (and often it was honoured more in the breach than in the observance, it must be said) was to give women the freedom to say no, something that was otherwise unheard of in the ancient world. Lifelong commitment meant that there could be no divorce, although a way out of this was found by allowing separation from bed and board in cases of cruelty and incompatibility, and annulment if it could be shown that the marriage was between people who were within the prohibited degrees of consanguinity and affinity. Since these degrees stretched to seven removes (later reduced to four), it was not difficult in a village culture to show that almost everyone was related within the prohibited range, so to some extent annulment served as a way round the prohibition of divorce. (It is important to remember that Henry VIII sought an annulment of his marriage to Catherine of Aragon and not a divorce in the modern sense, because that did not exist at the time.) After the reformation, matrimony ceased to be regarded as a sacrament and was no longer reserved for the laity, but although some clergy took advantage of their right to marry (granted by statute in 1549), by no means all did and clerical celibacy was common for another generation. Divorce however, remained unrecognised, and this is still the case – at least officially.

The last point mentioned by this article concerns some devotional practices that had grown up in the late middle ages concerning the reservation and exposition of the consecrated bread and wine of the Lord's Supper. These practices may have originated at an earlier date, but they became common after the Black Death, or bubonic plague, struck Europe in the years 1347-50. About a third of the population died, and in parts of England it was more like half. Such massive devastation inevitably produced a reaction, and one of the forms it took was an increasing, and often somewhat macabre, devotion to the body and blood of Christ. The doctrine of transubstantiation had made the consecrated bread and wine objects of special veneration in any case, but now they were put on display and people were encouraged to show the same veneration to them that they would have accorded to Jesus Christ in the flesh. Inevitably this led to superstition, of which the so-called 'black mass' was perhaps the most extreme example. Churches would be robbed and the reserved sacrament stolen so that it could be used in occult practices, something which everyone found outrageous but which was encouraged by a false devotion to material objects. The essential point is that the sacraments were not meant to be treated as museum pieces but to be used as part of the active proclamation of the Gospel. To do anything else with them was an abuse and was therefore to be forbidden by the church as inconsistent with the preaching of the Word of God.

Questions for discussion:

1. Is the concept of 'sacrament' a useful category in which to place baptism and the Lord's Supper?

2. What is the relationship between the administration of a sacrament and the reality which that sacrament signifies?

3. Can a person be a Christian without being baptised or receiving the Lord's Supper?

Key Bible Passages:

Matthew 28:16-20; Luke 22:14-23; John 1:19-34; Acts 2:37-41; 1 Corinthians 1:10-17, 10:14-21.

For further reading:

Barrett, C. K. *Church, ministry and sacraments in the New Testament.* Exeter: Paternoster, 1985.

Jeanes, G. P. *Signs of God's promise. Thomas Cranmer's sacramental theology and the Book of Common Prayer.* London: T. and T. Clark, 2008.

Martos, J. *Doors to the sacred, a historical introduction to sacraments in the Catholic church.* Garden City, NY: Image Books, 1982.

Spinks, B. D. *Sacraments, ceremonies and the Stuart divines: sacramental theology and liturgy in England and Scotland, 1603–1662.* Aldershot: Ashgate, 2002.

White, J. F. *The sacraments in Protestant practice and faith.* Nashville: Abingdon, 1999.

26. Of the Unworthiness of the Ministers, which hinder not the Effect of the Sacraments

Although in the visible Church the evil be ever mingled with the good, and sometime the evil have chief authority in the ministration of the Word and sacraments; yet forasmuch as they do not the same in their own name but in Christ's, and do minister by his commission and authority; we may use their ministry both in hearing the Word of God, and in receiving of the sacraments. Neither is the effect of Christ's ordinances taken away by their wickedness, nor the grace of God's gifts diminished from such as by faith and rightly do receive the sacraments ministered unto them, which be effectual because of Christ's institution and promise, although they be ministered by evil men.

Nevertheless it appertaineth to the discipline of the Church, that inquiry be made of evil ministers, and that they be accused by those that have knowledge of their offences, and finally, being found guilty by just judgement, be deposed.

The original context of this article was the problem created in the church by the immoral lives of some of its ministers. This was nothing new and can be traced right back to the Old Testament, where the story of Eli's two sons serves as a reminder of what will happen to those who abuse their calling before God (1 Samuel 2:22-36; 4:11-22). In the New Testament we read about people who abused their position in the church and we are warned to avoid them (2 John 7-11; 3 John 9-10; Jude 8-16). Of course all of us are sinners, and if this principle were pushed to an extreme, there would be no church at all. The article does not demand spiritual perfection, but it does expect that the standards of ministry laid down in 1 Timothy 3:1-13 and in Titus 1:5-16 as well as in other parts of the New Testament ought to be maintained in the church. It is the responsibility of the whole community to see that its leaders represent it in the right way, and if they do not, to remove them.

Much of the time, the criteria for removal from office are fairly straightforward. Anyone convicted of a crime, for example, would have to be dismissed. Similarly, someone who turned on the congregation and started abusing its members would also have to go. It would likewise not be possible for a man whose private life contradicted his public statements and responsibilities to carry on. Drunkenness, sexual immorality, profanity and the like are all grounds for discipline, the exact form of it depending on the gravity of the misdemeanours involved.

The church has always had a series of options available to it in such cases, not all of which are of equal severity. Sometimes, in cases of pastoral breakdown, it is enough to move a man to another parish and allow him to start again in a more congenial atmosphere. At other times, he might have to leave parish work and go into a non-parochial job, but still within the church. Occasionally he might be encouraged to resign or take early retirement. In extreme cases he might have to be defrocked and ejected from the ministry altogether. In the nature of things, cases like these are kept as confidential as possible and so it is not easy to find out how many there are, but those with experience in the field can testify that there is a working discipline of this kind and that it is usually quite effective when it is applied.

Trouble comes, of course, when it is not, and this is one of the biggest problems the modern church has to face. Today we are assailed on all sides by various forms of sexual immorality, and here it must be said that the church has tended to buckle and give way when it should stand firm. For example, it is now possible for divorced people to leave active ministry for a few years and then return to it, even when the cause of the divorce was closely connected with the ministry in the first place. It is not unknown for a clergyman to run off with a woman in the congregation, or even with a fellow minister, leaving a wife and family behind, and yet be rehabilitated a few years down the road and redeployed in a place where the original transgression is not known.

It is also possible, thanks to the ordination of women, for a clergyman to undergo a sex-change operation and carry on in his/her ministry as if nothing had happened, despite the doubts that inevitably surround the motives and morality of such things. Not long ago there was a case in England where a man decided to change his sex, despite his wife's opposition. He was not a clergyman, but what would have happened if he had been? More seriously still, practising homosexuals have been ordained and even consecrated as bishops in some places, and same-sex civil partnerships (so called to avoid the term 'marriages') are permitted among the clergy. It may be true that in such cases the clergyman or clergymen are asked to declare that they are 'celibate', whatever that is supposed to mean, but perception is as important as the reality and whatever may or may not be going on in private, the public image of the church is disgraced. Unfortunately, there are many who fail to see this, and think that such aberrations are the fruits of new 'discoveries' about human sexuality, as if promiscuity has not been around for a very long time! Sympathy for homosexuals is not the same thing as tolerance of deviant sexual practices, a distinction which is unfortunately lost on many people today, who seem to think that 'love' means accepting and allowing almost anything.

In the middle ages the clergy were put on a pedestal by the church itself and so naturally expectations of them were high – unrealistically so. There were plenty of men who failed to meet the demands placed on them and who lived in concubinage while officially claiming to be celibate. Some were dishonest and a few were criminals, though not nearly as many as later legend would have claimed. In such circumstances, it was only natural that lay people would be disgusted at what was going on and reject the ministry of those who were involved in such things. Unfortunately, the good suffered along with the bad in these cases, and it was this problem that the article intended to address. For example, what if I had heard the Gospel preached and was converted by the ministry of a man who later turned out to be an adulterer? Would baptism administered by such a person have any validity? Most of the recipients of that man's ministry would have been completely innocent and possibly ignorant of his misdeeds; should they be made to suffer because of his failings?

Here the answer of the church had to be no. The efficacy of the ministry does not depend on the worthiness of the minister but on the grace of God. If God has been pleased to use the deeds of wicked men to bring some good out of their evil then so be it. They will have to answer to him as their judge, but ordinary believers can rest secure in the knowledge that they have done what is right in God's eyes and been blessed accordingly.

Today it often happens that people who are newly converted turn against the church because they think they have been let down by it in some way. Especially if they have been baptised as infants and then not brought up as Christians, they are liable to feel that the whole thing was a charade. Most likely they will not know the minister who performed the baptism and will not take it out on him personally, but they will probably blame their parents for having succumbed to folk religion and gone through the motions without really believing a word of it. The hardest thing about this is that such critics may well have a point. There is undoubtedly a great deal of laxity in these areas and nobody, least of all truly committed Christians, would wish to defend it. But at the same time, who are we to judge the motives of others? How can we say for sure that God was not working in and through their ignorance to bring them to faith? If an unbelieving relative gives me a

Bible because he thinks I ought to have one and then I am converted by reading it, should I doubt my salvation (or the validity of the text) simply because of the way it reached me? Life is usually more complicated than we like it to be and there are many anomalies and loose ends that we cannot always account for. Why did Jesus choose Judas to be his disciple, when he knew that Judas would betray him? Why did he choose Peter for that matter, when he knew that Peter would deny him three times on the day of his trial and crucifixion? We would probably not do these things, at least not consciously, but who are we to think that we know better than Jesus did?

It should be said here that this article was not aimed primarily against false teachers, even if it can legitimately be applied to them. The reason for this is not that Thomas Cranmer thought that false teachers should be allowed to continue their ministry unmolested, but because the punishment reserved for them was far greater. In the sixteenth century a heretic was sentenced to death, as Cranmer would be only three years or so after writing these words (though technically for treason rather than for heresy.) Heresy is far worse than moral failure, because it touches the things of the spirit and not just the things of the flesh. The modern church is reasonably good at dealing with moral evil but it has largely forgotten that it must also preserve the orthodoxy of its faith. A philanderer who preaches the Gospel faithfully may be a hypocrite, but at least there is a chance that his ministry will bear fruit of eternal worth. A morally upright person, on the other hand, who preaches heresy can only do mischief, which may be all the greater precisely because he is so moral and upright in human terms. His ministry is unlikely to produce anything other than spiritual destruction and death and so must be avoided far more conscientiously than the former. Of course, neither is desirable, but given a choice between these two, the true believer must be able to discern which one is the lesser of two evils.

Having said all that, there is no excuse for tolerating either moral laxity or doctrinal deviance in the Christian ministry. It may be true that God's grace is able to overcome the defects caused by such things, but we also have a responsibility to make sure that both the preaching of the Gospel and its preachers are as pure as they can reasonably be expected to be. We are all sinners and make mistakes, but that is not a pretext for deliberately denying the truth or for consciously living in a way that the Bible condemns. There is all the difference in the world between a man like Apollos, who was insufficiently instructed in the meaning of baptism but otherwise perfectly sound in the faith

(Acts 18:24-28) and someone like Simon Magus, who thought he could buy the power of the Holy Spirit (Acts 8:18-24). The former was a believer with more to learn – like us all! – but the latter had no idea what the Gospel was all about and responded to it in a way that contradicted its very nature. When we meet that kind of thing, as we do whenever we come across ministers who openly reject the Christian faith by their teaching and lifestyle, we have a duty to protest and do what we can to remove them from the position of trust that they have abused.

Questions for discussion:

1. If an evangelist loses his faith, are those who came to Christ under his ministry truly converted?

2. How should ordinary Christians react when a bishop or ordained minister denies the Gospel?

3. Under what conditions, if any, should people who have resigned their ministry because of inappropriate behaviour be readmitted to it later on?

Key Bible Passages:

1 Corinthians 5; Ephesians 3:7-13; Philippians 1:12-18; 3 John.

For further reading:

Bridge, D. *Spare the rod and spoil the church.* Bromley: Marc Europe, 1985.

Evans, G. R. *Discipline and justice in the Church of England.* Leominster: Gracewing, 1998.

Under authority: The report of the General Synod Working Party reviewing clergy discipline and the working of the ecclesiastical courts. London: Church House Press, 1996.

White, J. *Healing the wounded: The costly love of church discipline.* Leicester: IVP, 1985.

27. Of Baptism

Baptism is not only a sign of profession and mark of difference, whereby Christian men are discerned from others that be not christened; but is also a sign of regeneration or new birth, whereby, as by an instrument, they that receive baptism rightly are grafted into the Church; the promises of the forgiveness of sin, and of our adoption to be the sons of God by the Holy Ghost, are visibly signed and sealed; faith is confirmed, and grace increased by virtue of prayer unto God. The baptism of young children is in any wise to be retained in the Church as most agreeable with the institution of Christ.

Baptism is the sign of entry into the Christian church, even though its origins are somewhat more complicated than that. There was no rite of baptism in the Old Testament, but it seems that in the inter-testamental period, some Jews practised ritual washing as a sign of repentance and cleansing from sin. The first clear evidence we have of it is in the life and career of John the Baptist, who proclaimed the coming of the Messiah and to whom Jesus himself went for baptism, somewhat to John's embarrassment (Matthew 3:13-15). As far as we know, Jesus did not baptise anyone himself, but just before his ascension into heaven, he commanded his disciples to go into the whole world, baptising the nations in the name of the Father, the Son and the Holy Spirit (Matthew 28:19). It is from there that the church's practice derives its authority and it is in the light of the great commission to go and preach the Gospel that we must understand it.

There are a number of things about baptism that we are not told and which have been controversial at different times in the history of the church. For one thing, we do not know if and when the disciples themselves were baptised. Presumably those who had followed John had been baptised by him, but what of the others? Did those who had received John's baptism have to be baptised again, and if so, by whom? Nor can we say for sure what was required of candidates for baptism. Some form of faith in Christ would seem to have been essential, but most accounts in the Acts of the Apostles suggest that baptism followed immediately on profession of faith, with little or no preparation for it. Some Samaritans appear to have been baptised only in the name of Jesus, not in the name of the Trinity, and so they had not received the Holy Spirit (Acts 8:14-17). How had this happened? Did it have something to do with the fact that they were Samaritans and not Jews?

Peter and John (a high-powered delegation) went to visit them, but they did not rebaptise them. Instead, it was enough for them to lay hands on the Samaritans and all was well. Is this how we are supposed to deal with what we might perceive as a defective baptism?

Above all, the New Testament does not tell us whether children were baptised along with their parents or not. There were certainly household baptisms, a practice which suggests that an individual profession of faith may not have been required of everyone, since it is hard to believe that an entire household would have professed conversion at exactly the same time. Perhaps they did, but this must be regarded as unproved. What we do know for sure is that the children of believers were regarded as holy, even if one of the parents was not a Christian (1 Corinthians 7:14). What implications does that have for baptism, if any? The unbelieving spouse was also regarded as 'holy', and presumably he or she was not baptised, so what does holiness mean in this case? Could a married woman have been baptised without her husband's knowledge or consent? Polemicists trying to prove that their view of baptism is the right one have proposed their own answers to questions like these, of course, but the truth is that we cannot say for certain one way or the other. What we do know is that some people thought their baptism gave them a certain cachet if it had been administered by the right person (1 Corinthians 1:10-17). Paul rebuked them for this, but how had such an idea arisen in the first place? What did these people think was happening to them when they were baptised?

In Romans 6:3-4 and again in Colossians 2:12-13, Paul tells us that baptism is a dying and rising with Christ, which has led some people to insist on immersion as the only proper way of administering the rite, even though Paul never said that. The evidence of ancient frescoes, for what it is worth, suggests that people went into the sea or a river and had the water poured over them when they were knee- or waist-deep in it. Other passages seem to suggest that baptism was essential for salvation (John 3:5), and there were certainly people in the early church who believed that. It led Augustine, for example, to say that water and blood flowed from the pierced side of Jesus when he was on the cross, in order to provide the means by which the believing thief next to him could be baptised and get to the paradise that Jesus had promised him! Like most people in his day, Augustine was a firm believer in baptismal regeneration, the conviction that baptism is the means by which a person is born again into the new life in Christ. In his *Confessions* he describes his own conversion after reading and being struck by Romans 13:14, but afterwards he tells his friend Alypius that they must go to the church and be baptised in order to be born again. Had that not happened already? We would say that it had, but Augustine obviously did not think so and saw the rite as something that had a power of its own that he needed in addition to his evident profession of faith. Did he believe that he would have gone to hell if he had died on his way to the church? Perhaps not, but that would appear to be the logic of his argument and behaviour.

Long before Augustine's time, some of the early church fathers had understood baptism as a kind of exorcism, and remnants of this still survive, as for example in the practice of signing the recipient with the sign of the cross in preparation for their future spiritual warfare. All the evidence suggests that baptism was of greater interest to the church fathers than the Lord's Supper was, but the controversies that arose over it were not those we might have expected and certainly not those that we are familiar with today. The most important of them concerned the validity of baptism administered by heretics. This was eventually resolved by saying that if the baptism was Trinitarian it must be accepted, regardless of who performed it. Even today it is possible for lay people to administer baptism, particularly in cases of necessity, but they are not allowed to preside at holy communion, which must seem anomalous to those who think that what applies to one sacrament must automatically apply to the other one as well.

The other major controversy that rocked the early church concerned post-baptismal sin. If baptism took away sin, what happened to those sins that were committed afterwards? Baptism itself could not be repeated, and so it seemed as though there was no remedy at all, apart perhaps from the baptism by fire, of which Jesus spoke (Luke 12:49-50). It is not hard to see why the early Christians interpreted this as martyrdom, which quickly became the sure route to heaven for those who could not rely on their own post-baptismal sinlessness. Another possibility, adopted by some, was to defer baptism to the point of death, though this could be risky if death were to come suddenly. In the end the problem was solved by saying that baptism took away *original* sin, preparing the soul for its spiritual journey through life in which it would have to contend with the many actual sins that a believer would commit after baptism. Those sins could be forgiven by relying on the means of grace offered by the church, and the whole system of merit theology developed on that assumption.

Infant baptism almost certainly became the general practice once it was accepted that it took away original sin but did not condemn the child to a life of post-baptismal perfection that he or she would be unable to achieve. Here we must bear in mind the high infant mortality rate, which put pressure on parents to make sure that their children would be in heaven if they died before coming to an age at which they could make a personal profession of faith and be held responsible for their actual sins.

By the fifth century what we think of as the traditional practice of the church was established and universal. For the next millennium and more, every child born in Western Europe (apart from Jews) was baptised as soon as possible after birth and integrated into the church's system of salvation by works. But when that system came under attack at the time of the Reformation, it was inevitable that the rites and ceremonies supporting it would also be called into question. Baptism was the first and therefore the most important of these, so we should not be surprised that it came under serious scrutiny, or that there were calls for a reform of traditional baptismal practices. At first, the Reformers did not think too much about the issue, but very soon they were forced to consider it because a small group at Zürich concluded, on the basis of Zwingli's teaching, that infant baptism was wrong and of no value. They therefore baptised themselves again (or, as they would say, for the first time) on the basis of their profession of faith, from which they were known as the 'rebaptisers' or Anabaptists. The early Anabaptists came in many shapes and sizes, and baptism was by no means the only thing that distinguished them from others, but it was the most fundamental – and perceived by the rest of the Christian world as the most subversive.

To minds steeped in the Augustinian tradition in which baptism was a cleansing from original sin, the Anabaptists were regarded as Pelagians, who believed that children were born innocent and only became sinners when they started to copy their elders. This was not a very accurate assessment of most Anabaptist theology, but it shows how their behaviour was perceived and why they were so disliked. In modern terms, they were like people who refuse to vaccinate their children on religious grounds, thereby exposing them to the risk of contracting terrible (and possibly even fatal) diseases. Why do that, many people ask, and deprive innocent children of the health and safety which they could otherwise have? This is how most Christians in the sixteenth century perceived the Anabaptists. Not only were they calling the basis of Western society into question, but they were putting their children in mortal danger because of their unwillingness to take advantage of the obvious and readily-available remedy for their original sin.

The mainline Reformers sensed that the Anabaptists were wrong, but it was much harder for them to explain why. When asked how he could square infant baptism with justification by faith, Martin Luther came up with the notion of 'infant faith' – a child responds with an instinctive trust that is acceptable to God as the ground of its justification. That seemed to be stretching things a bit, and soon other answers were being put forward to supplement (though not to deny) the notion of 'infant faith'. By interpreting the sacraments as signs of the Gospel, the Calvinistic Reformers believed that they had found a viable solution to the problem, and that is what we find outlined in this article.

The rite of baptism is explained as a sign of regeneration, which is related to it in the same way that a marriage contract is related to a marriage. (This is the meaning of the word 'instrument' used in the article.) A married couple wanting to prove their status would refer to their contract as evidence. Similarly, if they wanted to understand what their rights and obligations as a couple were, the contract was there to tell them. It was a fixed point of reference to which they could turn for encouragement, consolation and (if necessary) rebuke. Dishonouring the contract was possible, but breaking it was not because it was made 'till death us do part'. At the same time, a marriage is more than a contract. It is a living relationship which the contract can describe and defend, but which it cannot create or sustain. For that, there must be mutual trust and affection, which can only come from the contracting parties themselves. The difference between a good marriage and a bad one is not to be found in the contract, which is identical in every case, but in the way in which it is appropriated and internalised in the spirit and behaviour of the contracting parties. Once this is understood, what Cranmer had to say about baptism makes perfect sense. It goes like this:

1. The baptised person is grafted into the church.

2. The promises of forgiveness and adoption are visibly signed and sealed.

3. Faith (where it exists) is confirmed.

4. Grace is increased through prayer.

The principles are not restricted to infants, but as adult baptism was not common at that time and the Prayer Book did not make any provision for it until 1662, we may take it as read that Cranmer was thinking primarily of them. (It is true that the English translation of the article says 'young children' which does not necessarily mean babies, but the Latin *parvuli* makes it clear that infants are what it has in mind.) The first point means that the baptised child is brought within the church. This does not mean that he is saved, because the church is a mixed company of good and evil people (see article 26), but it does mean that he is exposed to the teaching which the church gives and hears the preaching of the Gospel to which he is expected to respond by being confirmed on profession of faith. The second point is the assurance that baptism contains the promise of forgiveness and adoption, which will be given to those who receive them in the right way – by faith. The promise is not to be equated with the actual gift, nor is it a guarantee that the gift will be rightly used once it has been given. It is a promise – the promise contained in the Gospel – but it will only become real as and when it is appropriated by the person to whom it has been made.

Baptism confirms faith because once the promise has been received it serves as a reassurance that it will be fulfilled. People who embark on married life seldom realise what they are letting themselves in for, and they discover the implications of their commitment as they go along. So it is with Christian faith. We begin with little idea of what it really means, but find out by experience. As we analyse that, we can turn to our baptism to see what it is that we have committed ourselves to and what we can expect in the future. As things start to work out in that way, our trust in the promises of God is strengthened and confirmed, because we know what is coming and see it unfolding in front of our eyes. Finally, the grace of God works more fully and deeply in our lives as we open ourselves up to him in prayer. Infants grow in it as their parents and godparents pray for them, and those who are truly saved will start praying for themselves as soon as they understand what it means. The prayers of a little child may be simple and naive, but they are not to be despised, because as Jesus said, it is the faith of a child which makes up the kingdom of heaven (Matthew 19:14).

What baptism cannot do is bring about real regeneration. If it could, there would be no need to preach the Gospel at all, since it would be enough just to pour water over everybody who comes along. If baptism could make people Christians, then there would be millions of people in the world who would be Christians without realising it, and often in spite of denying it. Bertrand Russell, for example, was baptised, but he openly denied that he was a Christian, so what was the effect of his baptism? Adolf Hitler was baptised, as was Josef Stalin. So what? Baptismal regeneration is a foolish and impossible idea, but that did not stop Henry Philpotts, Bishop of Exeter from 1831 to 1869, from trying to insist that it was the teaching of the Church of England. Philpotts was so insistent on this that he refused to institute George Cornelius

Gorham to the living of Brampford Speke in Devon because Gorham did not believe it. Philpotts was backed by a number of high churchmen and the Court of Arches, the supreme judicial body of the church, found in his favour, basing its conclusion on the Prayer Book's words 'seeing this child is regenerate...' following the act of baptism. But the words of the Prayer Book have to be interpreted in the light of the Articles, not the other way round, and read in context. Baptism is a *sign* of the regeneration that occurs when a person receives the Gospel by faith; the rite itself cannot cause regeneration to occur automatically. The Court of Arches' judgment was absurd and outrageous, and if it had been upheld, it would have contradicted the true doctrine of the Church of England and forced many sound believers to leave it. In the end, the judgment was overturned by the judicial committee of the privy council which had a clearer understanding of the Articles of Religion, and Gorham was vindicated, making it clear that baptismal regeneration is not the doctrine of the church.

Today there are few people who take the notion of baptismal regeneration seriously because the evidence against it is so overwhelming, but by the same token, there is much greater dissatisfaction with the practice of infant baptism than there once was. In a secular age, it often seems better to insist that each individual person should make his own profession of faith, and not be allowed to rely on something he has inherited from his parents but may not share or even fully understand himself. This feeling is perfectly understandable and we must respect it, particularly given the fact that the abuse of infant baptism is so widespread. At the same time however, we must remember that the promise of the Gospel of salvation is made to us and to our children (Acts 2:39), that Christian parents have a duty to bring up their children in the knowledge and fear of the Lord, and not allow them to 'make their own decision when they get older' as so many basically indifferent parents describe it. They also have a right to claim the promise that what God has given them he will preserve and protect. Christian children are a gift from the Lord, and while there can be no guarantee that they will necessarily accept the faith they have been brought up in, their parents have every right to walk in faith and trust him in this as in everything else. At the end of the day, infant baptism, like baptism in general, is a sign that is neither absolutely necessary for salvation nor productive of it, but a promise of what is waiting for those who respond to the preaching of the Gospel in faith.

> *Questions for discussion:*
>
> 1. What qualifications should a person have in order to be baptised?
>
> 2. Should a person who was baptised in infancy be re-baptised on profession of faith as an adult?
>
> 3. Does baptism make us Christians?

Key Bible Passages:

Acts 17:25-34; Romans 6:1-14; Ephesians 4:1-6.

For further reading:

Bridge, D. and D. Phypers. *Water that divides.* Leicester: IVP, 1977. Repr., Fearn: Mentor, 1998.

Ferguson, E. *Baptism in the early church: history, theology and liturgy in the first five centuries.* Grand Rapids: Eerdmans, 2009.

Marcel, P. C. *The Biblical doctrine of infant baptism.* London: James Clarke, 1953.

Spinks, B. D. *Reformation and modern rituals and theologies of baptism: from Luther to contemporary practice.* Aldershot: Ashgate, 2006.

Stott, John and Alec J. Motyer, *The Anglican evangelical doctrine of infant baptism.* London: Latimer Trust, 2008.

Thompson, D. M. *Baptism, church and society in modern Britain: from the Evangelical revival to 'Baptism, eucharist and ministry'.* Bletchley, Milton Keynes: Paternoster, 2005.

28.   Of the Lord's Supper

The Supper of the Lord is not only a sign of the love Christians ought to have among themselves one to another; but rather is a sacrament of our redemption by Christ's death: insomuch that to such as rightly, worthily and with faith receive the same, the bread which we break is a partaking of the body of Christ, and likewise the cup of blessing is a partaking of the blood of Christ.

Transubstantiation (or the change of the substance of bread and wine) in the supper of the Lord, cannot be proved by Holy Writ, but is repugnant to the plain words of Scripture, overthroweth the nature of a sacrament, and hath given occasion to many superstitions.

The body of Christ is given, taken and eaten in the supper, only after an heavenly and spiritual manner. And the mean whereby the body of Christ is received and eaten in the supper is faith.

The sacrament of the Lord's Supper was not by Christ's ordinance reserved, carried about, lifted up or worshipped.

Baptism was a controversial subject at the time of the reformation, but the arguments over it pale in significance when compared to those that surrounded the Lord's Supper. To this day, Protestants who practise infant baptism can have fellowship with those who do not and it does not constitute a barrier to co-operation in mission and evangelism, but the Lord's Supper is a different matter. The different views held about it divide the church and make it impossible for some groups of Christians to recognise others as fellow believers. Participation in this sacrament may be refused to members of other churches or rejected by them, even when their baptism is accepted as valid. In modern times, so central has it become to the worship and self-understanding of most major denominations that withdrawal from it, or refusal to partake of it (even for good and legitimate reasons) is often regarded as tantamount to leaving the church itself. So much is this the case that in many churches it is virtually impossible not to participate, because the worship is structured in such a way as to make such a refusal highly disruptive and embarrassing. What we think about it therefore matters in a way that our views of baptism do not. Celebrations of baptism are relatively infrequent and can often be avoided, but holy communion is something every churchgoer has to come to terms with in an immediate and personal way.

Different names have been used for this sacrament and unfortunately they have sometimes become badges of churchmanship in a way that has tended to compromise their use. For example, the Lord's Supper is a term now often associated with low church people and nonconformists, and so it tends to be avoided by others, which is a pity, since it is a Biblical designation which was widely used in the early church. Holy communion is more 'middle of the road' and therefore more widely used among Anglicans, and the term emphasises the important dimension of fellowship with Christ and with each other that the sacrament exemplifies (1 Corinthians 10). The term 'eucharist' ('thanksgiving') is now the ecumenically preferred name, but it suffers from being somewhat exotic, as the word is not otherwise used in most modern languages and few people other than specialists know what it means. Finally, there is 'mass', which is common among Anglo-Catholics and Roman Catholics, but which is the least descriptive and least suitable term of all. The word is a corruption of the Latin *missa*, which was adopted for the sacrament because at the end the celebrant dismisses the congregation with the words: '*Ite, missa est [ecclesia]*' ('Go, the congregation is dismissed'). In theological terms it is meaningless, but it has come to represent the Roman Catholic doctrine of the sacrament and is used almost exclusively by those who hold that position.

What exactly went on in New Testament times as far as this sacrament is concerned is not entirely clear. There was a connection with the Last Supper that Jesus ate with his disciples, but the two things were not identical, because the Last Supper was held before the crucifixion and not in remembrance of it. Similarly, there was a close link with the Jewish Passover, but again there were differences, because Passover was an annual event that commemorated the deliverance of the Israelites from Egypt whereas the Lord's Supper was much more frequent and also forward looking, remembering the death of Christ until he comes again and reminding us that it may happen at any time (1 Corinthians 11:26).

In 1 Corinthians 11 the Apostle Paul gives us a detailed account of how the service proceeded and his words have become central to Anglican liturgies everywhere, but although we have a form of words dating from apostolic times, there is much else that we do not know. For example, we cannot say whether the early Christians used leavened or unleavened bread. This became an issue in the early church, where the East regarded the West's use of unleavened bread as a Judaising practice and forbade it at the Council in Trullo (692). Nor can we be sure what sort of wine they used, fermented or unfermented, or perhaps both. This was not an issue in ancient times but has become one more recently, in that many Protestant churches use some type of grape juice instead of alcoholic wine and some feel quite strongly about it because of their more general opposition to the use of alcohol. Neither of these things really matters theologically, but it has to be admitted that rivers of ink have flowed over the centuries from people who were determined to prove the contrary. What is important is that the elements used should be bread and wine of some kind, since that is what the New Testament prescribes and what most clearly represents in visible form what the body and blood of Christ looked like. To substitute coffee and doughnuts, for example, may have no theological significance, but it breaks the visible continuity with the event being commemorated, and such substitutions should be avoided for that reason if for no other.

The early church continued to celebrate the Lord's Supper and came to regard participation in it as the ultimate sign of communion within and between churches. When communion was broken for some reason (usually heresy) admission to the Lord's table would be withdrawn and the offender would be expelled from the fellowship. As time went on, the practice of exclusion became more widespread, extending for example to unbaptised catechumens, who were ordered to leave at a point in the service before the consecration of the bread and wine began. To this day, Eastern liturgies contain a section known as the 'departure of the catechumens' which recalls this practice (although nowadays nothing happens and everyone stays put) and the Book of Common Prayer contains preliminary exhortations to the worshippers which may be regarded in a similar light. They are mostly ignored these days, but they are a serious attempt to exercise some discipline in the church and their effective disappearance is to be regretted for that reason.

What we do not know is who presided at the Lord's Supper, how often it was celebrated, or what else formed part of the worship. Somebody must have been in charge and logically this would normally have been the head of the local church, but this is a deduction from the standard practice of later times and we cannot claim to have New Testament authority for it. That said, there would have to be good reasons today for *not* following this custom, because of the danger of treating the sacrament in a casual and irreverent manner. That would certainly be against New Testament principles and ought to be avoided for the sake of decency and order in the church. It is important that there should be somebody responsible for overseeing what is going on so as to avoid abuses which can so easily creep into such an important act of worship.

In the course of the middle ages this sacrament became the central act of worship and the one at which the attendance of the laity was most strongly encouraged. It was by no means the only service however, and we have to remember that it was placed within a cycle of prayer that included many other things. The Book of Common Prayer provides for the service of Morning Prayer *and* the Litany to be said before Holy Communion, and the modern tendency to suppress the first two of these gives the wrong impression. Nowadays, more often than not, there is nothing other than Holy Communion available to the average worshipper, which was never the intention of the Reformers (or of the medieval church, for that matter).

In the sixteenth century there was a great variety of rites in use across Western Europe, which is surprising when we think of the drive towards administrative centralisation initiated by the papacy in the eleventh century and pursued relentlessly thereafter. The Reformation did not extinguish this variety, because there were many churches which sprang from it, each with its own rite, but it changed its nature. Whereas previously, local custom, the liturgical cycle and sometimes personal preference had decided the matter, after the Reformation each church, including the church of Rome, imposed uniformity on its own members. This was partly to ensure doctrinal unity but also to help lay people know which church they were attending. Roman Catholics and most Protestants tried to make the form of their worship correspond as closely as possible to their doctrinal beliefs, so that the outward appearance would proclaim the beliefs held by the congregation. Anglicans however, took a different approach. The Church of England maintained as much of the traditional ceremonial as it could but reshaped it into a Reformed theological mould. This was largely for pragmatic reasons, because the Reformers did not want to upset worshippers for the wrong reasons. Theologians may deplore this, but the fact is that an alteration in worship style is far more likely to split a congregation than heresy preached in the pulpit, which only a minority can understand. But move the pulpit, turn the communion table around, or dress the clergy in unfamiliar robes and everyone knows that something must be going on.

This was the essence of the struggle between the so-called Puritans in the English Church and the establishment, as represented by men like Cranmer. It was not a matter of doctrine, for Cranmer was just as Reformed as people like John Hooper and John Knox, whose views on questions of ritual were different from his. Cranmer did not really care about clerical dress or church furnishings. What mattered to him was the Gospel message, and if doing unfamiliar things distracted people and turned them against that message, he was against it. Far better, he reasoned, to let unimportant ceremonial things stay than to alienate people from the Gospel. Men like Hooper and Knox however, thought differently. To their minds, if a preacher dressed like a medieval priest then he *was* a medieval priest – clothes made the man! If Cranmer was serious about creating a Reformed ministry (which he was) then his ministers ought to look the part and wear academic dress (a black Geneva gown being preferred). Feelings ran so high that at one point Cranmer had Hooper arrested and put in gaol for not wearing the traditional vestments!

All this is liable to seem very strange to us, though the question of vestments still plagues Anglicans today. Officially, clerical dress has no theological significance and one look at the standard Catholic vestments tells us that they are relics of the past (whereas they were standard apparel in late Roman times). Even the Protestant replacements for them – scarf and hood, Geneva gown and so on – are passé nowadays and scarcely less exotic than the vestments are. The truth is that here we are dealing with an inheritance which most people no longer understand. In the sixteenth century and for a good while thereafter, there were laws that decreed what a person might or might not wear. Noblemen were allowed to wear furs, for example, but not peasants. The clergy lived in a society where everyone had a kind of uniform, and theirs was just one among many others. We have left that world behind now, but the idea of the uniform has survived and lack of imagination as much as misplaced traditionalism has kept the past alive in an unfortunate way. The result is that a controversy which should never have arisen is perpetuated by the very people who ought to know better – the clergy themselves! It should be said in passing that there is a good deal to be said in favour of a recognisable clerical dress, but no reason at all why this should reflect the habits of a bygone age.

When discussing the Lord's Supper, Archbishop Cranmer took it for granted that the celebrant would be an ordained priest (or bishop), that he would look the part and that he would follow the prescribed liturgical forms with only minimal variations permitted. These things were set out in the Book of Common Prayer, which must be consulted to see how the doctrine was interpreted in practice. In the Articles however, it was the underlying principles that concerned him most, and whatever we say about the rest must be said in relation to (and dependence on) what we find here.

First of all, Cranmer accepted that the Lord's Supper was a fellowship meal of believers and an opportunity for them to show their love for one another. This idea is very common today, and probably exaggerated in many cases, but it was less so in the sixteenth century, where the celebration of private masses, either by the priest alone or with only a tiny and select congregation (usually of noblemen and their families) was accepted practice. The reformers tried to do away with this by stressing the fellowship of the entire body of Christ around the Lord's table and so we must give this aspect of the matter its due weight.

Having said that however, Cranmer also believed that the heart of the sacrament was not the fellowship but the sacrifice which Christ had made on the cross and which formed the elements that gave it its core meaning. We have fellowship with one another not because we like one another or share common interests like bell-ringing or whatever, but because we have been redeemed by the broken body and the shed blood of Christ. If that is lost sight of, the sacrament loses its meaning and degenerates into something that no longer proclaims the Gospel. Furthermore, the article stresses that those who partake of the Lord's supper must do so with the right understanding and in the right spirit, since otherwise it will be of no benefit to them. This is a reiteration of the sacramental principle outlined in article 25 (see above), which is essentially that spiritual things are meant for spiritual people and have no meaning or effectiveness when applied to those who are spiritually dead.

When we take the bread and drink from the cup we partake of the body and blood of Christ, which means that we share in his suffering and death for our salvation. 'Sharing' in this case does not mean suffering and dying along with Christ in a literal sense, but participating in and benefiting from the spiritual meaning of his atoning sacrifice. We can only do this if we have heard the Gospel and responded to it. Stuffing ourselves with consecrated bread and wine, as some of the people at Corinth apparently did (see 1 Corinthians 11:21-22) is less than useless if we do not know what we are doing.

The bread and wine used in the sacrament relate to the body and blood of Christ in the same way as the water used in baptism relates to the cleansing power of the Holy Spirit in our lives. They are signs appointed by God to bring home to us the reality of Christ's suffering and death, and to remind us that salvation is a total experience. When we are raised from the dead, we shall be raised as bodies and not just as souls or spirits. God cares about our physical being and what we do with our body matters to him. It is certainly true that flesh and blood cannot inherit the kingdom of God but they are related to it in the way that a seed is related to the plant it produces after it is sown. The plant looks very different from the seed, yet without the seed there can be no plant. (1 Corinthians 15:35-55). How the one turns into the other is a mystery, but it is also a reality and the use of bread and wine serves to remind us of this.

At the same time however, the bread and wine must not be turned into something magical that destroys their nature and their purpose. If flesh and blood cannot inherit the kingdom of God, then the bread and wine that stand for Christ's flesh and blood cannot be part of it either. They are earthly means used to represent spiritual realities but are not transformed into them. This was the great error of the medieval church, which pushed its reverence for this sacrament to the point of saying that when the elements are consecrated by the priest they become the body and blood of Christ in 'real' terms. What this means is very hard for modern people to understand because the doctrine was worked out against a background of medieval philosophy which is no longer widely understood or accepted as valid. To put it simply, it rests on two fundamental principles:

1. Reality is spiritual and not material. Matter is at best a corruption of what is truly real and an imperfect guide to understanding it. Ideas and principles are 'real', but the way they work out in the world is corrupted by circumstances and therefore only a partial manifestation of them.

2. Everything that exists can be analysed in terms of its substance and its accidents. The substance is permanent and unchanging, invisible because it is 'real' (in the above-mentioned sense). Accidents on the other hand change all the time and are usually visible, being things like size, shape, weight, colour and so on. Bread, for example, comes in many accidental varieties, but the underlying substance is the same, since otherwise we would not recognise a pitta and a granary loaf, for example, as being both 'bread'.

In the traditional Roman Catholic view, Christ is 'really present' in the consecrated bread and wine of the Lord's Supper, which means that his body and blood are there in the shape of bread and wine. What came to be known as the 'miracle of the altar' and what theologians know as 'transubstantiation' means that, contrary to what happens in ordinary life, in the eucharistic act the accidents of bread and wine remain unchanged but the underlying substance becomes Christ's body and blood. In other words, it looks like bread, it feels like bread, it tastes like bread, but thanks to the power given to the consecrating priest, it is not bread any more but Christ's body, 'really present' in our midst.

Today nobody who knows what they are talking about accepts this idea because the philosophical outlook which underlies it is no longer scientifically tenable. It is not just that bread and wine cannot be changed in this way, but that the substance/accidents distinction is no longer accepted as valid. We analyse matter in a completely different way, and regard it as 'real' in a sense that ideas are not. In fact, it would not be too much to say that the modern mind conceives of 'reality' in a way which is almost the exact opposite of its medieval forbear. In the sixteenth century the medieval understanding of reality was already breaking down, but society at large had a harder time catching up with this. Henry VIII burnt people at the stake for denying transubstantiation, even many years after he had broken with Rome, because to him this was the heart of the Christian faith – Christ in us, the hope of glory. Only very slowly and painfully did people's minds change, which explains why the article (and especially the Prayer Book) go on about this at much greater length than seems necessary to us now.

Cranmer understood that transubstantiation was wrong because he realised that the Lord's Supper was a proclamation of the Gospel and conformed to the nature of a sacrament. For him, the 'real presence' of Christ was to be sought not in the elements of bread and wine but in the preaching of the pure Word of God and the faithful response of those who heard and received that Word. In that relationship, Christ speaks to his Spirit at work in our hearts, where the Spirit of Christ cries: 'Abba, Father' (Galatians 4:6). He is present in that relationship of faith and not in material objects that can be set apart and venerated. The articles that follow (29-33) elaborate on this theme and draw out the particular implications of it that are most relevant to our own worship, practice and understanding.

The last sentence of the article refers to various liturgical practices that had grown up in the later middle ages and that only make sense in the context of transubstantiation. If a priest really does have the power to turn bread and wine into Christ's body and blood, then it is understandable that the consecrated elements should be set aside, either for emergencies or for use when a priest is not present. This 'reserved sacrament' would then be an appropriate object of veneration, if not of actual worship, since it would be the real body and blood of Christ himself. In the fifteenth century the practice grew up of taking the 'reserved sacrament' on procession, not simply around the church but around the parish, so that the faithful could have an opportunity of paying their respects to it without going to mass. A special feast, Corpus Christi, was given over to this and fixed for the Thursday following Trinity Sunday, and to this day it is a big occasion in some Roman Catholic countries. But once the doctrine of transubstantiation was abandoned, these rituals ceased to have any meaning and were dropped by the Protestant churches. The article does not specifically condemn them, but it does point out that they have no Biblical warrant and the assumption is that they are therefore unjustified. Unfortunately, it has to be admitted that there are Anglican churches where the consecrated elements are reserved and devotional practices associated with that are encouraged. There is really no excuse for this and those who indulge in such behaviour ought to be challenged by being reminded that it is perilously close to idolatry, and not the true veneration of Christ that they imagine it to be.

Questions for discussion:

1. How should we prepare ourselves before coming to holy communion?

2. Should Christians who are not members of our church be allowed to receive communion?

3. How often should the Lord's Supper be celebrated in church?

Key Bible Passages:

Matthew 26:17-29; 1 Corinthians 11:17-34.

For further reading:

Bolt, P., M. Thompson and R. Tong. *The Lord's Supper in human hands: who should administer?* Camperdown, NSW: Australian Church record, 2008.

Cummings, O. F. *Canterbury cousins: the eucharist in contemporary Anglican theology.* New York: Paulist Press, 2007.

Gittoes, J. *Anamnesis and the eucharist: contemporary Anglican approaches.* Aldershot: Ashgate, 2008.

Marshall, I. H. *Last supper and Lord's supper.* Carlisle: Paternoster, 1997.

29. Of the Wicked which do not eat the Body of Christ in the Use of the Lord's Supper

The wicked, and such as be void of a lively faith, although they do carnally and visibly press with their teeth (as St Augustine saith) the sacrament of the body and blood of Christ; yet in no wise are they partakers of Christ; but rather, to their condemnation, do eat and drink the sign or sacrament of so great a thing.

This short article was not in the original Cranmerian compilation but was composed afresh in 1563. It was approved by the convocation of Canterbury, but the Queen (probably on the advice of some of her ministers) struck it out of the version she ratified, probably because she was afraid that it might be seen as taking sides in a controversy then raging among German Protestants. They were dividing into 'Gnesio-Lutherans', so called because they claimed to hold the authentic doctrine of Martin Luther, and 'Reformed' who also claimed to be interpreting Luther, but as he was understood by Philipp Melanchthon, Martin Bucer and John Calvin. The most important difference between these two groups, and a real bone of contention, was the way they understood the real presence of Christ in the eucharist. In his original text of article 28 (29 in the forty-two articles of 1553) Thomas Cranmer had taken the 'Reformed' side with a trenchant paragraph denying the 'ubiquity' of Christ's body after his ascension, something that was a major plank in the Gnesio-Lutheran platform. What Luther thought about ubiquity is hard to tell, because the controversy erupted after his death, but suffice it to say that those who objected to it believed that they were following Luther just as much as the 'Gnesio-Lutherans' did.

The 'ubiquity' controversy is hard to understand today, and perhaps the fairest thing that can be said about it is that the protagonists each started with a presupposition that seemed reasonable enough in itself, but when it was taken to its logical conclusion it excluded the other viewpoint. Thus, the Gnesio-Lutherans said that when Christ ascended to heaven he took his body with him, meaning that it was transformed into its spiritual and heavenly state. Because he was fully God and fully man, wherever his divinity was present his humanity was present also, albeit in this heavenly and spiritual manner. This enabled them to interpret the 'real presence' of Christ in the sacrament as including his body and blood, though not in the way the Roman Catholics understood it. The Reformed tradition, on the other hand, claimed that when Christ ascended into heaven, he took his body with him, but because a body has a defined space allocated to it, it did not merge with his divine nature. In their eyes, the ubiquitist view was a denial of the two-natures Christology of the council of Chalcedon, which said that the natures were united in Christ 'without confusion'. They could also quote such New Testament passages as the appearance of the risen Christ to Saul of Tarsus (Acts 9:3-6) and the visions of the Lamb seated on the throne in the book of Revelation, as evidence that even in heaven, the Son of God retained his visible humanity within the limitations imposed by his body. Of course, heaven is not a place in the physical sense, so it is hard to see where exactly Christ's ascended body would be located, but that is the sort of unanswerable question that this dispute led to.

The revisers of the articles dropped Cranmer's paragraph on the subject, which would have been much too inflammatory, and substituted this milder version instead. Even so, it was a hot potato at the time. It was put back into the Articles without alteration in 1571, perhaps because it was so obviously anti-Roman in its emphasis at a time when the unacceptability of Roman doctrine needed to be reaffirmed, but the German controversy was far from over and in the *Formula of Concord* which united the Gnesio-Lutherans and others sympathetic to them in 1577, the Anglican view was condemned outright, though without mentioning any names (VII, 66). The history of the interpretation and reception of this article are a reminder to us that although some in the Church of England tried to steer a middle course (the famous *via media*) between the so-called 'Gnesio-Lutherans' and the Reformed, they were ultimately unsuccessful because, when all is said and done, the Anglican position on the matter is Reformed and therefore incompatible with the line taken by the Gnesio-Lutherans.

The article quotes a passage from Augustine which comes from his *Tractates on John*, 26, which says exactly the same thing. Along with the Gnesio-Lutherans and the later *Formula of Concord*, the article agrees that those who eat and drink the sacramental bread and wine unworthily do so to their own condemnation, but they do not have any share in Christ or his benefits because all they are doing is consuming earthly substances. If the spiritual understanding is not there, the spiritual benefit cannot be received. Such hypocrisy is harmful, not because the consecrated elements have any power in themselves to hurt the recipient, but because the latter, being spiritually blind, has cut himself off from the grace of God and offended him by abusing his sacramental gifts.

From an Anglican point of view, the problem with the Lutheran doctrine is that if an unworthy person really does receive the body and blood of Christ, why do they not have a positive effect on him and win him over to faith? After all, we are told in the Scriptures to 'taste and see that the Lord is good' (Psalm 34:8) and it seems like a denial of God's sovereignty and power to suggest that this does not happen in this case – rather the opposite. Lutherans, of course, see the matter differently and the argument is stalemated by the existence of two distinct and ultimately incompatible approaches to the presence of Christ in the sacrament. At the end of the day however, both sides are agreed that only those who eat and drink in faith receive the intended benefits of the sacrament, and surely that is the most important thing.

Questions for discussion:

1. Should the church impose tests of faith or behaviour on members when they come to communion?

2. In what ways do unbelievers who profane the sacrament suffer as a result?

3. Should differences in the way we understand communion be a barrier to welcoming people from other churches at the Lord's table?

Key Bible Passages:

1 Corinthians 11:29-32; Hebrews 6:4-6.

For further reading:

Garcia, Mark A. *Life in Christ: union with Christ and twofold grace in Calvin's theology.* Milton Keynes: Paternoster, 2008.

Hein, K. *Eucharist and excommunication. A study in early Christian doctrine and discipline.* Frankfurt am Main: Peter Lang, 1973.

30.   *Of both kinds*

> *The cup of the Lord is not to be denied to the laypeople; for both the parts of the Lord's sacrament, by Christ's ordinance and commandment, ought to be ministered to all Christian men alike.*

This article was also added by the revisers in 1563 and it remained unchanged in 1571. At first sight it seems fairly obvious, and there is no doubt that in the New Testament and for many centuries afterwards, all Christians who received holy communion received both the bread and the wine. They may have received it by 'intinction' as is now the custom in the Eastern Orthodox churches – the bread being dipped in the wine and then given to the communicant – but that is a minor detail. The point is that both elements (or 'kinds' as they are called here) were given to everyone.

How and why this began to change is not entirely clear. The most plausible theory is that it was originally a question of hygiene. Medieval people did not understand anything about germs, but they knew that diseases were generally contagious and that it was not a good idea to drink from a common cup. As has happened again in recent years, the cup may have been temporarily withdrawn from the laity at first, in order to calm the fear of contracting disease, but after the Black Death that fear became overwhelming, and what had originally been a temporary measure became permanent.

Once that happened it was necessary to develop a theology to justify the practice of communion in one kind, especially after the practice was objected to by Jan Hus and his followers in Bohemia. They are called Utraquists, from the Latin word for 'both' and their doctrine, although it was nothing more than the ancient tradition of the universal church, was condemned at the council of Constance (Konstanz) in 1415, where Hus was burnt at the stake for heresy. By any standard, the judicial murder of Hus was a scandal, especially as he had been given a safe conduct to the council by the Emperor Sigismund, but the church could not resist the temptation to deal with him when they had him in their grip. The result was a revolt in Bohemia and the secession of large numbers of Utraquists (Hussites) from the church. Despite many attempts to crush them, the Hussites survived and so have a claim to being the first Protestants, a century or so before Luther (who acknowledged his affinity with them).

The theology that justified giving communion in one kind only said that because a body has blood in it, giving the communicant the body of Christ was in effect giving him two in one! It was also said that the priest took the cup as the representative of the people, thereby strengthening his sacral position in the church and making him a kind of mediator between the laity and God. The chief importance of this controversy was that it established the principle that the church, and in particular the papacy, had the right to modify Biblical practice if it saw fit to do so. That had already happened with the imposition of clerical celibacy in 1123, but this was more far-reaching. Compulsory celibacy was a discipline imposed on the clergy but not a doctrine, whereas communion in one kind, if not quite a doctrine in itself, nevertheless had serious doctrinal implications and was imposed on everyone except the clergy. It was a clear example of where Rome had erred, and done so in a blatant and shameless fashion. What is more, although there was pressure put on the church from within to restore the cup to the laity, this was actually resisted by the council of Trent, which went out of its way to reaffirm the practice of giving communion to the laity (and to non-celebrating clergy) in one kind only (Session 22, 17 September 1562).

Today, the Roman Catholic Church has gradually reinstated communion in both kinds, though it is still far from universal. However, it has not repudiated the theological arguments that justified abandoning it and it is hard to see how it can do so without undermining its own authority. For Utraquism was condemned by a general (ecumenical) council and therefore the condemnation is as infallible as the council itself was. One error has led to another and created a situation from which there would appear to be no retreat. Perhaps the most we can hope for is that the whole thing will be quietly forgotten as the ancient practice is restored to the place it deserves to occupy in the sacrament.

Communion in one kind only has recently resurfaced for reasons not unlike those which prompted it in the first place – the risk of infection. This can be a real problem, but there are other ways of solving it that should be explored. Some churches pour the wine into smaller cups which are then given to communicants, and this would seem to be the most sensible solution. In Scandinavia, those partaking of the sacrament will often bring a cup with them (supplied by the church!) and while they are kneeling at the communion rail, the minister will pour the wine from the chalice directly into it. The danger of contracting disease is eliminated, but the practice of receiving communion in both kinds is protected, as it ought to be in the light of Biblical teaching and precedent.

Questions for discussion:

1. To what extent should health issues affect the way we receive the bread and the wine in communion?

2. Does the person who presides at communion have a spiritual privilege that others do not share?

3. Is it ever right to use a non-alcoholic drink instead of wine for holy communion?

Key Bible Passages:

1 Corinthians 11:23-28; Hebrews 9:11-15.

For further reading:

Spinka, M. *John Hus' concept of the church.* Princeton, N.J.: Princeton University Press, 1966.

31. *Of the one Oblation of Christ finished upon the Cross*

The offering of Christ once made is that perfect redemption, propitiation, and satisfaction for all the sins of the whole world, both original and actual; and there is none other satisfaction for sin, but that alone. Wherefore the sacrifices of masses, in the which it was commonly said that the priest did offer Christ for the quick and the dead, to have remission of pain or guilt, were blasphemous fables and dangerous deceits.

This article was composed by Archbishop Cranmer in 1553 and remains virtually unchanged in its Latin form, the only addition being the word *blasphema* before *figmenta*, giving 'blasphemous fables' instead of 'forged fables' in English translation. Some other words were changed in the English version to bring it closer to the Latin original in two significant respects. The word 'propitiation' is used in English to replace 'the pacifying of God's displeasure' as a translation of *propitiatio*, and near the end the word 'guilt' replaced 'sin' as the translation of the Latin *culpa*. The changes make the English translation more precise in theological terms, but do not change the meaning of the original.

The purpose of the article is to define the nature of the relationship between the sacrament of the Lord's Supper and the historical event that it signifies. No-one doubts that the crucifixion of Jesus Christ at Calvary 'under Pontius Pilate' who was governor of Judaea from AD 26 to AD 36, was the great, final and complete atonement for sin that made the sacrifices offered in the temple redundant. Its effects were both qualitative and quantitative. Qualitatively, they were the propitiation for the sins of the world that was demanded by God's justice. This idea has frequently been attacked in modern times by people who reject the idea that the Son of God came to expiate the wrath of his Father against sin, but as Anselm of Canterbury once said to his servant Boso, these people have not given sufficient consideration to the seriousness of human sin in the eyes of God. Most of them are nice, middle class people who would never dream of harming anyone else deliberately, and they simply cannot conceive of how sinful they themselves really are. They accept that they are imperfect, but not that they are totally depraved and incapable of doing good in their own strength, so the message of the Gospel is lost on them. The God they worship is a heavenly gentleman, not the judge of all the earth and they do not seriously believe that he could or would ever reject people like themselves.

True Christians however, know only too well how desperate their condition is. They understand that God's wrath is actually a sign of his love and concern for them, since if he did not react in that way it would be a sign of his indifference to their behaviour, not of his approval of it. In their eyes, propitiation is not a pagan idea brought into Christianity by crude people with an even cruder understanding of God, but a necessary offering, revealed to ancient Israel in the Torah and fulfilled in Christ that recognises the seriousness of our sin and deals with it at the root. Satisfaction on the other hand, is more an indication of quantity. How many sins did Jesus pay the price for? The answer is – all of them! There is no sin that anyone has ever committed or ever will commit that the blood of Christ is unable to atone for. Some people may object that there is a sin against the Holy Spirit that will not be forgiven (Matthew 12:32), but that is because God has so decreed it, not because Christ's sacrifice is too weak to be able to atone for it. The universality of Christ's atonement makes any other sacrifice unnecessary, and those who pretend otherwise are in fact guilty of unbelief. Why would they suggest such a possibility, unless they rejected the adequacy of Christ's atoning work?

In this context, a distinction must be made between Christ's satisfaction for *sins* and his redemption of *sinners*. When speaking of the former, there can be no doubt that his atonement is universal in the sense just described – nobody can sin too much or too badly for the saving power of Christ, which is always sufficient to redeem them. But when it comes to the question of the redemption of particular sinners, a different logic applies. In the Old Testament, the high priest made atonement for the sins of the whole people, but the people were those who were in covenant relationship with God in response to the promise made to Abraham and in the context of the law of Moses which had been given to regulate it. The lamb that was slain in the temple did not atone for every sinner in the world and those outside the covenant did not benefit from it. This principle still applies in the New Testament. Christ died for those whom he has chosen for salvation, not for everyone without distinction. To think otherwise is to deny his sovereign power, because if Christ really had died for everybody, how is it that not everyone is saved? Have they got the power to resist the command of God? Saul of Tarsus did not have it, and it would be hard to think of anyone more resolutely opposed to the Gospel than he was before Christ met with him on the road to Damascus. How can we say then that basically indifferent people who do not care one way or the other have the power and determination to resist and defeat the will of

God for their lives?

Of course, those who reject the idea of limited (or 'definite') atonement do so because they do not want to think that we are all predetermined and have no free will of any kind. They do not want to be told that it is pointless to preach the Gospel because everyone who is chosen for salvation will be saved in any case and the rest are just a waste of time. They can point to the disastrous effects that such teachings have had in some places, where an exaggerated and false sense of predestination has produced ideas of racial superiority that have justified the oppression of those not lucky enough to be included among the elect. These objections are understandable and have some validity, but they are based on a misunderstanding. Our place as Christians is to do what Christ has commanded us – obedience is the key to putting faith into practice. He has told us to go to the nations and preach the Gospel to them. We do not know who will be saved and who will not be and it is not our place to judge or to guess this in advance. We are labourers who have been sent out to gather in the harvest that is waiting for us in the fields. There the wheat and the tares look alike and grow together, so that we cannot tell them apart in advance. The only way we might be able to distinguish them is by noticing that the wheat lets itself be picked whereas the tares tend to resist, but even that is not foolproof. Some wheat is more tenacious and takes more effort to gather, and tares slip in along the way. Our gathering is not perfect, but it is not for us to sort things out – that is the work of the judge who is the Lord of the harvest. What the doctrine of limited atonement does is remind us that there are both wheat and tares, sheep and goats, and that we cannot change one into the other however hard we may try. If we spend our time working on someone who turns out to be a tare (or a goat) we have no reason to feel disappointed or cheated of our reward because we have done our duty – that is all that is required of us. Yet having said that, we must also say that our mission is to go out and call those whom Christ has chosen for salvation, believing that he is already preparing them to receive the message of the Gospel and praying that we may be used to reap that harvest.

The article does not go into this in any detail, but concentrates instead on the Roman Catholic theology of the mass, which had recently been defined in some detail by the thirteenth session of the council of Trent (11 October 1551). It is not true, as many Protestants mistakenly believe, that Rome teaches that its priests add something to the sacrifice of Christ on the cross. Like us, they accept that this was, is and always will be the one and only full, perfect and sufficient sacrifice, oblation and satisfaction for the sins of the whole world. But in the Roman view, this sacrifice has now gone up to heaven with the ascended Christ, and thanks to the grace of God, it can be brought back down to earth so that we can have direct access to it through our priests. They have been given the power to transubstantiate bread and wine into his body and blood, and in the action of the mass, they re-present Christ's sacrifice both to the worshippers and to God. We cannot go back in time to Calvary, but thanks to the miracle of the altar we do not have to, because that sacrifice comes to us instead. The priest plays the part of Christ (an argument that is used by some Catholics to defend an all-male priesthood), the bread and wine are the sacrifice of Christ's body and blood and the communion table is an altar on which that sacrifice is made. Eternity comes into time and space, making the presence of Christ 'real' in our worship and experience. Once that is accepted, it is but a short step to saying that the priest can then offer Christ's sacrifice as a propitiation for our sins, because he holds that sacrifice in his hands. It is this that is objected to in this article. The sacrifice of Christ was made once for all on the cross, and is full, perfect and complete in itself. It cannot be brought back down to earth, not can a priest offer it to God on our behalf. Our sins are forgiven by Christ in heaven, not by priests on earth who can somehow gain access to his eternal sacrifice.

By admitting worshippers to the sacrament (or by refusing them permission to participate) the Roman Catholic priest could effectively control the gift of God's grace. Indeed, he has the responsibility to do so, by ensuring that those who come to communion have made their confession and prepared themselves adequately to receive the heavenly gift. To Catholic minds, this is the outworking of the promise of Jesus to his disciples after his resurrection: 'If you forgive the sins of anyone they are forgiven; if you withhold forgiveness from anyone, it is withheld.' (John 20:23). Of course, as we might imagine, the force of the Reformers' objection to this was directed more towards the power to withhold forgiveness than the power to grant it, but these are two sides of the same coin. The point is that it is a man who is empowered to decide who should and who should not be forgiven, and this they could not accept. Jesus said these things to his disciples only after he had breathed his Holy Spirit on them; it is his Spirit, in other words, and not the disciples acting independently, who pronounces forgiveness. We still do this today, but in the context of the preaching of the Gospel, not of controlling access to the sacrament. It is Christ who forgives or who withholds forgiveness, not his ministers, who may be allowed to proclaim it but who have no power to decide it one way or another. The

Roman church may object that it has been misunderstood on this point, but if so, it has only itself to blame. Its doctrine of the mass rests on a false foundation, and until that is cleared away, the 'misunderstanding' of which they complain is bound to remain.

Questions for discussion:

1. What is the relationship between the death of Christ on the cross and the sacrament of holy communion?

2. Does participation in holy communion bring us God's forgiveness or only remind us that we have it already?

3. Is it better to think of holy communion as a fellowship meal shared by Christians to celebrate their redemption rather than as a reminder of Christ's death on our behalf?

Key Bible Passages:

2 Corinthians 3; Galatians 3; Hebrews 9-10.

For further reading:

Jeffery, S, M. Ovey, and A. Sach. *Pierced for our transgressions.* Nottingham: IVP, 2007.

McKnight, S. *Jesus and his death: historiography, the historical Jesus and atonement theory.* Waco, Tex.: Baylor University Press, 2005.

Morris, L. *The atonement: its meaning and significance.* Leicester: IVP, 1983.

Peterson, D., ed. *Where wrath and mercy meet: proclaiming the atonement today.* Carlisle: Paternoster, 2002.

Stott, J. R. W. *The cross of Christ.* Leicester: IVP, 1986.

Of the Marriage of Priests

> *Bishops, priests and deacons are not commanded by God's law, either to vow the estate of single life, or to abstain from marriage; therefore it is lawful for them, as for all other Christian men, to marry at their own discretion, as they shall judge the same to serve better to godliness.*

The question of celibacy is one that goes back to the very beginning of the church. Jews did not encourage it, for the very obvious reason that the covenant was passed on from one generation to the next, and it was a major tragedy if a family in Israel were to die out. When that happened, as it occasionally did, special measures were taken to ensure that the family name would continue by adoption or union with another one (Numbers 36:1-11). In such a context, celibacy had no logical place and it was not formally practised in Israel at all.

Jesus however, had a different message. He himself was celibate and he was not afraid to say that there were people who had made themselves eunuchs for the sake of the kingdom of God (Matthew 19:12), something which must have shocked his hearers, who knew that no eunuch could be a priest in God's temple. Jesus also spoke of heaven in terms of virgins (Matthew 25:1) and the image is picked up again in the book of Revelation (14:4). Of course these images do not have to be taken literally, and they can be supplemented by others that take a different view, notably the one which portrays Christ as the bridegroom and the church as his bride (Revelation 22). Nevertheless, the fact that the language of virginity could be (and was) used favourably, whereas in the Old Testament the 'barren woman' was an object of pity, shows that we are talking here about something new. The Hebrew dispensation was one of inheritance over generations, but the Christian revelation focuses on the immediate present, the 'last days' as it is called (Hebrews 1:1), making physical procreation over an extended period of time irrelevant as far as maintaining the faith is concerned.

The Apostle Paul recommended celibacy for those who were able to practise it, though he did not condemn marriage and preferred it to a state of constant lust. There was to be no compulsion in this matter, and it appears from what we read in the Pastoral Epistles that church leaders were expected to be 'the husband of one wife' (1 Timothy 3:2; Titus 1:6). Presumably celibates were not excluded, but they would have been rare in village life and Paul may have thought that anyone deliberately abstaining from marriage ought to be a travelling evangelist, as he was. This suggests that he thought of celibacy as a gift to be used for the service of God, but not that everyone called to such service must necessarily practise it.

Later on, the issue of celibacy surfaced from time to time and was handled in different ways. Tertullian, the great Christian writer of North Africa, believed that there were three kinds of virginity, one which is natural from birth, one which is chosen after conversion, and one that is practised within marriage. He preferred the third of these because to his mind, the person who exposed himself to temptation but resisted it was greater than the other two who were not tested in the same way! Whatever we may think of this rather bizarre idea, it is important to remember that Tertullian thought it should apply to *all* Christians, not just to the ordained clergy.

In the course of the third century a new movement arose in the church which we know today as monasticism. This took different forms, but in every case it involved a separation from the world that was marked by vows of poverty, chastity and obedience. Monks and nuns (for monasticism was open to females as well as to males) were expected to live the life of the kingdom of heaven, where there was no marriage, on earth as a sign of the end times that were nigh. Theirs was meant to be what we today would call an 'alternative society' that modelled true Christianity in a world where compromise was inevitable for most people. Once Christianity was legalised and people started streaming into the church, standards inevitably dropped, and the monastic alternative was felt by many to be more necessary than ever. Most of the great church leaders of the time were celibates, whether or not they were monks in the strict sense. Augustine is famous for having abandoned his concubine (though not the son whom she had given him!) and chosen celibacy, despite its difficulty. Today we would probably advise him to regularise his relationship by entering into a lawful marriage and legitimising his son, but it is instructive to note that that option never seems to have occurred to him. To Augustine's mind, celibacy was the royal road to heaven, and so the concubine had to go, however hard and even unjust that may have been (or seemed) at the time.

Clerical celibacy did not enter the picture in a big way until the time of Gregory the Great, who was bishop of Rome from 590 to 604 (and incidentally was the pope who sent Augustine of Canterbury to establish the Church of England in 597.) Gregory was a monk himself, and he thought that all priests should follow his example. He tried to enforce this on the church, but in spite of some success, he was unable to make it a hard and fast rule. Later on, at the Council in Trullo held at Constantinople in 691–2, it was decreed that bishops must be celibate monks but that married men might be ordained as priests. However, if a single man became a priest or if a married man lost his wife after being ordained, he could not marry again, the compensation being that he would then make himself eligible for the episcopate! This rule still applies today, so that married Orthodox priests have no hope of being promoted to the episcopal dignity and bishops come to their dioceses from another world – the monastery, which does not always equip them very well for the problems they have to face. On the other hand, it does mean that an unsatisfactory bishop can be removed and sent back to the cloister, a practice which is not as uncommon as one might suppose.

The Western church never ratified the Council in Trullo and so its canons never became the norm in the area under papal authority. It was only with great difficulty that the popes were eventually able to impose celibacy as the rule for all ordained priests and bishops at the first Lateran council in 1123, and even then it took years to implement. In Ireland it failed completely and right up until the Reformation the Irish clergy, including abbots of monasteries, were usually married with children. Considering the vehemence with which the same Irish later opposed the Reformation that would have approved of that practice and regularised it, this situation can only be regarded as an amazing historical irony! Elsewhere, clerical celibacy enhanced the special status of the priest as the one empowered to dispense the grace of God, and (in theory at least) it liberated him from the family ties which could so easily compromise ministry in a village community. On the other hand, it was hard to be the only single man in the parish and concubinage was common and often accepted by the laity. From the church's point of view it meant that a priest could not pass on the revenues of the church to his children in the form of dowries (for the girls) or inheritances (for the boys), and so the land and money that had been given to the church over the centuries remained intact. On the other hand, people gradually came to see that concubinage was immoral and unworthy of men who were supposedly devoting their lives to the service of God, and it is noticeable that the main reason the Reformers gave for allowing clerical marriage was as a way of promoting 'godliness', by which they meant public moral behaviour.

At the time of the Reformation the rule of celibacy was one of the first to go, at least on the continent. Martin Luther married an ex-nun and many of his followers copied his example. Nevertheless there was considerable opposition to this from people who thought that

Luther, a monk and the nun he married had both broken the vow of celibacy that they had taken, and breaking a vow was then regarded as a very serious offence. Luther was forced to justify himself by saying that the vows he and his wife had taken were illegitimate, because there was no warrant for them in the Word of God. The dissolution of the monasteries soon put an end to the problem though, and from that time onwards Protestant ministers have been free to marry.

In England the road to clerical marriage was somewhat longer and more complicated. Henry VIII would not hear of it, despite his own rather impressive track record, and Thomas Cranmer, who had married in secret, was forced to send his wife away. It was not until 1549 that it became legal for clergymen to take a wife. Quite a number did so, as we know from what happened next. When Mary I ascended the throne in 1553 and took the country back to Rome, one of her main concerns was to weed out 'heretical' clergy, which in practice meant those who had married after 1549. It seems that as many as a third of those in active ministry were deposed in this way, which is astonishing evidence of how rapidly clerical marriage had taken hold. On the other hand, Queen Elizabeth I did not like married clergy, and certainly not married bishops, and it was not until 1691 that a married man became archbishop of Canterbury! Nor could fellows of Oxford and Cambridge colleges marry and retain their fellowship, a rule which was not relaxed until 1882, some years after university fellowships had been secularised.

Today clerical marriage is no longer an issue, at least not in the traditional sense, but other problems have come in that show how difficult a problem it can be. Divorce among the clergy is now common and same-sex civil partnerships are permitted with only minimal restrictions. A discipline that was still operative a generation ago now seems to have broken down and restoring it will be costly and difficult. Ordained women often bring a husband along with them, but he has no traditionally defined role in the parish and probably has a life of his own outside it. The same is increasingly true of clergy wives, many of whom have careers of their own and pay little attention to the church. That is their right of course, but it is hard to see why a parish would prefer a married clergyman to a single one if the married man's wife is never going to be there. The stability of the post-Reformation order of things has now given way to a much more fluid situation, whose final shape remains uncertain. A return to compulsory clerical celibacy seems very unlikely but some of the alternatives we now experience are even worse and it is most unlikely that we have heard the last word on this complex and ever interesting subject.

> *Questions for discussion:*
>
> 1. Should single Christians actively look for a marriage partner?
>
> 2. Is it right to expect higher standards of behaviour from the clergy than from ordinary Christians?
>
> 3. Should clergy who divorce be expected to resign their orders?

Key Bible Passages:

Matthew 19:1-12; 1 Corinthians 7; Ephesians 5:22-33; 1 Timothy 3:1-13.

For further reading:

Brown, P. R. L. *The body and society: men, women and sexual renunciation in early Christianity.* New York: Columbia University Press, 1988.

Olson, C. *Celibacy and religious traditions.* Oxford: OUP, 2008.

Parish, H. *Clerical marriage and the English reformation: precedent, policy and practice.* Aldershot: Ashgate, 2000.

Robertson, C. K., ed. *Religion and sexuality: passionate debates.* New York: Peter Lang, 2006.

33. Of excommunicate Persons, how they are to be avoided

That person which by open denunciation of the Church is rightly cut off from the unity of the Church, and excommunicated, ought to be taken of the whole multitude of the faithful as an heathen and publican, until he be openly reconciled by penance, and received into the Church by a judge that hath authority thereto.

Of all the articles of religion, this one must surely be the strangest to the modern mind. Who today has ever been excommunicated or met someone who has been? How on earth would we avoid such a person, and is this the right thing to do as a Christian anyway?

Questions like these come to our minds because we have had little or no experience of excommunication and do not really understand what is involved. In the sixteenth century it was very different. Excommunication had emerged as a weapon in the church's arsenal which was widely and effectively used to enlarge papal power. Pope Innocent III (1198–1216) excommunicated King John (1199–1216) and even placed England under the interdict, which basically meant telling the clergy to go on strike. That eventually brought John to heel and among other things was instrumental in leading to Magna Carta, which confirmed the liberties of the church (one of only three of its sixty-three clauses that are still in force today). Later on, abuse of the weapon blunted its effectiveness and by the time of the Reformation kings and other highly placed persons were able to ignore it most of the time.

It was a different matter though for those lower down the scale. There were ecclesiastical courts in England, which until 1858 administered what we would now call family law – matrimonial disputes, inheritance and even defamation of character, which was regarded as a spiritual offence because it was seen as an attack on someone's soul rather than on his body. Ecclesiastical courts also regulated the payment (or non-payment) of tithes, and those who were in arrears were often dragged before them and ordered to pay up. In addition, the ecclesiastical courts had jurisdiction over things like witchcraft and heresy, though these were somewhat less common than the more routine offences. If a person who was summoned to appear before an ecclesiastical court failed to turn up or found himself in contempt of it in some other way, he would be routinely excommunicated until such time as he made good his misdemeanour. Hard as it is to believe, this pattern remained the law until 1813, when excommunication was finally replaced by a writ of contumacy which lacked the spiritual sanction that excommunication had imposed.

Only when we understand this can we make sense of this article as it stands. An excommunicated person was supposed to be shunned by the community in order to encourage him to repent and mend his ways. If he found that he could not live or do business, necessity would soon compel him to give in, and it was regarded as an act of charity, not only to him but also to the wider community, to do as much as possible to encourage him in that direction. In order to be reconciled to the community, the excommunicated person would have to show evidence of his change of heart, which is what is meant by the reference to 'penance' here. Penance in this context is not to be understood as a spiritual merit, which might help the excommunicated person to get closer to God, but merely as an indication of his sincere regret for having disrupted the social order. The context is the reintegration of the offender into civil society and for that reason the effect of penance is purely secular. That does not make it any less important though, since Christians are called to live their present lives in the service of Almighty God, but neither is it in any way a claim on God's eternal mercy and forgiveness which is an act of free grace and not a reward for penance performed.

In its origins, excommunication has solid Biblical warrant. Jesus himself laid down a pattern of discipline, according to which a recalcitrant offender should be put out of the fellowship of the church after a serious effort to get him to mend his ways had been tried and failed (Matthew 18:17). This practice was reinforced by the Apostle Paul in 1 Corinthians 5:5, where excommunication is referred to as delivering a man to Satan for the destruction of his flesh! It was also applied to false teachers, who were not to be admitted in the church under any circumstances (2 John 10). There is therefore every reason for the church to practise this kind of discipline, and the fact that it was subsequently misinterpreted and abused is one of the great tragedies of Christian history.

It must however be remembered that this pattern of abuse was common to the whole of Europe and was often practised with great enthusiasm by Protestants as well as by Roman Catholics. The Anabaptists, who rejected state control of the church and would have regarded articles like this one as an attack on their religious freedom (as indeed it was), nevertheless were great enthusiasts for shunning people and continued the practice within their communities long after it had died out elsewhere. Even today, shunning still occurs among some of the stricter Mennonites and something very similar to it can also be found among some smaller Protestant bodies, like the Exclusive Brethren for example. But these are exceptions that can exist only because the groups concerned are effectively sealed off from the wider society and immune to the pressures that that society can exert. A mainline church like the Anglican one is in a different position and would probably discover that any serious attempt to exercise church discipline by excommunication would be counterproductive, to say the least.

Whether we like it or not, we have to admit that excommunication has practically died out among Anglicans, who would hardly know where to start if they wanted to revive it. Does the article have any real application today? The ecclesiastical courts continue to exist and in theory it is still possible to charge people with heresy and the like, but anyone who does this is liable to find himself on the receiving end of huge public criticism and will almost certainly do more harm than good. On the other hand, there are things that can be done to reaffirm the principle without creating such adverse publicity. One of them, which is actually quite common, is to close the church to the ministry of an unsatisfactory bishop. Incumbents of parishes in England are under no obligation to admit their diocesan bishop, and if there are good reasons for excluding him, then this should be done as a protest, if nothing else. Bishops who tolerate homosexual practice for example, or who openly deny orthodox beliefs should certainly be shunned in this way and the point be made that such behaviour is not acceptable to the godly.

Another means of protest is the withholding of the parish quota or share which the diocese expects to receive. There is no statutory obligation to pay this, and a parish has every right not to do so, even without a good reason. That should not be encouraged of course, but if circumstances demand it, there is nothing like putting the financial squeeze on to make the authorities sit up and take notice. Of course none of this should be done in a spirit of pique or at the behest of individuals who may be waging private vendettas of their own. Extreme measures should be reserved for extreme cases, or their effectiveness will be diminished, as happened with excommunication in the middle ages.

In the public sphere nowadays, excommunication usually takes the form of a boycott, or sanctions imposed against a country than has defied international norms of behaviour. In the days of apartheid in South Africa many people thought it was right to avoid having any dealings with that country, and Barclays Bank, which was a major investor there, was actually forced to pull out as a result of popular protest in the United Kingdom and elsewhere. This was unfortunate though, not least because Barclays was doing more than most companies to train black people in South Africa to work in banking and industry, and when it left the country this process was set back by many years. At the time, moreover, many of those best placed to know what the effects would be objected to sanctions, because they hurt those they were intended to help and only hardened the resolve of the local leaders to keep up their defiance of world opinion and become as self-sufficient as they could. On the surface, joining in the boycott looked like the Christian thing to do, but underneath things were much more complicated and many sincere believers argued the exact opposite. Politically-motivated forms of excommunication seldom work in the way they are meant to do and are a dubious form of discipline at best. Of course not all protests are political and there may be good reasons for not buying the products of a company engaged in destroying rain forests, or that pays its workers starvation wages in a third world country where there are no effective labour laws. But once again, matters are seldom as simple as they are made to appear, and the church ought to be very careful before endorsing any form of official sanction. Similar considerations apply to organisations that may seem to contradict Christian values of one kind or another. The General Synod of the Church of England has tried to tell church members not to join or vote for the British National Party, on the ground that it was racist, but interestingly, a number of people objected to this as an illegitimate interference in the political process. Hard as it may be to imagine a Christian voting for the BNP, it is even harder to imagine the church excommunicating it.

Where more narrowly theological matters are concerned, Christians have to exercise their discretion in a different way. Nothing obliges us to buy books that deny Christ or patronise bookshops that sell them. We have every right to protest at television programmes that misrepresent the Christian faith or permit behaviour that is unbecoming. Recently the British Broadcasting Corporation has been forced to rein in some of its presenters because of the bad language they use and the vulgar behaviour they sometimes indulge in, and this has been widely seen as a good thing. Perhaps it is, but it should not be confused with the ancient practice of excommunication, which was intended to be a healing process of reconciliation for the visible church and not as a means of punishing those who had transgressed certain social norms. Even in ancient times, theologians saw no connection between excommunication and witch hunting, which was treated in a completely different way, and we should not make that mistake now.

A persistent problem, which has never been satisfactorily solved, concerns the moral and spiritual discipline of individual members of the church. The old ecclesiastical courts were expected to deal with this and they did so with some vigour until 1640, when conflict between the king and parliament on this issue (among others) led to a crisis. As England headed into civil war, the church courts lost their powers of discipline, which were only patchily revived after the restoration in 1660. Nowadays there is still a system in place for disciplining members of the clergy, though it is rarely used, but there is no effective way of keeping the laity in check. A man or woman known to be committing adultery, for example, can be denounced and shunned by the rest of the congregation, but he or she cannot be formally excommunicated, because there is no mechanism for doing so. In such cases, one would hope that common sense would prevail and that the offending person or couple would withdraw from the church of their own accord, but if this does not happen, there is precious little that anyone can do about it. The fact of the matter is that if a minister were to refuse communion to such people it is he, and not they, who would be subject to church discipline! This is an absurd situation, of course, but it is the result of a history of excess in the opposite direction, which has now resulted in the complete loss of effective clerical control over the laity.

Perhaps one day it will be possible to devise a way to discipline lay people in order to protect the integrity of the church's collective witness, but so far no satisfactory solution to this problem has been found. One difficulty (which is probably insuperable) is that in the modern world, it would be very easy for someone who has been subject to disciplinary measures in one congregation to leave it and go somewhere else, with no questions being asked. People already tend to find the church that suits them, and this trend would probably just increase if ever disciplinary action was attempted against individual church members.

Questions for discussion:

1. Is excommunication a realistic form of discipline in the modern world?

2. On what grounds should a church exclude a person from membership?

3. How much should a church do to achieve reconciliation when division has occurred?

Key Bible Passages:

1 Corinthians 5; 2 Corinthians 6:14-18; Galatians 6:1-5; 1 Timothy 1:3-17.

For further reading:

Logan, F. D. *Excommunication and the secular arm in medieval England: a study in legal procedure from the thirteenth to the sixteenth century.* Toronto: Pontifical Institute of Mediaeval Studies, 1968.

Richardson, W. L. *Walking together: a congregational reflection on Biblical church discipline.* Eugene, Oreg.: Wipf and Stock, 2007.

Vodola, E. *Excommunication in the middle ages.* Berkeley, Calif.: University of California Press, 1986.

34. *Of the Traditions of the Church*

It is not necessary that traditions and ceremonies be in all places one or utterly like, for at all times they have been divers, and may be changed according to the diversity of countries, times and men's manners, so that nothing be ordained against God's Word.

Whosoever through his private judgement willingly and purposely doth openly break the traditions and ceremonies of the Church, which be not repugnant to the Word of God and be ordained and approved by common authority, ought to be rebuked openly, (that others may fear to do the like,) as he that offendeth against the common order of the Church, and hurteth the authority of the magistrate, and woundeth the consciences of the weak brethren.

Every particular or national church hath authority to ordain, change and abolish ceremonies or rites of the Church ordained only by man's authority, so that all things be done to edifying.

The question of tradition is one that has been present in the church since New Testament times. Jesus attacked the scribes and Pharisees of his day because they had developed traditional practices and interpretations of the Biblical text that effectively undermined their true meaning (Matthew 15:3-6). Later on there were disputes about the validity of certain practices in different local churches, notably the question of when Easter should be celebrated. Some thought it should be tied to the Jewish Passover, whereas others believed that it ought logically to fall on a Sunday, because that is the day on which Christ rose from the dead. Easter controversies raged for centuries, and even today they have not been resolved to everyone's satisfaction. The Eastern churches continue to celebrate it according to a different calendar and there has been considerable resistance to change, precisely because it is by now an ancient and hallowed tradition!

In the early centuries there was no attempt to impose a single rule on every local church, with the result that different practices emerged in different places. It is possible that some of them went back to the apostles themselves, but if they are not recorded in the New Testament we cannot be sure about that. The Scriptures provide a fixed rule and certain testimony that oral transmission cannot equal, and for that reason it is unsafe to rely on the latter for support unless there is Biblical backing as well.

In the Eastern churches, tradition was fixed fairly early on and has acquired enormous importance, so much so in fact, that many of the splits that have occurred within them have been the result of changes in traditional practices, many of which are very minor. The Western churches have always been more flexible, but Rome (in particular) has used the concept of 'tradition' to impose non-Biblical beliefs and practices on the church to which Protestants, and sometimes also the Eastern Orthodox, have objected. The Anglican position, like that of other Protestant churches, is that only what is mandated by Scripture is immutable. Everything else is of secondary importance and may be changed if circumstances so require. At the time of the Reformation it was necessary to throw out a number of things that had accumulated over time but that were getting in the way of the Gospel. Shrines, pilgrimages and a host of dubious devotional practices were abolished, however ancient and popular they may have been.

On the other hand, the sixteenth century also witnessed a trend towards greater uniformity, and the Roman Church did its best to stamp out local and national peculiarities in favour of a common rite that would embrace the whole church. The Tridentine mass, which was introduced in 1570 and remained the official liturgy of the church for four hundred years, was intended to be universal, so that a Catholic could go into a church anywhere in the world and participate in the worship. The continuing use of Latin was also justified on this basis, because it allowed people to join in to a degree that would have been impossible if local languages were used instead. All this has changed dramatically in the past generation and Rome cannot now be accused of imposing uniformity in the way that it did in the past, but it remains to be seen whether this will last or whether a new kind of uniformity will eventually be imposed from the top as it was after the council of Trent.

In the Anglican world things have followed a similar pattern, though with some notable differences. The Reformers objected to the Catholic concept of uniformity, insisting on the right of every national church to make its own liturgical and administrative arrangements, which included the abolition of episcopacy. Some people will find it hard to believe now, but in the sixteenth and seventeenth centuries, the Church of England did not insist that other churches should have an episcopal structure and was happy to receive continental Protestants who were not episcopally ordained into its ministry. It was only much later, for reasons of politics and prejudice more than anything else that this policy changed to the one that has become familiar to us now.

Within England however, attitudes to local traditions were very different. When Archbishop Cranmer issued his first Prayer Book in 1549, he prefaced it with the following remark:

> ...whereas heretofore there hath been great diversity in saying and singing in churches within this realm; some following Salisbury [Sarum] use, some Hereford use, and some the use of Bangor, some of York, some of Lincoln; now from henceforth all the whole realm shall have but one use.

So much for the legitimacy of local diversity! The Prayer Book was not in itself traditional, though it contained traditional elements. It was something radically new, not least in the provision it made for congregational participation through the medium of the English language. It was not intended to defend practices hallowed by time but to impose a uniformity made all the more necessary because of the danger that local practices might be used to conceal resistance to the changes of doctrine that the Reformation had introduced. The Church of England went through four Prayer Books before finally settling on the 1662 version (the others were issued in 1549, 1552, 1559 and 1604). Even that was not finally canonised until 1689, when a proposed liturgy of comprehension, designed to include the majority of dissenters, was rejected. By then of course the Prayer Book had become traditional and developed a resistance to change that was not overcome until the twentieth century.

Having allowed for the mutability of tradition by lawful means, Cranmer went on to make the point that individuals who made their own adjustments to it were stepping out of line and damaging the church by introducing controversy and division. In his day that was a fairly minor problem, but it grew to enormous proportions in the late sixteenth and early seventeenth century, eventually leading to civil war and a disruption of the national church that continues to this day. The difference between the Puritans, as the more radical reformers came to be called, and their establishment opponents lay in the way in which they understood the phrase 'not repugnant to the Word of God' contained in this article. To many Puritans this meant that anything that could not be proved by an appeal to Scripture should be rejected, especially if it reminded people of Roman Catholicism. Things like kneeling to receive holy communion became major issues of dispute between those who thought it was wrong in principle and those who thought that it did not matter one way or the other, but because it was traditional, it ought to be kept. This was not a difference of doctrine but of attitude to the right application of a commonly agreed principle. People with a theological education tend to find this sort of thing puzzling and tedious, but ordinary worshippers notice little differences and are usually more bothered by them than by seemingly abstract theological debates. In the seventeenth century this difference of outlook, combined with the well-founded suspicion that the authorities who were trying to impose uniformity were unsound in matters of doctrine, led to an *impasse* in which the two sides talked past each other and finally came to blows because neither was prepared to give the other the benefit of the doubt.

Today we live in a world where tradition is at a discount and novelty is all the rage. Forms of worship and even beloved hymns have been jettisoned or changed beyond all recognition, sometimes for trivial reasons, such as the perceived need to replace 'thee' and 'thou' with 'you', even though 'you' does not rhyme with the same words that 'thee' and 'thou' rhyme with, making it necessary to alter hymns much more than would otherwise be the case. People who know the traditional words find this annoying. They also dislike the modern version(s) of the Lord's Prayer, which now can no longer be prayed in common as it used to be because different people use different forms of it. In this case, however, the power of tradition has proved strong enough to keep the old words alive as an alternative in modern worship services, even though this is a linguistic anomaly that is deplored by the modern advocates of uniformity.

Here there is no simple answer. When modern forms of worship are imposed there is usually a traditionalist backlash that should be, but often is not, properly accommodated. This problem is much worse in overseas Anglican churches than it is in the Church of England, where traditional forms are protected by law. Other Anglican churches have actually expelled members who have refused to go along with change, something that sounds excessive to many people in England but which, it must be said, would have been the policy of the Reformers as well.

The difference of course is that the Reformers were motivated by doctrinal considerations in a way that is not true today. Modern liturgists have agendas ranging from patristic fundamentalism, which opts for anything that can be shown to be properly ancient, to a political correctness that sometimes extends to the point where masculine pronouns cannot be used to refer to God, even though that is clearly the Biblical practice. Most of what they have come up with is trite, banal, doctrinally ambiguous and eminently forgettable, but that does not stop the march of 'progress', with the result that the church has now lost not only its uniformity, but its sense of cohesion as a body of believers sharing a common faith.

The right of a national church to alter its ceremonies, which the revisers of 1563 added to Cranmer's original article, is not contested today, but it is applied in ways that would have horrified the Reformers and which have done nothing to further the mission of the Gospel or of the church. This has become a serious matter in parts of the Anglican Communion, where the exercise of this right to change things has been invoked by some people to allow practices that others regard as contrary to the Christian faith. In some places it may involve an injudicious attempt to include customary rituals and symbols in Christian worship as a form of indigenisation, without considering what the effects of this (usually well-meant) practice may be. In other places however, it has been used to overturn such 'traditions' as an all-male ministry, with the result that some Anglican ordinations are no longer accepted as valid throughout the Communion. In cases like this one, the right of the local church to alter its ceremonies has been taken to an extreme which threatens the unity of the church as a whole, and it has become a matter of urgency for Anglicans to decide what the limits of legitimate diversity are. The principle will no doubt be retained, but it will be have to be more carefully defined in future if the Anglican Communion is to survive as a coherent entity.

Questions for discussion:

  1. What are the essential ingredients of Christian worship?

  2. How much variety should there be in the services of any particular congregation?

  3. To what extent should we use forms of worship recognised or approved by the church as a whole?

Key Bible Passages:

John 4:9-24; Romans 14; 1 Corinthians 10:23-33; Colossians 2:16-23.

For further reading:

Atkinson, N. *Richard Hooker and the authority of Scripture, tradition and reason: reformed theologian of the Church of England?* Carlisle: Paternoster, 1997.

Carson, D. A., ed. *Worship by the book.* Grand Rapids: Zondervan, 2002.

Dillistone, F. W., ed. *Scripture and tradition.* London: Lutterworth, 1955.

Peterson, D. *Engaging with God: a Biblical theology of worship.* Leicester: Apollos (IVP), 1992.

Skillrud, H. C., J. F. Stafford and D. F. Martensen. *Scripture and tradition.* Minneapolis: Augsburg, 1995.

35. Of Homilies

The second Book of Homilies, the several titles whereof we have joined under this Article, doth contain a godly and wholesome doctrine, and necessary for these times, as doth the former Book of Homilies, which were set forth in the time of King Edward the Sixth; and therefore we judge them to be read in churches by the ministers, diligently and distinctly, that they may be understanded of the people.

1. Of the right use of the Church
2. Against peril of idolatry
3. Of repairing and keeping clean of churches
4. Of good works, first of fasting
5. Against gluttony and drunkenness
6. Against excess of apparel
7. Of prayer
8. Of the place and time of prayer
9. That common prayers and sacraments ought to be ministered in a known tongue
10. Of the reverent estimation of God's Word
11. Of almsdoing
12. Of the nativity of Christ
13. Of the passion of Christ
14. Of the resurrection of Christ
15. Of the worthy receiving of the sacrament of the body and blood of Christ
16. Of the gifts of the Holy Ghost
17. For the rogation days
18. Of the state of matrimony
19. Of repentance
20. Against idleness
21. Against rebellion

This article is the updated version of a much shorter one that Archbishop Cranmer included in 1553. It was made necessary by the production of a second book of *Homilies* to complement the first one, which appeared as early as 1547 and can rightly be regarded as the first step in the Edwardian Reformation that followed. To us it does not seem odd that a doctrinal programme should be set out in a series of sermons or lectures on the subject, but that was unprecedented at the time, even among the continental Reformers. By putting the teaching of the church in a form that could be readily communicated to ordinary worshippers, Thomas Cranmer solved the most important problem facing him as archbishop of Canterbury, which was getting his message across. Those who read books and took the decisions were a small élite centred on London and the universities, but the rest of England was *terra incognita* to them. Most of the rural clergy had no idea what was going on and many were unsympathetic to change – any change. They had not been trained to preach, did not have the education or resources they would need to prepare a sermon and in many cases lacked the motivation that such preparation would have demanded. So the answer was to do the work for them, to provide ready-made sermons that could be read from the pulpit. This had the added advantage of guaranteeing uniformity, because everybody would hear the same message. Some of the homilies (as the sermons were known) were too long to be read all at once, and so they were broken down into sections that could be used over a series of weeks.

The first book of homilies was written by a number of different people, but most of them remain unknown to us. Cranmer himself wrote four of them, Thomas Becon wrote one and Catholic traditionalists wrote the second and the sixth. The titles of those homilies are not given in the article but were as follows:

1. A fruitful exhortation to the reading of Holy Scripture (Thomas Cranmer)
2. Of the misery of all mankind (John Harpsfield)
3. Of the salvation of all mankind by only Christ (Thomas Cranmer)
4. Of the true, lively and Christian faith (Thomas Cranmer)
5. Of good works annexed to faith (Thomas Cranmer)
6. Of Christian love and charity (Edmund Bonner)
7. Against swearing and perjury
8. How dangerous a thing it is to fall from God
9. Against the fear of death
10. Concerning good order and obedience
11. Against whoredom and uncleanness (Thomas Becon)
12. Against contention and brawling

The first five are summarised in the Articles and can be used as a commentary on them, as long as it is remembered that they were composed first and the Articles came later. This may explain why the third homily is referred to in the Articles as the homily on justification, which is not its actual title. The others are more to do with the practical consequences of Christian living which does not make them any less important of course, though they have fewer points of contact with the theological definitions found in the Articles.

The value of homilies as a means of getting the message across was appreciated by the Catholic side, which produced its own collection, recycling the second and the sixth from the earlier book, under the auspices of Bishop Edmund Bonner of London in 1555. Copies of it still exist but it is not widely known or read, because it was part of the Marian reaction against the Reformation and therefore died with her in 1558.

The second book of homilies appeared at the same time as the revised version of the articles in 1563, which is probably why their (then unfamiliar) contents are listed in detail here. Once again, several of them can be regarded as commentaries on specific articles, and at least one (number 16 on the gifts of the Holy Spirit) is an expansion of the rather meagre article 5. The twenty-first homily was added in 1571 in response to the excommunication of the queen by the pope in the previous year. In the bull of excommunication, the pope had incited the queen's subjects to rebel and even to assassinate her, an outrageous command that appalled even the most Catholic rulers of Europe, like Philip II of Spain.

The homilies are seldom read today and many Anglicans are unaware of their existence, which is a pity. They are obviously products of their time and many of them seem long-winded to modern ears, but with some pruning and adjustment they can still be very effective and moving today. Whether they should be preached as they stand is an open question, but much of the material in them can be adapted for modern use without too much difficulty and the clergy, in particular, can get good sermon material from them. On the other hand, some of the details contained in them are now outdated and many of the historical statements which are quoted as fact would no longer be so regarded by modern scholars. There are also instances where beliefs and practices of the pre-Reformation church are accepted without comment, and no homily should be cited as an authority for Anglican doctrine if it can be shown to go against one of the three official formularies of the church.

The homilies were out of print for many years but they are now once again available in an attractive edition (though unfortunately lacking an index) and are waiting to be rediscovered by the modern church. Here there is real scope for further research to be done on a significant but sadly neglected part of the Anglican heritage.

Questions for discussion:

1. What is the purpose of having a sermon in public worship?

2. Are sermons the most effective way of teaching Christian doctrine today?

3. What makes a sermon 'good'? How long should it be?

Key Bible Passages:

Romans 10:5-21; 2 Corinthians 4:1-15; 2 Timothy 4:1-8.

For further reading:

The homilies appointed to be read in churches. Edited by John Griffiths (1859). Rev. by Ian Robinson. Bishopstone: Brynmill and Philadelphia: Preservation Press, 2006.

Ash, C. *The priority of preaching.* Fearn: Christian Focus, 2009.

Stott, J. R. W. *I believe in preaching.* London: Hodder and Stoughton, 1982.

Wabuda, S. *Preaching during the English reformation.* Cambridge: CUP, 2002.

36. Of Consecration of Bishops and Ministers

The book of consecration of archbishops and bishops, and ordering of priests and deacons, lately set forth in the time of Edward the Sixth, and confirmed at the same time by authority of Parliament, doth contain all things necessary to such consecration and ordering; neither hath it anything that of itself is superstitious or ungodly. And therefore, whosoever are consecrated or ordered according to the rites of that book, since the second year of the forenamed King Edward, unto this time, or hereafter shall be consecrated or ordered according to the same rites; we decree all such to be rightly, orderly and lawfully consecrated and ordered.

This article deals with what is known as the ordinal, which is the way in which the general principles of ministry laid down in article 23 are applied to the actual forms that ministry takes in the Anglican Communion. The ordinal is the form used for the making of bishops, priests and deacons that was attached to the first Prayer Book of 1549 and then, in a slightly revised form, to the second Prayer Book of 1552. Since that time it has survived without alteration to the present day, although modern revisers have updated the language and reordered the contents as they have with the Prayer Book itself. It should be noted that although it is always printed with the Book of Common Prayer (and is therefore easily available) it is not, strictly speaking, a part of it, and church legislation has always treated it as something distinct.

That point has to be made in relation to this article, which in its original form contained an introductory statement commending the 1552 Prayer Book and treating the ordinal as an appendix to it. The revised article says nothing about the Prayer Book, and by mentioning the second year of King Edward VI, which ran from 28 January 1548 to 27 January 1549, makes it clear that it is referring in the first instance to the original text, as well as to the revised version that appeared three years later. The reason for this is that there was some dispute about the status of those who had been ordained between 1549 and 1552 and it was necessary to include them under this heading.

The importance of the article lies in the fact that the Anglican ordinal differs from the Roman Catholic one that it replaced. Ministers of the Church of England were not priests in the Roman sense, ordained to offer eucharistic sacrifices on the altar of the church during the celebration of mass. Rather they were called to be pastors and teachers, as were the ministers in other Protestant churches. This was not seriously questioned until the nineteenth century, when the rise of Anglo-Catholicism prompted some people to argue that there had been no substantial change at the time of the Reformation and that Anglican clergy were therefore identical both in form and in substance with their Roman counterparts. Cold water was poured on this idea by Pope Leo XIII, who in his bull *Apostolicae curae*, published on 18 September 1896, declared Anglican orders to be null and void, largely because of what he called their 'defect of intention'. Put in layman's language, what this means is that Anglicans are not ordained as mass-priests, so they are not mass-priests in the way that Roman Catholic clergy are. Anglo-Catholics have never accepted this, of course, and have tried to have the bull overturned at various times, though without success so far. We may be grateful to the pope for his clarity on this point, because the claims of high church Anglicans about the supposed 'catholicity' of Anglican orders are false, and rejected by the papacy with good reason. We do not want our clergy to be mass-priests, and are glad that they are not officially recognised as such by those who are in a position to know what they are.

In practice, ecumenical contacts in recent years have produced a situation in which the churches accept each other's ministers for the purpose of contact and dialogue and leave the disputed questions to one side. Anglicans do not regard Roman orders as invalid, and do not re-ordain priests who join the Anglican church, though of course the opposite is not the case. Much the same applies to the clergy of the Eastern Orthodox churches who become Anglicans, though once again, not in reverse. The main practical effect of this is that neither Rome nor the Eastern churches can regard the Anglican Communion as a fully Christian church, however polite they may be in ecumenical conversations.

Unfortunately, Anglicans tend to adopt the same condescending attitude towards ministers of other Protestant churches, especially if they have not been episcopally ordained. This has caused problems in inter-church relations, though it has not prevented the union of Anglicans with other Protestants in India, for example. More recently, local ecumenical projects and shared ministry schemes have allowed ministers of other denominations to function in an Anglican context and it is possible that, given time, the issue will cease to be a barrier to church union with them. This possibility is strengthened by the fact that modern scholarship has demonstrated that the Ordinal's claim that there were three distinct orders in the early church is inaccurate.

Archbishop Cranmer was not lying about this, of course, because in his day people did not realise this. In the nineteenth century however, it became clear from research into the matter that the first generations of Christians did not recognise any real difference between bishops and priests, and that the Greek words for them (*episcopos* and *presbyteros*) were more or less synonymous. It is true that in time, the college of presbyters in the churches started to refer to their president as the bishop and that the terms became differentiated as a result, but the sort of claims that have been made in modern times about the so-called 'historic episcopate' and the need for episcopal ordination have been shown to lack any solid foundation in the evidence from earliest times and have therefore been quietly sidelined or dropped altogether. This has made it much easier to recognise other forms of ministry and has helped to overcome the feelings of resentment which episcopalian snobbery has caused in the past.

Matters are complicated however by the fact that those who pay little attention to the 'validity of orders' tend to pay little attention to doctrinal orthodoxy either. They relate well to Protestant ministers whose theology is as liberal as theirs is, but not to others who are more orthodox. In particular, the ordination of women is something shared among liberals but objected to by conservatives in every denomination. This creates a situation in which a liberal Anglican will probably be more willing to admit a liberal Presbyterian (and especially a liberal Presbyterian woman) to his pulpit than a conservative Anglican who does not share his views on this subject. Conservative Anglicans, for their part, would never dream of letting liberal ones into their pulpits, and would certainly prefer fellow conservatives from other churches, regardless of how they were ordained. Within the Anglican Communion, conservatives cannot conscientiously recognise the ministry of ordained women, even if their ordination is within the parameters laid down by the ordinal. This creates a situation which in England is called the 'two integrities', whereby different groups of clergy and churches operate without direct contact with each other. The possibility of consecrating women bishops creates a problem here, because whereas both groups can accept a male bishop, the conservatives cannot accept a female one, and of course, the collegiality of the house of bishops is inevitably impaired if some of its members do not recognise some of the others.

Modern developments have destroyed the collegiality of the ordained Anglican ministry, a fact which is only slowly being recognised across the Anglican Communion. Matters came to a head in 2008, when an openly practising homosexual bishop from the American Episcopal Church was not invited to the Lambeth Conference of Anglican bishops, but objectors (on both sides) pointed out that it was unfair to single him out. The trouble, of course, is that the liberals want him to be included along with everyone else, whereas the conservatives want his supporters to be excluded along with him. At bottom, the issue is one of doctrinal orthodoxy, not of orders as such, but unless and until this is recognised, it is unlikely that the problem will be satisfactorily resolved.

The ordinal deals with three orders of ministry that were inherited from the medieval church, but there were others that had a less exalted status, like subdeacons, readers, acolytes, doorkeepers and so on. These disappeared at the Reformation but over time they were replaced by others of a similar kind. Today we have lay readers and deaconesses, although with the ordination of women, the latter are gradually dying out. There are also locally ordained ministers who may be in holy orders, as the first three are technically called, but whose ministry is confined to a circumscribed area. In other Anglican churches there are catechists whose job it is to teach people and lead services where no ordained clergyman is available to do so. Neither the Ordinal nor the Articles has any objection to this kind of thing, and it is important for us to recognise how useful and necessary they can be in certain circumstances. Every member of the church can have a ministry of some kind, and none is better or worse than any other. The only principles that must be retained in all circumstances are the need for appropriate training and for public recognition, so that everyone knows who is doing what and why. Beyond that we are free to develop whatever forms of ministry we think are needed and do not have to rely exclusively on those who are formally ordained into one of the three officially recognised 'holy orders'.

Questions for discussion:

    1. Should the church have a body of specially ordained ministers?

    2. To what extent should people not specially ordained be allowed to lead public worship?

    3. What qualifications should the church look for in those who are ordained?

Key Bible Passages:

1 Corinthians 9:13-14; 1 Timothy 5:17-22; Titus 1:5-2:15.

For further reading:

Bullock, F. W. B. *History of the training for the ministry of the Church of England.* 3 vols. St Leonards-on-Sea: Budd and Gillatt, 1955–1976.

Echlin, E. P. *The story of Anglican ministry.* Slough: St Paul Publications, 1974.

Pennington, E. L. *The Episcopal succession during the English reformation.* Windsor: Savile Press, 1952.

Tavard, G. H. *A review of Anglican orders: the problem and the solution.* Collegeville, Minn.: Liturgical Press, 1990.

37. Of the Civil Magistrates

The Queen's Majesty hath the chief power in this realm of England, and other her dominions, unto whom the chief government of all estates of this realm, whether they be ecclesiastical or civil, in all causes doth appertain, and is not, nor ought to be, subject to any foreign jurisdiction.

Where we attribute to the Queen's Majesty the chief government, by which titles we understand the minds of some slanderous folks to be offended; we give not to our princes the ministering either of God's Word or of the sacraments, the which thing the injunctions also lately set forth by Elizabeth our Queen doth most plainly testify; but that only prerogative which we see to have been given always to all godly princes in Holy Scriptures by God himself, that is, that they should rule all estates and degrees committed to their charge by God, whether they be ecclesiastical or temporal, and restrain with the civil sword the stubborn and evil doers.

The Bishop of Rome hath no jurisdiction in this realm of England.

The laws of the realm may punish Christian men with death for heinous and grievous offences.

It is lawful for Christian men, at the commandment of the magistrate, to wear weapons and serve in the wars.

This article is a revised and much expanded version of the one written by Archbishop Cranmer in 1553. It was adopted in 1563 and left unchanged in 1571, and in its current form its intention is to define the relationship between church and state in a situation where the head of the state also plays a similar role in the church.

In the sixteenth century, every Western European state had an established religion, which until then had been that of the Roman Catholic Church. The papacy had long tried to claim jurisdiction over these states and their rulers, while allowing them the freedom to operate within their own defined sphere of competence. For example, the popes did not try to raise armies without the consent of secular rulers, because warfare was regarded as their province and not his. But when the call came from the east for help against Muslim aggression, the papacy did not hesitate to call for a crusade which it supervised even if the clergy did not normally lead the armies into battle themselves. Popes also claimed the right to levy taxes and did all they could to secure what was in effect a form of diplomatic immunity for the church and its clergy. Whether or not a priest could be tried in the king's court for a civil offence and punished by the state if found guilty became a major bone of contention that was only resolved in favour of the state after many centuries of bitter argument. In England, problems like this led to the introduction of what was known as 'benefit of clergy', a device which guaranteed at least special treatment for those in holy orders. In time, benefit of clergy was diluted to the point where it could be granted to anyone who could sign his name, and even to women, but its origins remained clear and the privilege was not abolished until 1827!

England stood out in medieval Europe because it was a highly centralised state that punched well above its weight in international affairs. We forget, for example, that the country was able to wage war against France for over a hundred years, always on French territory and often very successfully, despite the fact that France had about four times as many people and was far richer. The secret was organisation; English kings could rely on their subjects whereas French ones were never sure, especially since the English kings were technically numbered among them! This meant that it was harder for the papacy to gain a foothold in England than it was elsewhere. Parliament granted the church a defined sphere of jurisdiction in 1316 but the church's attempts to make heresy a capital crime punishable by burning at the stake were frustrated until 1401, because only the church could decide who was a heretic, and the king would not let his authority over his subjects be weakened in that way. One of the beneficiaries of this was John Wycliffe, who in spite of his condemnation for heresy was able to retire from Oxford and die in his bed unmolested by the church.

By the early sixteenth century, papal claims to universal jurisdiction were more theoretical than real, but the Roman curia retained its role as an appellate court in ecclesiastical cases. In particular, this meant that Rome could decide matrimonial questions, which is what sparked off the quarrel that was the immediate cause of Henry VIII's break with it in 1534. This is such a well-known event that it is easy to forget that there were other factors involved which would probably have led to a similar break at some point. The most fundamental one was that English law was incompatible with Roman law on a number of points, and the church operated on principles derived from the latter. (It is interesting in this connection to note that the United Kingdom today often has difficulties with the European

Union for essentially the same reason – the legal systems of the two entities are different and in many ways incompatible.) There was also the fact that the pope was distant from England and unfamiliar with it, and that the papacy was falling under the influence of secular rulers closer to home, especially the Habsburg emperor of what was still the Holy Roman Empire. The papacy did not see itself as the religious expression of that empire, of course, but it could easily be seen that way by others, and submission to the popes called into question the independence of states that did not recognise the emperor as their ruler. It is not an accident that when Henry VIII decided to break with Rome, he did so by declaring that the realm of England was an 'empire' in its own right.

In 1534 Henry VIII got the church and parliament to declare him the 'supreme head in earth' of the Church of England, and that was the title used by Cranmer in his article of 1553. Elizabeth I however, was sensitive to the objection that Christ alone was head of the church, and so she called herself 'supreme governor' instead. The difference may not have meant much in practice, but it did have important theological implications which are spelled out in this article. These may be summarised as follows:

1. The monarch has supreme jurisdiction in both civil and ecclesiastical cases. This means that church and state cannot be played off against each other by the claims of rival authorities.

2. The monarch has no authority in internal church affairs and is not a minister of Word and sacrament. She has no power to ordain the clergy or to oblige the church to accept any doctrine not contained in Holy Scripture. This may be contrasted with the situation in Germany, where secular rulers were often regarded as bishops of the church and took an active role in its internal affairs. Even in modern times, Scandinavian churches have been forced to accept women ministers by state decree, something which would be inconceivable in England.

3. England is an independent country and no foreign power has any jurisdiction within it. This has been modified somewhat by adhesion to the European Union and international treaties of various kinds, but this is a voluntary surrender (or pooling) of sovereignty which can, at least in principle, always be withdrawn.

4. The clergy are members of the commonwealth and subject to the civil laws. They may be granted special privileges in respect

of their function in society, but they are not a class apart and cannot claim exemption from secular jurisdiction on that ground.

5. The state may introduce the death penalty and oblige its citizens to serve in the army, neither of which is the province of the church.

This last provision calls for some comment. The church was never entirely comfortable with the death penalty and officially at least, it stood for peace and not war. Admittedly there were many occasions when these principles were flouted, but they were abuses and recognised as such. Clergymen were not even allowed to sit on a jury because they were not supposed to sanction the death penalty, which was in frequent use until the nineteenth century. (It is interesting to note that, now that the death penalty has been abolished, so has the clerical exemption from jury duty.)

The state however, has a different function to perform and is not bound by the same principles as the church is. The theological ground for this is that the church represents the eternal kingdom of God in the world and must therefore do its best to reflect that, whereas the state is a purely temporal institution whose authority is established by, and limited to, temporal affairs. Like it or not, the world is in the grip of Satan and secular rulers who are Christians must come to terms with that fact. It is all very well to believe in peace, but pacifism is not a realistic option in a fallen creation. There have always been groups of Christians who have advocated it, but they have only been able to exist and maintain their principles because they are small and because the majority has been prepared to tolerate them. The Quakers, for example, were allowed to set up an officially pacifist colony in Pennsylvania, but at the time of the American revolution, this privilege was withdrawn by the Continental Congress which could not allow such a large and important body of people to declare themselves neutral non-combatants.

Today this is an issue mainly when it comes to the nature of the church's involvement in politics. It is probably unwise for clergymen to get involved in secular affairs unless they have to, but the church is often under pressure to take a stand on things like military involvement in foreign countries and so on. Ideally, it has to be against warfare, but this is not always a practical option and it would certainly be wrong for it to urge soldiers to desert their units, or to persuade its members not to pay their taxes, as a way of opposing government policies. So-called 'ethical investment' is another difficult area, partly because the business world is too complex for simple decisions about this to be made on any consistent basis, and partly because what is right in one circumstance may be wrong in another. For example, it is right to insist that our free democracy should be heavily armed, so as to protect its freedom and the peace of the world. Failure to do this could have the most dire consequences, as people discovered in the 1930s, when European dictators took advantage of the prevailing pacifist mood to deprive weaker countries of their independence and in the end to precipitate a devastating world war. On the other hand, it must be wrong to supply third-world dictators with weapons so that they can oppress their own people. The trouble is that the companies that supply weapons to both responsible democracies and to tin-pot dictatorships are often one and the same!

It is sometimes said that disestablishment would change this situation and make the role of the church much easier, but there is no evidence to support this. In many African countries, disestablished churches are deeply involved in local politics, often (though not always) for the better. In the United States, churches can also be very political, but there it seems to be more for the worse (though again not always). In Western European countries the likelihood is that the church's electoral base is too small for its voice to make any difference, and even when that is not the case, people have a way of separating their religious commitment from their politics in disconcerting ways. We have seen this in the former Yugoslavia, where Roman Catholics and Eastern Orthodox people have cheerfully slaughtered each other and gone to church to celebrate it, and of course much the same thing is true in Ireland, where the different paramilitary groups have a well-recognised religious affiliation, whatever they (or the churches) might claim to the contrary. Issues of religion and politics are not necessarily resolved by separating church and state, and in any case the church must still decide where the boundaries lie and do its best to maintain them.

The injunctions to which the article refers were a series of measures designed to instruct the clergy how to implement the changes brought about by the Reformation. The first set of these was issued by Henry VIII in 1536, and was quickly followed by a second (and more detailed series) in 1538. They were repeated and extended further when Edward VI came to the throne in 1547, and issued again, with further substantial additions, by Elizabeth I in 1559. The main injunction referred to here is no. 28 (identical in substance to no. 33 of the Edwardian injunctions issued in 1547), which reads as follows:

Also, whereas many indiscreet persons do at this date

uncharitably contemn and abuse priests and ministers of the church, because some of them (having small learning) have of long time favoured fantasies rather than God's truth; yet, forasmuch as their office and function is appointed of God, the queen's majesty willeth and chargeth all her loving subjects that from henceforth they shall use them charitably and reverently, for their office and ministration's sake, and especially all such as labour in the setting forth of God's holy Word.

The ministry of word and sacrament was never given to an officer of state, and certainly not to the monarch. In fact, English monarchs have had a lower status within the Church of England than their continental counterparts had within the Roman Catholic church, where they were usually allowed to take communion in both kinds (unlike their subjects). The last monarch to attempt to put pressure on the church in matters of doctrine was Charles I. In a way this may be unfortunate, since his son Charles II favoured a broader comprehension of Puritan dissenters than the church itself was willing to allow, and had it been forced to accept the king's wishes, the great ejection of Puritan ministers in 1662 might never have taken place. But both then and in 1689, when comprehension was once again in the air, the king was forced to defer to the wishes of the church as expressed in the convocations of the clergy.

At the same time, the state has taken seriously its rôle as the protector of the church, as this was understood by the Reformers themselves, who liked to quote Isaiah 49:32 ('kings shall be your foster fathers and queens your nursing mothers') as their justification, and who had no hesitation in referring to Edward VI as the 'new Josiah' or to Elizabeth I as the 'new Deborah'. The state's nursing rôle can be seen in the grant of certain financial privileges (the most famous of which is known as Queen Anne's bounty) which have enabled it to carry on its mission more effectively, but also by intervening at times when it appeared that the church itself was veering off-course. The best-known example of that occurred in 1928, when parliament rejected the proposed Prayer Book on the ground that it would have reintroduced practices and even beliefs that had been rejected at the time of the Reformation. Parliament still exercises this rôle today to a limited extent, and in other parts of the Anglican Communion state authorities and courts have sometimes been called in to adjudicate disputes which the church has been unable to resolve for itself. It is also true than in many countries the church continues to benefit from forms of state aid (such as tax exemptions) which carry on the tradition established in sixteenth-century England.

Questions for discussion:

1. Should the church submit to state laws that go against its teachings?

2. What relationship should the church try to have with the state?

3. Should church leaders take sides in political debates?

Key Bible Passages:

Matthew 22:15-21; Romans 13:1-7; 1 Peter 2:13-17.

For further reading:

Broadhurst, J., ed. *Quo vaditis? The state churches of northern Europe.* Leominster: Gracewing, 1996.

Hill, M. *Ecclesiastical law.* 3d ed. Oxford: OUP, 2007.

Holloway, D. *Church and state in the new millennium.* London: Harper Collins, 2000.

Partington, A. *Church and state. The contribution of the Church of England bishops to the House of Lords during the Thatcher years.* Milton Keynes: Paternoster, 2006.

Taylor, J. A. *British monarchy, English church establishment and civil liberty.* Westport, Conn.: Greenwood Press, 1996.

38. Of Christian Men's Goods, which are not common

The riches and goods of Christians are not common, as touching the right, title and possession of the same, as certain Anabaptists do falsely boast. Notwithstanding, every man ought, of such things as he possesseth, liberally to give alms to the poor, according to his ability.

Communism is one of those beliefs that is a good idea in theory but does not work in practice. 'From each according to his ability, to each according to his need' is a noble aspiration, and in some contexts it works – within the family for instance, where it has long been accepted that the younger and healthier members ought to look after the old and infirm ones. This is a clear Biblical principle, and in the form of social welfare it is extended to cover people who do not have a family or church network they can rely on in this way.

Unfortunately, human nature being what it is, it is also true that there are plenty of people who think they can manipulate the system to their own advantage and live high on the labour of others. There will always be abuses of this kind, and some of the most spectacular examples can be found in underdeveloped countries, where the local élite banks the foreign aid money in safe havens around the world and aspires only to live in luxury, either at home or, if things get too hot, in exile on the French Riviera or somewhere like that. Denizens of council estates who practise benefit fraud may be less able to wallow in luxury, but the principle is the same, and those clever enough to know how to work the system can live quite well at the taxpayer's expense. When this kind of thinking is extended to an entire society, the effects can be disastrous. Anyone who has ever lived in a Communist country will know that it will contain a large number of people who have little incentive to work. Everybody has a job and is looked after to some extent, so there is no need to do anything much. Those with drive and ambition may actually be dangerous because they are liable to get restless and dissatisfied with the *status quo* and seek to introduce a social order that would allow them to rise above their fellow citizens.

Here the church is in an ambiguous position. On the one hand, there is the parable of the labourers in the vineyard, which tells us that those who have worked all day will get the same reward as those who have entered at the eleventh hour (Matthew 20:1-16). This is obviously true in the kingdom of heaven. The thief on the cross who confessed his faith in Jesus will have the same reward as the Apostle Paul, who spent years preaching the Gospel and founding churches, often in the teeth of considerable opposition. Is this fair? In worldly terms, no, but it is the message of the Gospel. We cannot think of the kingdom of heaven as a society based on merit, because if it were, none of us would ever get there. That does not exclude the possibility that there are gradations of reward in heaven, but whatever these are, they are determined by the grace of God and not by human achievements.

On the other hand, ownership of resources in this world is an incentive to use them responsibly. People will look after their own gardens, but will not usually volunteer to clean the city parks, because the parks are not their responsibility, even if they can be said to 'own' them in some sense. No better means than this has ever been found to ensure the right use of the world's goods, and even if it means that some people end up with more than others, in the end it must be regarded as the better solution because of the superior results it so obviously produces. (Again, anyone who believes in the superiority of public ownership should take a look at the dilapidated state of communal facilities and spaces in Communist countries.) What should the proper relationship be between the individual and the community?

The New Testament church had to face this question right at the beginning. At Jerusalem the first converts spent a lot of time together and shared their goods in common. There does not seem to have been any directive compelling them to do this. Rather, they were probably motivated by their enthusiasm and idealism. Unfortunately, it did not last long and as the episode of Ananias and Sapphira tells us, the urge to hang onto private property was too strong to resist (Acts 4:32-5:11). The whole experiment ended in tears and the church quickly reverted to the same kind of lifestyle that everyone else lived, at least as far as the ownership of property was concerned.

At different times in the history of the church there have been similar impulses pushing people towards a form of communism. Monastic life was based on that principle, though it also involved great personal sacrifice and cannot be regarded as a social norm. At the time of the Reformation, many Anabaptists took it up, and in some cases their descendants have maintained it to this day. They have succeeded to some extent, but their success has come at the price of cutting themselves off from the wider society. That can hardly be an option for the church as a whole and was deplored by the Reformers as an escape from the world that was the very opposite of true Christian discipleship. Today there are sects and other small groups which practise communism, at least for a time, but often some scandal occurs and the communities that live in this way break up.

When the Apostle Paul established churches in the Gentile world, he did not create communities of that kind. There were certainly household churches that must have been closely knit, and Paul's own activities as a tentmaker with Priscilla and Aquila show that they helped each other out in business. But they did not pool their resources, and sometimes they did not even pay their pastors a salary. Paul boasted that he never took a penny from the Corinthians, but always paid his way when he was among them (2 Corinthians 11:8). On the other hand, he was not ashamed to beg for money in order to help other people. His last recorded missionary journey around the Aegean Sea was designed to collect funds for the Jerusalem church, which was suffering hardship during a famine, and as he records it, the giving was generous. This is how he envisaged Christians helping one another, and it is this that the article lays down as the norm for us today.

Charitable giving has a long history, and we have every reason to be grateful for the millions who have sustained it over the years. It may be less in evidence in Western societies, now that there is widespread affluence and state security for those in need, but it is still very obvious in the third world, where Christian relief agencies are among the most responsible and most active. The difficulty here is to give without being accused of proselytism, and yet at the same time make it clear that we see our charitable work as an extension of our commitment to the Gospel. If it is hard to preach to people who are naked and starving, it is cruel to feed and clothe their bodies without paying any heed to their souls. We do not want what are known as 'rice Christians', converts who come to the church mainly for what they can get out of it but neither can we be happy about putting our beliefs aside. If that happens, the good being done for people in this world may smother the good which needs to be done for them as they prepare to go to the world to come, whose ambassadors on earth we are. It is not always easy to choose between them, but for Christians the Gospel must come first and the consequences of sticking to that priority must be worked out later in a way that is truly gracious and loving to all concerned.

Key Biblical Passages:

Acts 4:32-5:11; 2 Corinthians 8-9; Galatians 6:4-10.

For further reading:

Finn, R. D. *Almsgiving in the later Roman Empire: Christian promotion and practice (313-450).* Oxford: OUP, 2006.

Garrison, R. *Redemptive almsgiving in early Christianity.* Sheffield: JSOT Press, 1993.

MacIntyre, A. C. *Marxism and Christianity.* London: Duckworth, 1995.

Marsden, J. J. *Marxian and Christian utopianism: toward a socialist political theology.* New York: Monthly Review Press, 1991.

Pullopillil, T. *Church, private property and the scheduled castes.* New Delhi: Intercultural Publications, 1998.

39. *Of a Christian Man's Oath*

As we confess that vain and rash swearing is forbidden Christian men by our Lord Jesus Christ, and James his Apostle; so we judge that Christian religion doth not prohibit, but that a man may swear when the magistrate requireth, in a cause of faith and charity, so it be done according to the Prophet's teaching, in justice, judgement and truth.

The last article deals with a confusion which is surprisingly common in some circles and which needs to be sorted out in people's minds before prescribing the right approach that should be taken. Swearing as we experience it in everyday life is what the article calls 'vain and rash swearing', that is to say, the use of profane language for no real purpose other than to let off steam. Taking the Lord's name in vain is expressly forbidden by the third commandment (Exodus 20:7) and this crude but very common form of it must be avoided by Christians. Jesus warned his disciples against it (Matthew 5:33-37) and so did the Apostle James (James 5:12), both of whom are mentioned here. There is even a homily written against it (the seventh in the first book published in 1547.) The prophet referred to is Jeremiah, who wrote: 'If you swear "As the Lord lives" in truth, in justice and in righteousness, then nations shall bless themselves in him, and in him shall they glory.' (Jeremiah 4:2).

At a more serious level, it is also possible to swear an oath or take a vow which, while perhaps not rash in this sense, is nevertheless foolish and ultimately illegitimate. In the middle ages, it was common to send young children into monasteries and convents, where they were obliged to take vows of celibacy before reaching the age of puberty and possibly with very little understanding of what they were doing. The Reformers rightly regarded this as an abuse, and denounced the practice. There is also the famous Old Testament case of Jephthah, who swore that if he won the battle against the Ammonites he would sacrifice to God the first thing that came out of his house on his return. That turned out to be his daughter, who showed her greatness of spirit by submitting to death rather than dishonouring her father, but the tenor of the story clearly shows that this was a very irresponsible thing to do (Judges 11:29-40).

There is however, another kind of swearing which is very different from these and to which there can be no valid theological objection. This is the kind of thing that we do when taking public office or when giving testimony in a courtroom. The oath is a public affirmation that we shall tell the truth, the whole truth and nothing but the truth and perjury in such circumstances remains a major criminal offence to this day. Oaths of this kind were authorised by the law of Moses (Deuteronomy 6:13) and Jesus had no objection to them (Matthew 26:63). The Apostle Paul was steeped in this culture and made frequent references to oath taking in the course of his ministry (Romans 9:1; 2 Corinthians 1:23; Galatians 1:20). In a world where lying is the norm and where some people find it difficult to know what the truth is, so corrupted have their minds become, the administration of justice and civil affairs generally would be impossible without them because we would never know whom we could trust.

But what if we could get away from this twisted world and live in a society where everyone was straightforward and honest? Would oaths be necessary then? In medieval times, monks were forbidden to swear oaths, because it was claimed that they had entered such a society and that they would necessarily tell the truth. As monastic discipline spread to the clergy, so too did this idea, and in documents of the period we find the phrase *in verbo sacerdotii* (on the word of the priesthood) which was deemed to be the equivalent of an oath taken by a lay person.

Whether or not priests and monks could be relied on to tell the truth, the idea that it was possible for Christians to live in an entirely truthful way was attractive to some people, including many Anabaptists, who forbade oath-taking among their members. Unfortunately, this prohibition was seen in the outside world as a loophole that allowed Anabaptists to be dishonest and escape their social obligations. This was not their intention of course, but in a society where trust was based on oaths and vows ('a gentleman's word is his bond') refusal to take part in them was bound to cause suspicion. It was a form of what we would today call super-spirituality and many Christians fall into it one way or another. For example, it is not uncommon for Christian organisations to be rather loosely run, without much accounting or accountability. An unscrupulous person can get into such circles and do great harm, which has sometimes happened, and the honest Christian people who thought they could trust everyone lose out as a result. Sometimes Christians work for other believers without a contract, which can also lead to trouble when expectations become blurred and remuneration is erratic or inadequate. The employee has no avenue of redress open to him and may be accused of being unspiritual if he complains about being badly treated.

Here as elsewhere, Christians must accept that legal norms and standards are there to protect them, and not to make life difficult. They must not think that they are above suspicion merely because they are Christians, and anyone who claims such a thing must be firmly resisted and excluded from the fellowship if he refuses to play by the rules. We are all sinners, after all, and nothing is gained by ignoring or denying the consequences of that. Of course we must not become hard and legalistic either, but that is another problem. Rules and regulations often have to be interpreted broadly so as to respond adequately to exceptional cases, but that is not the same thing as trying to do without rules altogether. In the end it is the combination of the wisdom of the serpent and the harmlessness of the dove that is called for, in the right proportions and in the right circumstances. If we remember that rule we shall be well-equipped to know what we are dealing with in the world and how we should apply our principles in the situations we are called to face every day.

Questions for discussion:

1. Should Christians protest against the use of profane language on television?

2. To what extent should we tolerate conscientious objectors who will not swear an oath or salute the flag when expected to do so?

3. What punishment should there be for lying under oath?

Key Bible Passages:

Luke 1:68-79; Hebrews 6:13-20.

For further reading:

Bray, G. L. *The oath of canonical obedience.* London: Latimer Trust, 2004.

Condren, C. *Argument and authority in early modern England: the presupposition of oaths and offices.* Cambridge: CUP, 2006.

Hughes, G. *An encyclopedia of swearing: the social history of oaths, profanity, foul language and ethnic slurs in the English-speaking world.* London: M. E. Sharpe, 2006.

Schlesinger, H. J. *Promises, oaths and vows: on the psychology of promising.* London: Taylor and Francis, 2008.

Ziegler, Y. *Promises to keep: the oath in Biblical narrative.* Leiden: Brill, 2008.

Appendix 1: Official declarations about the Articles

On 11 May 1571 the following declaration was appended to the Articles:

> This book of Articles before rehearsed is again approved, and allowed to be holden and executed within the realm, by the assent and consent of our Sovereign Lady Elizabeth, by the grace of God, of England, France and Ireland Queen, defender of the Faith etc. Which Articles were deliberately read and confirmed again by the subscription of the hands of the archbishop and bishops of the upper house, and by the subscription of the whole clergy of the nether house in their Convocation, in the year of our Lord God, 1571.

In December 1628 King Charles I issued the following declaration, which is still prefaced to the articles:

> Being by God's ordinance, according to our just title, Defender of the Faith and Supreme Governor of the Church within these our dominions, we hold it most agreeable to this our kingly office and our own religious zeal, to conserve and maintain the Church committed to our charge in unity of true religion and in the bond of peace; and not to suffer unnecessary disputations, altercations or questions to be raised which may nourish faction both in the Church and commonwealth. We have therefore, upon mature deliberation, and with the advice of so many of our bishops as might conveniently be called together, thought fit to make this declaration following :
>
> That the Articles of the Church of England (which have been allowed and authorized heretofore, and which our clergy generally have subscribed unto) do contain the true doctrine of the Church of England agreeable to God's Word; which we do therefore ratify and confirm, requiring all our loving subjects to continue in the uniform profession thereof, and prohibiting the least difference from the said Articles, which to that end we command to be new printed, and this our declaration to be published therewith.
>
> That we are Supreme Governor of the Church of England, and that if any difference arise about the external policy, concerning the injunctions, canons and other constitutions whatsoever thereto belonging, the clergy in their convocation is to order and settle them, having first obtained leave under our broad seal so to do; and we approving their said

ordinances and constitutions, providing that none be made contrary to the laws and customs of the land.

That out of our princely care that the churchmen may do the work which is proper unto them, the bishops and clergy, from time to time in convocation, upon their humble desire, shall have licence under our broad seal to deliberate of, and to do all such things as, being made plain by them, and assented unto by us, shall concern the settled continuance of the doctrine and discipline of the Church of England now established; from which we will not endure any varying or departing in the least degree.

That for the present, though some differences have been ill raised, yet we take comfort in this, that all clergymen within our realm have always most willingly subscribed to the Articles established; which is an argument to us that they all agree in the true, usual, literal meaning of the said Articles; and that even in those curious points in which the present differences lie, men of all sorts take the Articles of the Church of England to be for them; which is an argument again, that none of them intend any desertion of the Articles established.

That therefore in these both curious and unhappy differences which have for so many hundred years, in different times and places, exercised the Church of Christ, we will that all further curious search be laid aside, and these disputes shut up in God's promises, as they be generally set forth to us in the Holy Scriptures and the general meaning of the Articles of the Church of England according to them. And that no man hereafter shall either print or preach to draw the Article aside any way, but shall submit to it in the plain and full meaning thereof; and shall not put his own sense or comment to be the meaning of the Article, but shall take it in the literal and grammatical sense.

That if any public reader in either of our universities, or any head or master of a college, or any other person respectively in either of them, shall affix any new sense to any Article or shall publicly read, determine or hold any public disputation, or suffer any such to be held either way, in either the universities or colleges respectively; or if any divine in the universities shall preach or print anything either way, other than is already established in Convocation with our royal assent; he, or they the offenders shall be liable to our displeasure, and the Church's censure in our commission ecclesiastical, as well as any other; and we will see there shall be due execution upon them.

Canon A5 of the Church of England, adopted in its present form in 1964, states:

The doctrine of the Church of England is grounded in the Holy Scriptures, and in such teachings of the ancient Fathers and Councils of the Church as are agreeable to the said Scriptures.

In particular, such doctrine is to be found in the Thirty-nine Articles of Religion, The Book of Common Prayer, and the Ordinal.

(It should be noted that the Book of Common Prayer referred to here, as well as the Ordinal, are those approved for use in 1662.)

Appendix 2: Subscription to the Articles

When the Articles of Religion were first drawn up in 1553 no provision was made for any form of subscription or assent to them on the part of the clergy, perhaps because it was assumed that official approval of them would be enough to make them enforceable. Ten years later the story was the same, and no attempt was made to pursue the matter any further. In 1571 however, the approach was different. The queen had been excommunicated by the pope on 18 February 1570, and the revised Articles were part of a wide-ranging response to that. The papal bull of excommunication had called on all loyal Catholics to rebel against Queen Elizabeth, even to the point of seeking her assassination. This made it necessary to ensure the complete loyalty of those entitled to preach in the church, so that they could not use their pulpits against her.

As a first step in countering this, all existing preaching licences were cancelled with effect from 30 April 1571 and every preacher had to apply for a new one. Preaching licences had originally been introduced in 1407 in an attempt to combat Lollardy and they were retained after the Reformation, albeit for a different purpose. In 1571 intending preachers were obliged to subscribe to the Articles which had just then been approved by the convocation of Canterbury (an approval subsequently ratified by the convocation of York) and this requirement passed into law.

In 1583 the newly-appointed Archbishop of Canterbury, John Whitgift, issued three articles of his own, insisting that '...none be permitted to preach, read, catechise, minister the sacraments or to execute any other ecclesiastical function, by what authority soever he be admitted thereunto, unless he first consent and subscribe to these articles following, before the ordinary of the diocese...'. The first of these articles reaffirmed the royal supremacy, the second, the Book of Common Prayer and the Ordinal, and the third, the Thirty-nine Articles, in the following terms:

> That he [the subscribing clergyman] alloweth the book of Articles of religion, agreed upon by the archbishops and bishops in both provinces, and the whole clergy in the convocation holden at London in the year of our Lord 1562 [1563 by modern reckoning], and set forth by her majesty's authority. And that he believeth all the articles therein contained to be agreeable to the Word of God.

In 1603 King James I ordered the composition of a new set of canons, which was completed the following year and which remained in force until modern times. Canon 36 took over Whitgift's three articles and extended them to cover lecturers and readers in divinity, not only in the universities but also in every parish church, where many had been appointed to do the work of preaching and catechising. In addition, canon 36 devised a form of subscription as follows:

> I, N. N., do willingly and *ex animo* subscribe to these three articles above mentioned, and to all things that are contained in them.

This pattern remained unaltered for more than 250 years, and the surviving subscription books bear witness to the fact that, with very few exceptions (probably due to negligence), every clergyman did in fact subscribe as required. There were always objectors – in the seventeenth century, many puritans opposed the practice because to them the Articles were inadequately Reformed, while in the eighteenth century Latitudinarians wanted greater intellectual freedom than the Articles allowed. However, it was not until the middle of the nineteenth century that objections were raised to an extent that could no longer be ignored. A commission was appointed to examine the question and it recommended a change in the form of subscription, which took effect in 1865 (on 29 June in Canterbury and on 5 July in York).

The revised form of words ignored the royal supremacy and combined the second and third articles as follows:

> I, A. B., do solemnly make the following declaration: I assent to the Thirty-nine Articles of Religion, and to the Book of Common Prayer, and of ordering of bishops, priests and deacons; I believe the doctrine of the united Church of England and Ireland, as therein set forth, to be agreeable to the Word of God: and in public prayer and administration of the sacraments, I will use the form in the said book prescribed, and non other, except so far as shall be ordered by lawful authority.

The general tone and arrangement of the oath shows that liturgical deviations were the main concern of those who devised it, which reflected the troubles of the church at that time. Subscription to the Articles was softened somewhat, but not substantially altered, since it was still necessary to affirm that they were 'agreeable to the Word of God'. The oath was slightly modified on 1 January 1871, when the Church of Ireland was disestablished (the words 'united' and 'of Ireland' being removed), but otherwise it remained in force for just over a century. In preparation for a major revision of the 1603 (1604) canons, the Archbishops' Commission on Christian Doctrine undertook a lengthy study of the question of subscription to the Articles, which resulted in a published report entitled *Subscription and assent to the 39 Articles* (London: SPCK, 1968). The recommendations of this commission were implemented in what is now canon C15, which contains the form of subscription now used. Unlike earlier forms, mention of the Articles is now confined to the words of the person administering the oath, although the one taking it is still expected to affirm what is stated in the administrator's preface. Since 7 May 1969 the form has been as follows:

> **Preface:** The Church of England is part of the one, holy, catholic and apostolic church worshipping the one true God, Father, Son and Holy Spirit. She professes the faith uniquely revealed in the Holy Scriptures and set forth in the catholic creeds, which faith the church is called upon to proclaim afresh in each generation. Led by the Holy Spirit, she has borne witness to Christian truth in her historic formularies, the Thirty-Nine Articles of Religion, the Book of Common Prayer and the Ordering of Bishops, Priests and Deacons. In the declaration you are about to make will you affirm your loyalty to this inheritance of faith as your inspiration and guidance under God in bringing the grace and truth of Christ to this generation and making him known to those in your care?
>
> **Declaration of Assent:** I, A. B., do so affirm, and accordingly declare my belief in the faith which is revealed in the Holy Scriptures and set forth in the catholic creeds and to which the historic formularies of the Church of England bear witness; and in public prayer and administration of the sacraments, I will use only the forms of service which are authorised or allowed by canon.

By this form of words, the Church of England has been able to satisfy those who still uphold the authority and integrity of the Thirty-nine Articles (not to mention the other sources of doctrine and worship listed in the Preface) without allowing them to hold other members of the church accountable for their failure to do the same. For example, the revised oath allows the person taking it to dissent from the view that the Bible is the written Word of God; all that is necessary is to believe the 'faith which is revealed' in it, whatever that means. It would certainly be possible, as modern scholarship makes plain, to reject large portions of Scripture, and perhaps even the entire Old Testament, as superfluous to this revealed faith, which presumably focuses on the mission and message of Jesus Christ. Nothing is said about using the Book of Common Prayer, or even about subscribing to the Ordinal; it is enough to 'use only the forms of service which are authorised or allowed by canon', a phrase so vague that it can now include almost anything. It is not even certain whether the 'catholic creeds' include the *Quicunque vult* or not, though presumably they ought to, if article 8 is any guide.

In this context, affirming that the 'historic formularies of the Church of England bear witness' to the faith revealed in the Holy Scriptures is not as weak as it may sound at first sight. We know exactly what the formularies are and according to the declaration, we are also expected to affirm that they really do reflect Biblical revelation, though in what way or to what extent is unclear. We may therefore conclude that although the words of affirmation are weak and fall short of the declaration of assent expected from 1571 onwards, the position of the Articles is parallel to that of the other written sources of our faith and doctrine. It is therefore wrong to suggest that they have been relegated to the sidelines in a way that other things have not, or that anything else has been singled out for a prominence it did not already have. In other words, the Articles still possess the same *relative* authority that they have always had with respect to Scripture and the creeds; it is the way that authority is viewed and enforced (or not enforced) in the church at large that has brought about their eclipse at the present time. On the other hand, if things change and the church returns to a point where it once more accepts the authority of its doctrinal sources *ex animo*, then there is every reason to believe that the Thirty-nine Articles will also be rehabilitated and once more become an honoured part of the church's theological inheritance.

For the time being, assent to the Articles of Religion, as to the other parts of our historic inheritance, must rely on the conscience of the person making the affirmation. No doubt this has always been so, but until 1865 (or perhaps 1969) it was possible to challenge the veracity of this in a court of law. That can no longer be done, but we are still called to be true to our consciences before God, and if we want to be Anglicans, then we ought to accept what the Anglican Communion has always believed and taught. We do not claim to be in full or exclusive possession of the truth, but we do believe that we have received enough light to walk by, and that our first duty is to walk in love according to that light. The Thirty-nine Articles of Religion are part of what we have received and, as the wording of the classical subscription has it, they are 'agreeable to the Word of God.' For that reason we are called to follow their teaching and do our best to put it into practice in the life of the church, so that when the final harvest comes, Christ the king will look at each one of us and say: 'Well done, good and faithful servant; enter into the joy of your Lord.' (Matthew 25:21).

Index of Scripture References

The numbers in the index are those of the articles under which the texts appear.

Reference		Article	Reference		Article
2 Corinthians	6:2	4	1 Timothy	1:3-17	33
	6:14-18	33		2:1-7	18
	8-9	38		2:8-3:13	22
	10	23		2:10-15	20
	11:8	38		3:1-13	26, 32
Galatians	1:1-17	23		3:2	32
	1:20	39		5:17-22	36
	2:1-14	19		6:12-16	8
	2:15-21	11	2 Timothy	1:6-14	8
	2:17-21	14		3:1-17	20
	2:20	15		3:13-17	6
	2:20-21	11		4:1-8	35
	3	31	Titus	1:5-16	23, 26
	3:10-14	15		1:5-2:15	36
	3:10-23	10		1:6	32
	3:15-25	7	Hebrews	1:1	32
	3:28	20		4:12	6
	4:6	5, 28		4:14-5:10	15
	6:1-5	33		5:8	15
	6:4-10	38		6:4-5	16
Ephesians	1:1	22		6:4-6	29
	1:1-10	17		6:13-20	39
	1:4	17		9-10	31
	2:1-3	13		9:11-15	30
	2:1-10	25		11	7
	2:6	4		12:2	15
	2:8-10	12	James	2:17-26	12
	2:10	17		2:19	3
	2:11-12	13		5:12	39
	2:19-22	19		5:14-15	25
	3:7-13	14, 26	1 Peter	2:8	17
	3:8	11		2:9-10	19
	4:1-6	27		2:13-17	37
	4:8	3		3:18	3
	4:8-10	3		5:1-4	23
	4:9	3	2 Peter	1:3-11	17
	4:17-32	10		1:21	6
	5:22-33	32		2:1-9	19
Philippians	1:12-18	26		2:12	17
	1:19-26	14,22	1 John	1:5-10	15
	1:20-23	3		2:1-17	16
	2:5-11	2,8		3:5	15
Colossians	1:15-20	2	2 John	7-11	26
	1:21-23	11		10	33
	2:9	2	3 John		26
	2:12-13	27		9-10	26
	2:16-23	34	Jude	1	22
	3:3	4		1-7	8
1 Thessalonians	4:13-18	22		1-25	19
	4:14-17	3		4	17

Reference		Article
Jude	8-16	26
Revelation	2-3	19
	14:4	32
	17:8	17
	22	20, 32
	22:7	17
	22:20	17

LATIMER PUBLICATIONS

LATIMER PUBLICATIONS

CPSIA information can be obtained at www.ICGtesting.com
Printed in the USA
LVOW06s1615270714

396249LV00001B/384/P